STAGES OF THE
FOURTH VOYAGE
1502–1504

D0251164

11°

CARIBBEAN SEA

10°

Nombre de Dios
(Bastimentos)

Portobelo

Colón

(Panama
Canal)

9°

Panama City

GULF OF PANAMA

8°

80°   79°

The Voyage of
the Vizcaína

THE Voyage OF THE Vizcaína

THE MYSTERY OF CHRISTOPHER COLUMBUS'S LAST SHIP

Klaus Brinkbäumer
and
Clemens Höges

Translated from the German by
Annette Streck

Harcourt, Inc.
ORLANDO   AUSTIN   NEW YORK
SAN DIEGO   TORONTO   LONDON

www.HarcourtBooks.com

This is a translation of *Die Letzte Reise: Der Fall Christoph Columbus*

Library of Congress Cataloging-in-Publication Data
Brinkbäumer, Klaus.
[Letzte Reise. English]
The voyage of the Vizcaína: the mystery of Christopher
Columbus's last ship/Klaus Brinkbäumer and Clemens Höges;
translated from the German by Annette Streck.—1st U.S. ed.
p. cm.
Includes index.
1. Vizcaína (Ship) 2. Columbus, Christopher—Travel—America.
3. America—Discovery and exploration—Spanish. 4. Shipwrecks—Panama.
5. Panama—Antiquities. I. Höges, Clemens. II. Streck, Annette. III. Title.
E118.B75 2006
970.01'5—dc22   2005030790
ISBN-13: 978-0-15-101186-5 ISBN-10: 0-15-101186-9

Text set in Dante
Designed by Kaelin Chappell Broaddus

Printed in the United States of America

First U.S. edition

A C E G I K J H F D B

CONTENTS

The Voyage of
the *Vizcaína*

CHAPTER I

The Wreck in
the Bay of Playa Damas

The village of Nombre de Dios has few inhabitants, slightly over three thousand; nobody seems to have made an accurate count. It has a whitewashed church, symbol and relic of the former colonial powers, and eight bars, most of them devoid of clientele. Signs reading "Se Vende" hang outside shacks and half-finished buildings; the signs look as if they have been hanging there for some time. Plastic chairs are scattered here and there under trees. The owners of the bars can be frequently found propped up along the counters of their establishments, drinking the beer themselves. There are no jobs to be had in Nombre de Dios, nor are there any tourists. The women wash clothes in the muddy waters of the local river. In sum, Nombre de Dios, which is situated on Panama's Caribbean coast, about fifteen miles east of the larger town of Portobelo, seems to be on the wrong side of what some might call "civilization."

Nombre de Dios's remoteness was doubtless one reason almost no one reacted when in late 2001 an American treasure hunter named Warren White posted an announcement on the Internet that he had found the *Vizcaína,* one of the ships that had gone on Christopher Columbus's fourth, and final, expedition to the New World in 1502. White's discovery made a few headlines—CNN offered a brief spot on it—but then, fairly quickly, things went quiet. One reason might have been that every year, it seems, someone somewhere announces a sensational discovery involving Columbus—a document, a ship's bell, an original logbook, and even, occasionally, a shipwreck. Over time archaeologists and Columbus scholars have grown thick-skinned about these claims; most of the time they simply ignore them. For good reason: most turn out to be hoaxes. Treasure hunters routinely inflate the importance of their finds. After all, a cannon from one of Columbus's ships would fetch significantly more on the open market than one from practically any other wreck. Moreover, Warren White did not help his cause. He had earned a reputation among archaeologists for being one of those treasure hunters who favored using explosives on wrecks, believing that this method more effectively and efficiently freed up the coins and gold hidden beneath the heavy timbers and sediment.

White was not the first or only one to claim to have found the wreck, which, many say, local fishermen had known about for years—it was lying a couple of dozen feet below the surface. Another American expatriate living in Panama named James Norris, who was in the process of buying a dive center near Nombre de Dios called Diver's Haven, felt he had earned that privilege. In the summer of 1996, Norris went scuba diving in various locations in the bay of Playa Damas, places where locals had assured him he would find the most fish—a draw for potential diving clients. He swam directly over the wreck, which, he said, he knew immediately was old. He told his son, who in turn—according to Norris—told Nilda Vázquez, a local real-estate agent and the original owner of Diver's Haven. Nilda Vázquez, for her part, denied Norris's claim of discovery. She maintained that she had heard about it from Warren White, while also insisting that she had been the one to tell White that it might be the *Vizcaína*. (At the time, Norris and Vazquez were involved in a bitter legal dispute over the purchase of Diver's Haven.) Of the three claimants, Vázquez remains most intimately involved in the issue of discovery and ownership, as we shall see. In any case, it is little wonder that historians and Columbus experts discounted the rumors surrounding the discovery of the wreck. Who would have had any reason to believe James Norris, embattled owner of Diver's Haven, or Warren White, the treasure seeker from Miami, or a local real-estate agent named Nilda Vázquez, particularly when so many professionals have tried and failed to find vessels such as the *Vizcaína*?

Almost everyone involved in underwater archaeological research has, at some point, gone in search of one of Columbus's ships. They represent the Holy Grail of the Western Hemisphere. Columbus lost nine ships in the four voyages he made to the New World. There are clues as to where they might lie. For example, archaeologists know that the *Santa María,* Columbus's flagship for the first voyage to America, sank on a calm night, while the crew and the Admiral of the Ocean Sea—the title Columbus had been given by King Ferdinand and Queen Isabella—were asleep. One of the ship's boys was at the helm as the *Santa María* drifted along the coast of Hispaniola, now the Dominican Republic, and then ran aground on a sandbank. Columbus used wood from the ship to build the first fortress in the New World, La Navidad, traces of which have been unearthed. However, no part of the *Santa María*'s hull has ever been found. Columbus lost the *Gallega*—another ship that went on his final voyage—in a battle against natives near the Río Belén, on the north side of what is now Panama, and approximately 125 miles due west of Nombre de Dios. For months researchers from Texas A&M University searched for the *Gallega*. They dredged the river and the estuary and at one point very nearly half the bay of Belén but came up empty-handed.

Lacking physical evidence, experts know fairly little about what these ships looked like. Most depictions date from decades later and tended to be shaped by the artists' imaginations. Most resemble the kind of ships that contemporary sailors would like to imagine went to sea in the fifteenth century. No constructional drawings survive—no detailed descriptions and no sketches.

Nonetheless, some facts about these ships do exist. We know, for example, that the *Santa María* was a cumbersome but stable old tub known as a *nao*. Hard to maneuver, it was ill-suited for a voyage into unknown waters under variable winds. Columbus scholars have concluded that he generally liked to sail on caravels, ships measuring between sixty and seventy-two feet in length and featuring a mainsail, two or three smaller masts, and a small castle at the stern. He preferred them because they were comparatively fast and reliably stable. Unlike the *Santa María,* which could only sail straight before the wind—meaning with a tailwind—caravels could sail in crosswinds. On the other hand, caravels had disadvantages in terms of space; a crew as large as fifty had to live on a sixty-five-foot ship for an entire year; there was no head and no galley. Not even the Admiral of the Ocean Sea had his own cabin and was forced to sleep under the quarterdeck with the crew. But those facts represent nearly the totality of knowledge. Seafaring in the Age of Discovery, as it is called, remains a deep mystery. "We know more about Greek or Roman ships than about the ships of the discoverers," said Filipe Castro, a nautical archaeologist at Texas A&M University.

Wrecks from the period are so precious because, like all wrecks, they are time capsules; an entire era freezes the moment disaster befalls a ship. Therefore it would be wrong to say that no one took notice when Warren White announced he had discovered the *Vizcaína.* Some were waiting for exactly a discovery such as this. They may have doubted whether this actually was the *Vizcaína,* but it seemed excitingly plausible that it might be a caravel from the same period. And were that the case, it would be the first caravel ever found, offering answers to many of their questions: about how the ships were built, or the masts designed, or what kind of cannonry they carried, or how fast they could go, or how were they laden, or how the crew ate and slept. Were it authentic, the wreck off Nombre de Dios might reveal even more about the era, such as how the shipbuilders treated their wood and where the timber came from (indicating, for example, the state of trade relations between Spain and other European na-tions). Remains of the provisions on board would reveal how the sailors lived. From the ballast rocks on board, experts would be able to draw conclusions about the ship's route (seafarers always bunkered ballast as and when required and usually collected heavy stones from beaches near to where they were anchored). Franck Goddio, a French marine explorer who is a celebrity among wreck divers, explained, "A sunken ship is like a well-corked mes-sage in a bottle from a long bygone era. During excavations on land, you will generally find more recent deposits above your actual objective. That often leads to utter confusion. But under-water, we have bundled information about a particular point in time." To Goddio, wrecks are more than time capsules. They are "time machines."

The Nombre de Dios caravel would offer a view into the greatest era of exploration in human history, the age during which fears and superstitions were being replaced by knowledge; when experience and technology gained greater weight than lit-eral interpretation of the Bible. Here was when the world began to mature into what we know it as today. If this wreck turned out to be the *Vizcaína,* some believe it would rival in significance the discovery of the *Titanic,* the *Bismarck,* the *Bounty,* the *Whydah* (the only documented pirate wreck ever discovered, off the coast of Cape Cod), the SS *Central America* (which contained California gold rush bounty), or any of the galleasses and galleons of the Spanish Armada.

Wrecks tell tales—of dreams and tragedies, humility and megalomania. There could be no greater story than that of the rise and fall of Christopher Columbus, Admiral of the Ocean Sea, discoverer of the New World. His was a swashbuckling white-knuckle adventure, a tale of grand visions and equally grand illu-sions, the greatest imaginable triumph and the most poignant failure. That story, such as we have it today, has been recon-structed almost exclusively from evidence found in correspon-dence, court documents, and his log (not the original, which has been lost, but a later transcript). Were it truly the *Vizcaína*, the Nombre de Dios wreck could solve so many puzzles.

In early 2003 a white motorboat sped through the placid blue waters of the bay of Playa Damas and approached the village of Nombre de Dios. Having reached a certain spot, the man driving the boat, Jesse Allan, shut off the engines. He announced they had arrived at the site. Allan is an imposing figure. Originally from Grand Junction, Colorado, he had spent twenty-four years in the U.S. Army, eventually retiring as a master sergeant, pay grade E-8. Allan hadn't been, however, your average infantryman. His specialty had been hostage release. He served in Vietnam twice, and then was posted in Taiwan before being sent to Beirut in the 1980s. Later he operated out of Syria and in Turkey, which served the military base for all operations in Iraq. Eventually Allan arrived in Panama, the base of operation for U.S. military activities in Central and South America. When he was scheduled for relocation to Africa, Allan said he told his superiors that he had had enough—enough of the parachute jumps, the hand-to-hand combat, the collateral damage; and he had enough money to lead a good life in Panama. "America was a foreign country to me. Panama had become my home."

Panama, the land bridge between South and North America, has a population of around three million and consists of some thirty thousand square miles, making it slightly larger than South Carolina. It also has somewhere around twelve hundred miles of coastline and of course is bordered by the Atlantic Ocean on one side and by the Pacific on the other. Until 1914 the Río Chagres provided the only water channel between the two oceans. Sailors were forced to make their way through miles and miles of the jungle on foot. In 1914 the fifty-one-mile Panama Canal was completed. Controlled by the United States for many decades due to its strategic importance as a link between East and West, its being a waterway between Asia and Europe, the canal brought Panama nearly half a billion dollars in revenue each year. Nonetheless, most Panamanians felt that as long as the U.S. controlled it, they were a mere pawn of a greater power; ownership of the canal became a matter of nationalist pride on both sides. Eventually, on December 31, 1999, American soldiers withdrew and the canal became the property of Panama. Soon after that Jesse Allan opened a diving center near Portobelo. He called it the Twin Oceans Dive Center.

Allan maintained he had also known about the wreck off Nombre de Dios for years. Fishermen, he said, had told him about it. So one day he took a boat out and brought along some metal detectors. "It was old, no question about it; there were lots of cannonballs made of stone. But because we found no plates, forks, knives, bottles, or coins, nothing that you would normally find at the site of a wreck, we thought that this wreck had already been plundered." Naturally, Allan had heard the rumors that it might be the *Vizcaína*—it was the kind of news that tends to get around quickly in the diving world—but he, for one, didn't believe them. He was acquainted with Warren White—he occasionally went diving with him—and knew how White operated. Like many Columbus experts, Allan was well acquainted with the letter Columbus had written in 1504 to the Spanish crown, stating that he had abandoned the *Vizcaína* "near Portobelo."

"Nowadays, you need an hour to get from Nombre de Dios to Portobelo," said Allan, "but in those times it meant a day's journey. You don't write 'near Portobelo' if you're referring to a bay that's fifteen miles away."

Of course, to the Europeans the bay didn't yet have a name, at least not a name that would have meant anything to Queen Isabella of Spain. Moreover, Columbus no longer considered either the ship or the bay of any great importance in the scheme of things. At the time he wrote the letter, he was stranded in Jamaica without a ship and delirious from malarial fever. The key portion of Columbus's letter to Queen Isabella reads as follows:

> *I sailed in the name of the Holy Trinity on the night of Easter Monday in ships that were rotten, leaky, and worm-eaten, leaving one of them (the Gallega) at Belén with a number of objects*

*and another (the Vizcaína) at Belpuerto. I had only two left,
which were in as bad a state as the others and without boats or
stores. In these I must sail seven thousand miles of sea or die on
the way with my son and brother and all these men.*

Many have wondered whether these sentences written some
five hundred years ago offer anything that could either substantiate or disprove the theory that the wreck lying in the bay of Playa
Damas off Nombre de Dios was the *Vizcaína*.

That is why a team of explorers was on that white motorboat
in 2003. They were the first ones to take the rumor seriously and
assess the wreck. One member of the team was a Belgian diving
instructor named Karl Vandenhole, an experienced ocean diver
who once operated a dive shop in Hamburg, Germany, where he
now works as an underwater cameraman for German television.
Vandenhole always knows the latest news about shipwrecks. He
had been in Panama on the trail of the legendary pirate Henry
Morgan when he'd heard about the alleged discovery of the *Vizcaína*. He quickly obtained the necessary papers and organized an
expedition.

Accompanying Vandenhole was a contractor named Klaus
Keppler. Keppler has earned his living salvaging cranes and
yachts and working on water-treatment plants. But his greatest
diving passion has always been reserved for the really big finds:
the sunken ships of Henry Morgan or the so-called gold fleet of
Mexico explorer Hernán Cortés. Naturally, anything involving
Christopher Columbus fits that category. Keppler would admit
that he is a treasure hunter, though he is not the kind that blows
up wrecks. His latest company venture is called Sea Explorer,
which engages in professional treasure hunting. It took him a few
years to make it work, as the research was so time-consuming.
"But once you've found that rhythm of research, negotiation,
searching, salvaging, restoration, and exhibition," he explained,
"once you've organized everything so that you're constantly making progress somewhere in the world, then it's the best job in the

world. Then you get so close to the discoverers that you feel like a discoverer yourself." Keppler has found ships like Morgan's *Jamaican Merchant,* as well as submerged airplanes and yachts. He is also one of the few treasure hunters who has managed to remain on good terms with archaeologists; he cooperates fully with governments and universities. He admitted that his line of business had its shady sides. "There are some six hundred companies in this business worldwide, and apart from twenty or thirty, they're all bandits."

The divers rubbed shampoo onto their masks to keep them from fogging up and put on diving suits, gloves, weight belts, vests, and finally masks and fins. Then they looked at each other, signaled, and slipped into the water. The waters of the Caribbean Sea were warm and calm; the waves break some distance off from this spot. Though the strong currents and the sandy ocean floor can limit visibility, experienced divers know how to compensate. No sooner had they let the air out of their vests than they sank straight to the site.

The wreck lay in the sand twenty feet down. At first glance it looked like a bright green mound, and it was very hard to tell whether what lay strewn about were stones or pieces of coral. Measured, the mound was thirty-two feet long and ten feet wide. When most people think of sunken ships, they picture ghostly gangways and decks through which divers swim; or of hulls that divers hover beside, perhaps in the company of a school of curious fish; or of ropes and chains covered in brightly colored coral. Those kinds of shipwrecks are made of steel, however, and have probably sat on the ocean floor for only a few years, at most a few decades. This wreck was striking in part because it was so unspectacular.

Diving presents the very antithesis of a high-speed sport. Everything changes under water; initial impressions count for little. The divers began to circle the mound, examining the exact position of the formation. They ran their hands over the debris.

Slowly they began to comprehend what they were seeing. The top layer, the green layer, consisted of deposits that occur naturally when a ship has been immersed in salt water for extended periods of time. Underneath this layer, however, were more interesting things. Interlocked anchors lay at the bow—surprisingly large anchors for a caravel, if that's what this proved to be. The bow pointed toward the beach in a southwesterly direction, at precisely 240 degrees. Diving slowly toward the stern, they saw cannons protruding from the green mound, trained in every direction. On this first dive alone, they counted thirteen cannons, of various sizes and types. There were both heavy cannons and smaller ones. The manner in which they were piled on top of one another suggested that at least some had been cargo. Records indicate that the first ship Columbus lost in Belén was the *Gallega* and that before it sank he redistributed its load among the three remaining ships.

Digging deeper, they found pottery shards and stone cannonballs, also of various dimensions, strewn across the seabed. Among them were pebbles, stones used as ballast in the days before sailing ships were equipped with stabilizing keel fins. They fanned their hands across the seabed, making the sand swirl off and revealing the timbers, long planks with narrower ribs set at a ninety-degree angle and secured by round wooden pegs. Even at first glance they could see these planks were riddled with channels and holes, the handiwork of the *Teredo navalis,* or shipworm, just as Columbus had indicated in his letter.

The divers spent two hours in the water on that first dive. At that kind of depth, they didn't need to be particularly careful. Surfacing divers usually make a safety stop at sixteen feet, to reduce the level of nitrogen in the blood. This wreck lay in such shallow water that a decompression stop was unnecessary. They ascended in a matter of seconds. Even before clambering back into the boat, they began discussing what they had seen.

"That thing is old, really old," said Keppler. "The wood isn't studded; there's no metal down there."

Worms posed one of the greatest problems for Spaniards exploring the Caribbean; the creatures literally ate their ships from under them. So much of a scourge had *Teredo navalis* proven that in 1508 the Spanish royal family issued a decree, requiring that the timbers of any ship sailing to the New World be sheathed in lead. The absence of lead suggested that this ship had been built early enough to have gone with Columbus.

———

Columbus called his fourth expedition to the New World El Alto Viaje, the "High Voyage." It would be his last. On his first, in 1492, he had landed on a tiny island of the Bahamas that he had named San Salvador. That first expedition had been an intimate affair; being a foreigner and an immigrant, he had been entrusted by the Spaniards with only three ships. He returned a hero. Promoted to commander, he was given a larger fleet for his second voyage, which he launched with great fanfare in 1493. The second voyage was a failure. His crew mutinied, the natives whom he had hoped to bring back to Spain died in the hulls of his ships, and he failed to find gold. All Columbus brought home to Queen Isabella were coconuts, some amulets (stolen from the natives), and a few grains of corn. Nevertheless, he set off on yet a third voyage. From this one he returned in chains. The new governor of Hispaniola, the island that five hundred years later would come to be shared by Haiti and the Dominican Republic, had had Columbus arrested and deported.

That was why so much was riding on the fourth journey. Columbus needed the High Voyage to reestablish his reputation, to confirm that he was a visionary, a great admiral, a statesman. It would demonstrate that the natives were willing to enslave themselves. It would prove that he had found gold. And finally, most importantly, it would establish the existence of a channel linking the Pacific and the Atlantic, a link between Cuba and China. Columbus's role model in all this was Marco Polo, the Venetian who in his writings had described the straits leading from China to the

Indian Ocean. Marco Polo had been referring to the Strait of Malacca, as it turned out, the sea passage between Malaysia and Indonesia; Columbus was thousands of miles away from that part of the world but apparently anticipating something along the lines of the modern Panama Canal.

On February 26, 1502, Columbus petitioned Ferdinand of Aragón and Isabella of Castile for a fleet. On March 14, the Spanish crown not only granted his request; they ordered that Columbus sail westward with all possible speed, for "the present season is very good for navigation." This would mean the month of March, when hurricane season begins to loom over the Caribbean. The promptness with which the royal family granted Columbus's request led Columbus biographer and naval historian Samuel Eliot Morison to conclude that Isabella, who had once admired Columbus for his courage, was only too glad to be rid of him, as soon as possible and perhaps forever.

The fleet was ready to sail within two weeks. Columbus had requested brigantines, shallow-drafted vessels with square-rigged lateen sails that could sail upriver and handle traversing winds. At the time brigantines were considered the very latest thing. Instead, he had to make do with what was chartered for him: four caravels with square-rigged mainsails. Columbus and his son Fernando—who was later to write a biography of his father—sailed on the largest, the seventy-ton flagship the Admiral had named the *Capitana*. The ship belonged to Mateo Sánchez from Seville. Sánchez had struck a most favorable deal when he chartered the ship out for 54,000 *maravedís* a month (based on the price of gold in 1502, this would now convert to somewhere around $7,500 per month). Diego Tristán, who had accompanied Columbus on his second voyage, captained the ship. The crew consisted of two officers, fourteen sailors, twenty ship's boys, seven carpenters, and a trumpet player, whose services would probably be called upon to create a dignified impression when the *Capitana* anchored before the palace of the emperor of China.

The fleet also included the aforementioned *Gallega,* which had an additional fourth mast attached to the foot railing on the stern. The sail was no bigger than a flag and would confer minimal wind advantage, but an expedition such as this depended upon such small advantages. The *Gallega* belonged to one Alonso Cerrajano from La Coruña and cost 50,000 *maravedís* per month to charter (roughly $7,000). The crew of twenty-six, fourteen of them ship's boys, was captained by Pedro de Terreros, who had accompanied Columbus on all four voyages to the New World and who was the Admiral's most loyal ally.

The *Santiago de Palos,* rechristened the *Bermuda* by Columbus, was the third vessel in the expedition. Although her captain, Francisco de Porras, was considered to be an inexperienced sailor, he also happened to be the brother of the mistress of the treasurer of Castile, and the treasurer of Castile was paying for the expedition. Then as now, connections helped. The *Bermuda* had a crew of thirty-one men, among them Porras's brother, Diego, scribe and notary to the royal family. To offset the weaknesses in personnel on the bridge of the *Santiago de Palos,* Columbus had also sent his own brother Bartolomeo.

The fourth ship was the *Vizcaína.* The *Vizcaína* was said to have had three masts and a loading capacity of fifty tons. At the outset of the voyage, it had belonged to Juan de Orquiva, who chartered her out for 42,000 *maravedís* a month (around $5,800). She was captained by Bartolomeo Fieschi, the Admiral's friend and the scion of one of the largest and wealthiest clans in Genoa. The Fieschi family had exerted a dominant influence on the politics and economic life of Genoa for decades, far greater than that of the Columbus family, who were rather humble. But out on the open seas, their statuses were reversed: Columbus was in command and Fieschi his subordinate. The twenty-five-man crew of the *Vizcaína* included boatswain Martín de Fuenterrabía, coxswain Juan Pérez, eight sailors, ten ship's boys, a chaplain named Fray Alejandro, and three private individuals. The sailors had received their pay six months in advance, while the captain earned 4,000 *maravedís* a month, about $560.

The ships set off on April 3, 1502. They put in at the port of Casa de Viejo, where the planks were scrubbed thoroughly and all four vessels coated in pitch. The crew knew what awaited them in the New World. Foreknowledge did them no good. Not one of the ships returned to Spain.

———————

After the first day of diving to the wreck off Nombre de Dios, during which a number of artifacts from the wreck had been brought to the surface, Keppler willingly offered his impressions of what they had seen. He was lounging in a hammock suspended on the landing platform of Jesse Allan's Twin Oceans Dive Center, located a mile and a half outside Portobelo. Twin Oceans is part of the Coco Plum Resort. Despite the name, the rooms there are simple, consisting of a bed, a sink, and a shower with feeble water pressure. People who come here are not looking for luxury; they are looking to dive. And the best place to hang out, literally, is in one of the hammocks on the landing platform.

Keppler was curious about some rounded knives they had found lying on the wreck. "Cutlasses?" he wondered out loud. "Why would Columbus need cutlasses? Let us assume that thing out there really is the *Vizcaína*. Why the cutlasses?"

This was one of those puzzles that always crop up as soon as a wreck has been discovered. There are a number of ways to solve these puzzles. You can scour the libraries for photos, sketches, maps, and three-dimensional images of the wreck. Or in the case of a wreck lying in shallow water, such as this one, you can build a bulkhead and slowly pump out the water, salvage the wreck, and then restore it. That, however, would take years. And some mysteries might still remain unsolved—such as the one involving these sickle-shaped knives, for example. Keppler weighed the possibilities for us. "Maybe Columbus thought he would be sailing through narrow channels in India and be involved in close combat with junks. Maybe they were just part of the load. Or maybe they were intended for bartering or for the settlement of India. We might never find out."

Before coming to Panama, Keppler had read everything about Columbus he could get his hands on, with particular emphasis on original documents: a log from the Admiral's first voyage, his letters, and reports written by Columbus's son and by Columbus's comrades. "Columbus was an expert at utilizing the knowledge available at that time. He had a plumb bob, hourglasses, a cross staff used to measure latitude by lining up the sun with the lower edge of the horizon, and he understood Arabian astrology. It is impressive to see how far he got with all this knowledge. On the other hand, he was very pigheaded and obstinate, much too set in his ways. There were solutions and possibilities that he just didn't see because he preferred to believe his own lies."

Like Nombre de Dios, the town of Portobelo today is fairly run-down: a few bars, houses with crumbling walls and corrugated-iron roofs. Eerily, skulls lie strewn around the grounds of the cemetery; inhabitants have stopped caring about proper burial of the dead. Yet the town is nonetheless beautifully situated: nestled beside a bay, surrounded on all sides by hills covered with jungle vegetation. Once Spain's main shipping center in the New World, Portobelo still features the ruins of three fortification rings and a huge tonnage of old cannons. The town was virtually impregnable from the sea, which is why Henry Morgan seized Portobelo by land. Around 1670 four hundred of his buccaneers stormed one fortification after another, gaining a triumphant victory for England. Today the town draws pilgrims from all over the country. Some crawl to the San Felipe Church on their knees in veneration of the Cristo Negro, the Black Jesus, Panama's most famous shrine.

Columbus arrived in Portobelo some five hundred years ago, hence the reason explorers have traditionally set out from here to look for the wreck of the *Vizcaína*. Nothing was ever found. That doesn't necessarily mean that a wreck isn't lying somewhere off Portobelo. The seabed is extraordinarily muddy. A ship can be buried under ten or fifteen feet of silt and never be discovered.

The next day, their second day at the Nombre de Dios site, the divers had come to a few conclusions about what they'd seen. "I always try to put myself in the position of the person who lost the ship," said Keppler. It was clear to him that the ship had not run aground but sank, the bow facing the beach. "Maybe Columbus anchored in an offshore wind to transfer the load or to scuttle the ship. He probably anchored one of the other ships directly next to it." Sailors call this technique, when ships are anchored so close together that they touch, "yardarm and yardarm."

The sea was calm and visibility excellent. The divers measured the cannonballs and anchors. They found thirteen falconets (small breech-loading swivel guns) and three mortars, lying intertwined. After five centuries in the water, they had grown together to form one great big lump and were impossible to separate by hand.

During a break Keppler offered his assessment. "There are cannons lying underneath the anchors. That doesn't make any sense, unless the anchors were lying above deck and the cannons were below as part of the load. The load is much like that of a cargo ship or like a vessel that has taken on the load from other ships. There are too many cannons for too few cannonballs. The rump is in excellent shape. The ribs are tightly drawn; the ship was stable. It is well built."

At two o'clock that afternoon, clouds began to gather and the sea turned choppy. Down at the site, visibility had deteriorated, and the current and the waves were making the sand swirl. The divers might have been able to feel their way along the wreck, but they could no longer see much of anything. So they reassembled on the boat, eating sandwiches and drinking water. Karl Vandenhole had spent the day looking for metal fittings in the wood, carefully sweeping the sand aside and feeling his way along the planks. Again, they had found no metal. "There are these fat stone cannonballs," he noted. "How long did the Spaniards sail off with stone cannonballs?" "Until the early sixteenth century," replied Carlos Fitzgerald. Fitzgerald is an archaeologist from Panama City who had arrived that afternoon. Given that the bad weather had forced the team to postpone their dive, Fitzgerald suggested that he take the team of divers back to Portobelo. He wanted, he said, to show them some other treasures.

At a bend in the road near the entrance to the harbor of Portobelo sits a flat, red-roofed building surrounded by a wire-mesh fence. Outside are eight concrete tanks, each half-filled with fresh water. These tanks, explained Fitzgerald, contained the first artifacts salvaged from the wreck in the bay of Playa Damas. One tank contained clay shards, the second pieces of wood. Ballast stones had been collected in the third, stone cannonballs in the fourth. The largest of the tanks contained all the heavy artifacts—the cannons, swivel guns, cutlasses, and anchor chains. A glance at the cannons told them some were quite antique—they featured a breechloader that needed to be removed after every shot—and others were modern wrought-iron cannons. All in all, the team counted five different types of cannons.

"What a mess," grumbled Keppler. He then offered a theory about the hodgepodge of weapons before them. "That's just like Columbus. He was badly equipped and he'd also taken on board the weapons from the *Gallega*."

Every artifact carried an identification tag. The one marked "Z 42," for example, was a falconet, a small cannon used in the sixteenth and seventeenth centuries. Still, Keppler's team was startled to find that these artifacts were so vulnerable, their tanks protected only by wire-mesh fencing. Nobody had treated them for preservation; nobody had worked on them; nobody had even thought to note down where they had been taken from the wreck. There was one paltry sketch and no map. Carlos Fitzgerald expressed his outrage to his guests. "This is potentially Panama's cultural heritage, one of the most important wrecks of all time.

They might not realize it now, but the way people are handling this is amateurish."

What the team had discovered was that at this point, though in its infancy, the Columbus project was already being buffeted by rivalries between organizations, in particular the Instituto Nacional de Cultura, the National Cultural Institute, called INAC for short, and a small company called Investigaciones Marinas del Istmo, or IMDI for short. INAC was located in the capital, Panama City, and its officials claimed to have an archaeological interest in wrecks such as this. They wanted to excavate the ship and see it restored. Furthermore, they said, they planned to build a museum that would benefit the population of Panama. Run by the state, INAC has, many believe, all the shortcomings of a governmental organization. Carlos Fitzgerald, for example, who now teaches in Panama City but who worked for INAC for many years, had effectively ignored the wreck until he got a call from Vandenhole.

IMDI was founded by Nilda Vázquez and her son Ernesto Cordovez, to assert their claim to all wrecks found off the Panamanian coast. To this end, they had obtained a permit from the Ministerio de Economía y Finanzas, the Ministry of Economy and Finance. IMDI wanted to ensure that the wreck would be exploited for maximum financial gain. IMDI's majority shareholder is Gassan Salama, who was at this point the governor of the province of Colón and known as a savvy entrepreneur inside Panama's "free trade zone."

Nilda Vázquez lived just a few feet away from the freshwater tanks. Her house boasted a magnificent view of the bay of Portobelo. There were photos on the wall inside, one of them showing her standing with fabled American treasure diver Mel Fisher. Vázquez had studied journalism at Florida State University, then returned home to manage a restaurant. When the Americans left Panama, she had opened Diver's Haven; later she went into real estate. "Everything has its price," she liked to repeat.

"Nobody in this country thinks ahead, and that is why this country is in such a state," she told us. Vázquez used to work for

INAC, running a museum. She had contacts and that is why the IMDI treasure hunters were able to obtain a permit from the former INAC director, entitling them to "exclusive rights to conduct archaeological exploration." This was according to Saturio Segarra, IMDI's attorney. He showed us the contract, which stated only that they had been granted the right to produce a video documentary. There was no mention of salvaging or conservation or exclusivity. Because the government had failed to act when the shipwreck was first discovered off Nombre de Dios, a very real and urgent problem had presented itself. The artifacts were the rightful property of INAC and the state of Panama, but they remained in the hands of the treasure hunters from IMDI, which owned the house with the freshwater tanks just outside Portobelo.

There was immediate worry they would announce that the cannons had belonged to Columbus, then put them on the open market. "We will see" was Gassan Salama's comment when asked about this. "After all," he added, "we have invested money, and we want our money back."

The wreck presented a classic case of the conflict that exists everywhere between archaeologists and those seeking a profit. One side calls the other thieves and looters, and the other considers its rivals snobs and sticklers. One wants to devote years to doing the detective work and be rewarded with fame through publications; and the other wants adventure, money, and fame. Both sides hate each other. Here in Portobelo, Fitzgerald the archaeologist and Vázquez the treasure hunter railed against each other. Fitzgerald quoted from a "legally binding" resolution dating back to October 2001 that stipulated that all shipwrecks found off the coast automatically belonged to Panama's national cultural heritage. Vázquez countered that her rights to the shipwreck off Nombre de Dios were much older.

"Nilda's whole house is stuffed full of coins and cannons she's stolen from the ocean floor," Fitzgerald informed us solemnly.

"Did you know that he's gay?" whispered Vázquez.

Squabbling aside, legal action had already been filed, ensuring that Fitzgerald and Vázquez would probably never find common ground. When Fitzgerald had announced his intention to show the artifacts in the freshwater tanks to Keppler's team, he had been forced to show his papers to Segarra and endure, he said, an hour of shouting and yelling. Discussions tend to be quite vocal in Panama. Fitzgerald eventually did gain access to the tanks, and now he could hardly contain himself. He climbed in and started pointing things out.

"This will provide us with so many results over the next few years," he explained. "Here, for example, there's a tiny leftover bit of burnt honey on this piece of ceramic. We can have that chemically analyzed and—with a little luck—we can determine its origin and age. The same goes for the wood. Or the stones."

Fitzgerald was not a Columbus aficionado nor much of an admirer. "He was so brutal, so merciless, and so self-righteous. But," he added, "as someone who shaped the history of the world, he has to be of interest to every historian and every archaeologist." When Columbus landed in Panama, he changed the face of the country. "Between one and two million people died from war and disease at that time," said Fitzgerald. "Tribes like the Cuevas disappeared entirely, and others were forced to move further east. No," he concluded, "one cannot say that Columbus is venerated in Panama."

Yet as Fitzgerald stood among all the artifacts in the tanks, the pieces of wood that were crumbling because of wormholes, he could not help himself. "I really feel a connection with the history of my country." Then he climbed out of the tanks, was subjected to a little more verbal abuse from Nilda Vázquez, and departed.

A few days later, the team prepared for its final dive off Nombre de Dios. Klaus Keppler heaved the scuba tank on his back, pulled on his gloves, adjusted his mask and fins, and picked up his knife. He retrieved three pieces of wood, cutting them out of the wreck, and collected a few ballast stones and some pottery shards. Once back on shore, the items were wrapped in cellophane and placed in a cooler, then driven to the German Embassy in Panama City. With "Im Dol 2-6, Berlin" printed on the address label next to the words "Diplomatic Cargo," the wood from Nombre de Dios was shipped off to the German Archaeological Institute in Berlin.

There are people who perform tasks that take years before revealing whether their labors have been successful or in vain. Dr. Karl-Uwe Heussner has such a job. He is a dendrochronologist, an expert at determining the age and origin of wood.

When the cooler from Panama arrived in March 2003, Heussner removed a small piece of wood from it, cut off a sample, and placed it under a microscope. "This one's a close call," he announced immediately. Heussner, sporting a long beard and tousled hair, studied prehistory at Humboldt University, located in former East Germany, before joining the Academy of Sciences in East Berlin; he became part of the German Archaeological Institute in 1988. His windowless office contained stacks of files. The computer monitor flashed with graphs and curves. On the table was a Leica ICA microscope.

Dendrochronology dates trees through their rings. Each year as it grows, a tree adds a layer of wood to its trunk and branches. These rings are produced by the tree's absorption of oxygen and other materials from the atmosphere. After experts like Heussner "read" these rings, they can sometimes draw conclusions about the environmental conditions that produced them—indicating changes in temperature and levels of moisture. Many millions of wood samples have been examined all over the world by dozens of institutes and research centers, and the results are millions of curves and graphs that can now be used for comparative studies. An ideal specimen for a dendrochronological analysis would have plentiful annual rings, which would in turn be capable of producing a nice graph and exact values. The bark has to be intact, revealing the youngest tree ring. If this is the case, the wood can be precisely dated. If the wood sample happens to have been sawn off at an angle to the tree rings, however, rendering the number of tree rings too low, it becomes difficult to classify and date the wood. "We need at least fifty rings. One hundred would be better," said Heussner.

He immediately identified the first Panama sample as North European oak. This would seem only logical in the case of a Spanish ship. During the fifteenth century, Spain imported most of its oak wood from the Baltic. Heussner then counted the tree rings. "Thirty-five," he concluded. "That won't help us." The second and third samples turned out to have even fewer rings, thirty and twenty-one, respectively. "Unfortunately, we can't do anything with them," said Heussner. "It's hopeless. We can't classify them." Two of the wood samples were packed up again and sent off for carbon-14 analysis at the Christian-Albrechts-University in Kiel, located in northern Germany.

Professor Consuelo Varela knows that learning anything concrete about Columbus's voyages depends to some degree on chance. She is a senior researcher at the Institute in Spanish and Hispanic-American Archival Sciences in Seville and married to fellow professor and Columbus expert Juan Gil. For forty years Varela has made Columbus the focus of her work. While chain-smoking heavy Ducados cigarettes, Varela recounted stories about the life of the explorer, digressing from time to time but never losing sight of the larger context. She offers her reasons for why the times had produced a man like Columbus and indeed launched the whole Age of Discovery.

By the end of the fifteenth century, Europe had survived decades of epidemics and wars; its inhabitants hungered for luxury. "It was an era of great expansion," Varela explained. Gold had become a precious commodity, especially to the churches. Europeans needed slaves to work the fields, and they needed whale oil to illuminate their expanding cities. These were riches that could only be supplied by seafarers and whalers. As the demand for these goods grew, so did the need for men who could maneuver ships and find countries to satisfy these demands. "This was the best time ever for sailors," said Varela.

For years Columbus's fourth voyage had interested Varela no more than his other three journeys. Historians knew the identity of the significant people on board with him, but the lesser figures were forgotten as the files themselves became lost. In 1985 Varela was researching in the Archivo General of Spain's old fortress city of Simancas. There she found shelves laden with literally tons of paper, most of it unsorted and unexamined: deeds of ownership, receipts, transcripts of legal proceedings, freight lists, and court rulings. Contained within them were centuries' worth of information about daily life and business, committed to paper because someone at the time had considered them noteworthy. Now these documents were extremely fragile; many were so worn that they crumbled to dust when Varela tried, as carefully as she could, to separate the pages.

Varela had searched through the archives without knowing precisely what she was after. She rummaged through a pile of letters—of no great significance—to the Spanish royal court. Many were folded tightly, as was the custom in those days. Buried in the pile was a piece of paper that was not a letter. On it were columns of figures and dates. After studying the list, Varela realized that it contained the names of all the crew members on the fourth journey, information that had been missing for centuries. It was a sensational find because of the detail. The columns provided not merely the names of everyone aboard Columbus's four ships but also their respective tasks, ages, and wages. The list included five people named Colón: Columbus himself, his brother Bartolomeo, his son Fernando, as well as his nephews Juan Antonio and Andrea—leading Varela to conclude that this fourth voyage was very much a family venture. She noted that Columbus had made a subtle distinction between the inner circle of his family and his more distant relatives. He himself, Fernando, and Bartolomeo were listed under the surname Colón, the name under which Columbus hoped to found a new dynasty to rule the New World. The nephews, however, went under his old name Colombo, the name belonging to Columbus's father and the name that the Admiral of the Ocean Sea apparently no longer wanted to bear.

"The Spaniards always kept an eye on the finances," said Varela, which is why she and her husband have always stressed the importance of following the money trail. Bookkeepers often proved more reliable sources of information than the explorers themselves, who were primarily interested in fashioning their own legends. The list that Varela had discovered in 1985 told of the lives and deaths of the men who sailed to Panama with Columbus. Crew lists were important for disbursement of wages, as the crown paid sailors daily rather than on a weekly or monthly basis. Amassing riches was the administrators' prime objective in financing this voyage. The officials were therefore painstakingly accurate about noting when precisely a sailor had died or who had jumped ship and shacked up on an island with a native girl. No work also meant no wages for relatives back home in Spain.

Juan Gil explained that this crew list also suggested the drama taking place behind the scenes, exposing the extent of Columbus's downfall, especially when weighed against other documents, such as the one Gil had found several years before. It was a letter from Columbus, involving the weaponry that would go aboard the ships on this fourth voyage. "Columbus clearly begs for exactly forty-eight cannons," explained Gil. "That makes twelve cannons for each of the four ships. But from the crew list, we know that he had only three cannoneers on board. Two served on the *Capitana* and one on the *Santiago*." These cannoneers were specialists. "A cannon couldn't be fired by just anyone." Columbus would certainly have needed more gunners to operate the forty-eight cannons he had requested. Gil concluded that the Admiral had not received anywhere near as many people and cannons as he would have needed. "That shows just how much his reputation had suffered. His fame was waning. Maybe the men just didn't want to sail with him anymore."

Nobody at the court of Castile really knew who was responsible for what they termed "the Indies." They argued over expenses. Everyone wanted gold; nobody wanted to incur debt.
"Due to this complexity, until now nobody has attempted to draw
up a list of payments for this voyage," Varela told us. In one of
her articles, she wrote: "Apart from the regular payments, crew
members customarily signed over the rights to their wages to
each other, leading to a vast number of unsorted and incomplete
facts, particularly when they involved a person who traveled on
more than one voyage."

In the archive at Simancas, Varela came across a report by
Diego de Porras, the crown's official scribe or notary during the
fourth voyage. Porras kept a four-month account of advance payments and listed the crew according to their respective positions—captain, officers, carpenters, sailors, soldiers, and ship's
boys. His report indicated that 139 men sailed with Columbus on
his fourth voyage. This number posed a problem for Varela. One
document indicated the name of one Diego Alvarez, but he was
nowhere to be found in other lists. Eventually Varela concluded
that this must refer to Diego "El Negro," the slave belonging to
Diego Tristán. The documents also mentioned the "tailor Baltasar," whose real name was presumably Baltasar de Aragón, a
seaman who had lent money to a number of sailors and who was
therefore listed as a creditor.

Over the years Varela has unearthed many details. She has discovered, for example, that the *Capitana* had officially been christened *La Gracia de Dios* and that the *Santiago de Palos* also sailed
under the name *Bermuda*. "We were able to find 146 crew members as well as four or five that are doubtful, but that is eleven
more than in Porras's crew list, so we come up with an exact figure of 150," she explained proudly. "Just as Colón says."

After being treated and prepared, the wood samples from the
coast of Panama were sent through the particle accelerator at
the Leibniz Laboratory for Radiometric Dating and Isotope Research at the University of Kiel during the summer of 2003. The

accelerator, which resembles an oil tank with some odd-looking curves to it, sits in a vast room (room 6), in which the humidity remains at a constant 50 percent and the temperature measures precisely seventy degrees. We noted that there were three emergency exits. The machine itself featured a number of warning labels, signs carrying symbols of lightning flashes. "Switch OFF if Alarm Sounds," they read. The accelerator activates three million volts, forcing particles to fly through its curves at initial speeds of 370 miles per second and ultimately accelerating to ten times that speed.

Professor Pieter Meiert Grootes was the man in charge. Originally from Holland and now in his sixties, he studied isotope physics and mass spectrometry and spent seventeen years working at the University of Washington in Seattle, doing research on the global climate and the Antarctic. The rooms here in Kiel are labeled "AMS Samples" (room 10) or "Target Production" (room 8). The corridors seem endless, and the whole place smells like a hospital. Grootes did his best to explain in layman's terms what C_{14} analysis was. Carbon-14 dating is a method of determining the age of certain archaeological artifacts of biological origin up to about five thousand years old. The radioactive carbon that is contained in the atmosphere has remained at a virtually constant level for thousands of years. Carbon usually contains twelve atoms—six neutrons and six protons—as well as six electrons. Some nuclei have seven neutrons, and these comprise C_{13}. And there are nuclei with eight neutrons, which are unstable and break down—hence C_{14}. The method determines age by the rate of decay, or the half-life of carbon. After 5,730 years, half of the remaining C_{14} material will have decayed, and after 11,460 years only a quarter is left. And so on. "If you have reference values, data, tables, then you can compare how much C_{14} is left and how much C_{14} must have existed in the first place," explained Grootes. "That is how you can measure how much time has passed. That is basically what radiocarbon age determination does."

Analysis begins with a chemical process. C_{14} nuclei are produced through cosmic radiation. Grootes explained that "if you isolate the outermost ring, you get a sample of the atmosphere during the last year of growth." Wood has to be turned into graphite, pure carbon, so carbonates and many other additives have to be eliminated from the sample. In order to do that, the sample is first cleaned with a 1 percent solution of hydrochloric acid, then sodium hydroxide solution, and finally with hydrochloric acid again. Each step takes four hours and has to be done at sixty degrees. What remains after all the cleaning is the pure cellulose material, enclosed in a quartz vial together with copper oxide and silver. As Grootes explained, "The sample is then vacuum-pumped until all the air disappears, and then an oven burns all the organic material, leaving us with CO_2, nitrogen oxide, sulfur oxide, and halogen compounds. Silver is added, for silver has cleaning properties; it binds sulfur oxide and the halogen compounds."

That, in a nutshell, is how a wood sample gets turned into a CO_2 gas sample. Iron and hydrogen turn CO_2 into a minute amount of graphite; this graphite gets pressed into a small container that is then fed into the particle accelerator. The primary objective is to measure the relative frequency of neutrons and protons. The carbon is bombarded with cesium ions, which produces negative carbon ions. This beam is accelerated and sent through magnetic fields, whereby the lighter particles are deflected more strongly than the heavier particles. At the end you count the number of C14 ions that have made it to the finish. The entire process takes about five weeks.

Grootes's team had labeled the two wood samples from Panama "KIA 20251" and "KIA 20252." Both wood samples originated from the same woodblock but were around twenty-five rings apart. A few weeks later, the results came in: KIA 20251 dated to between 1445 and 1472. And KIA 20252 dated to between 1449 and 1489. In his report Grootes wrote that the difference would suggest the year in which the tree was felled, and hence that, with a probability of 68.3 percent, "the wood dates back to a time period between 1469 and 1487. If you combine both values, then you get a pretty exact distribution, which would put the formation of the outermost wood ring at between 1470 and 1486. One can well imagine that a ship was built using this wood maybe in 1490, and that the ship was no longer seaworthy in 1502. It doesn't prove that the ship belonged to Columbus, but it is an indication that it could have belonged to Columbus. At any rate, it doesn't prove that it couldn't have belonged to him."

Filipe Castro and Donny Hamilton, among the most prominent underwater archaeologists working today, decided to weigh in. Hamilton, born and raised on his father's junkyard in Levelland, Texas, is president of the Institute of Nautical Archaeology. One of his professors at Texas A&M and one of the world's foremost experts on Iberian shipwrecks, Castro was born in Santarém, near Lisbon, the son of a veterinarian. Hamilton spent ten years in Jamaica, working underwater until he had excavated substantial portions of the sunken city of Port Royal, the last home of Henry Morgan and the place where the pirate rulers of the sea once gambled away their gold and spent the rest on drink. Although Hamilton was on sabbatical from Texas A&M working on a book about Port Royal, he and Castro went to Panama in September 2003 to examine the shipwreck in the bay of Playa Damas.

"The best part is when all the excitement dies down and you dive for the first time," said Castro. He explained what he and Hamilton would be looking for. "In the long term, two things are important. One is the future work with the wreck. That is why we will examine the underwater visibility, the current, the ocean bed, basically how we will be able to work here." He was already thinking ahead to the logistics of a future archaeological excavation. "We are talking about a project here that could take up to five years: one year for the underwater work, four for conservation," he explained. "You're talking about a team of sixteen people and costs of at least a million and a half for the cranes, ships, and containers if you want to transport the entire wreck to Texas and back at some stage."

Castro's other priority was a preliminary assessment of the

wreck. "For a long time, ships were the most complex things people ever built. We want to assess the importance of this wreck and see what else we can find, how many artifacts, how much wood."

Hamilton and Castro stayed underwater for two hours, knowing that their assessment would carry tremendous weight in the world of underwater archaeology. When they finally resurfaced, they looked ecstatic. Instead of climbing back into the boat, they treaded water, talking enthusiastically.

"That is a fantastic site," Hamilton shouted. "There are huge wooden beams, these anchors, and two big fat bombards. This ship is old. Very old." And then he dove again.

"The anchors are extraordinarily large," said Castro. "Actually they're too big for a fifty-ton ship. That's an incredible arsenal down there."

Hamilton resurfaced and removed his mask. "The way the cannons are lying there, it's as if the ship had tilted to the starboard side first and the cannons had rolled over."

"They're not loaded. You can see that even through all the incrustations. These cannons were part of the load," added Castro.

Then they both dove down to take yet another look. Diving down to the bow of the wreck and the crisscrossed anchors, they needed, they later told us, only a few minutes to make their discovery. They saw three anchor rings. The third was covered in incrustations and coral and was hard to detect. Previous divers, none of whom were novices, had only seen two anchors. Hamilton and Castro took exact measurements, diving from cannon to cannon, feeling their way carefully along the timbers, measuring the thickness of the beams. A difference of a few centimeters can be quite substantial.

As soon as they had resurfaced, Hamilton and Castro began discussing the site. Their preliminary assessment was that the ship was old and that it was Spanish; they could tell that immediately from the wood, the shards, and the weapons. They also announced that it was in fantastically good condition. Three ships from the Age of Discovery have been found in the New World; this was by far the best preserved of the three.

"A sensation," enthused Castro. "It's a ship that definitely has to be examined, excavated, and conserved with the utmost care," added Hamilton. "We can't afford to make any mistakes." Up to this point, the two experts hadn't mentioned a word about whose ship it might have been.

"Columbus, Columbus, Columbus." Castro grinned broadly. "I'll commit myself to a time frame of fifty years. This ship sank in the first half of the sixteenth century, more likely in the first quarter. It certainly does look like this could be the oldest ship ever found off the coast of the Americas."

"The shards and the weapons look archaic compared to the European standard," said Hamilton. His first assessment—"Spanish, early sixteenth century"—tallied with Castro's, but he added, "The anchors seem too large. The planks are thick; it could have been a larger ship, but we still don't know enough. We do know that Columbus didn't have much money and was forced to scrounge around for his equipment. So it is feasible that he just took any anchor he could get."

"We don't know enough to say that it's probably Columbus's ship. But we do know enough to say that it is possible. And logical," said Castro.

"We're scientists. We would rather prove that it's his ship than merely claim that it's his ship," added Hamilton.

Proving it means resolving the thorny problem of semantics. In his 1504 letter, Columbus had written the ship had sunk "near Portobelo." In his logbook he reported that he had lost the *Vizcaína* in Portobelo. "Portobelo" is the one constant in the written evidence. Diego Méndez de Segura, one of his men, wrote "Portobelo." Even Columbus's son Fernando noted, "We held on our course till we reached Portobelo; there we had to abandon the *Vizcaína* because she was drawing much water and because her planking was completely riddled by the shipworm." According to three original sources, the *Vizcaína* sank in Portobelo, a day's journey from the bay of Playa Damas, even under full sails.

Consuelo Varela remained open to the possibility. "Yes, it could still be the *Vizcaína*. At least the location doesn't rule it out."

Varela and her husband, Juan Gil, work together, though they don't always come to the same conclusions. Varela posited that the "Portobelo" mentioned in the log and the biography might refer to the whole region. After all, the readers for those writing these letters or travelogues lived in Europe. Neither the *Vizcaína* nor the location of her final resting place would have been of any particular importance. What mattered was that a ship had been lost and that it had not been due to a mistake on Columbus's part. Varela further pointed out that as Fernando had been a child when the *Vizcaína* sank, he had written his father's biography some thirty years after the event (it wasn't published until 1571). "It is quite possible he couldn't remember exactly where it happened."

Gil shook his head thoughtfully. He couldn't get beyond the fact that all the sources indicated Portobelo.

The couple went to Nombre de Dios to view the wreck. A local fisherman took them out to the site on a small boat. Varela and Gil are scholars, however, not divers, so they examined it from the surface. Gil thought that the wreck was too large to be the *Vizcaína*. He conceded, however, that he couldn't be sure.

The fate of the *Vizcaína* reflects the mysteries that continue to swirl around Columbus himself. Scholars have argued about his national origins and his religion, about the maps he used. Even where he first touched land in 1492 remains in dispute, as is the issue of where his remains lie buried today, as we shall see. To those of us looking at him five centuries after his death in 1506, we cannot help but wonder whether he could have fully comprehended the enormity of his discovery. His life has captured the imagination of so many for so long. Many believe that at last we are edging closer toward answering at least some of these questions. First, however, we need to tell his story.

———

CHAPTER 2

Man Without a Home, Man Without a Name

The Admiral, although endowed with all the qualities that his great task required, chose to leave in obscurity all that related to his birthplace and family. . . . Just as most of his affairs were directed by a secret Providence, so the variety of his name and surname was not without its mystery.

—From Fernando Colón's biography of his father, published in 1571

The wind swept down the Apennine gorges, across concrete piers, over rusty quays and the potholed freeway that runs along what used to be the beach before Genoa's city fathers decided that a bypass would better serve the city. The airport is small and shabby. There isn't even enough room above the main portal to provide the full name of the man after whom the airport is named, so it reads: "Aeroporto C. Colombo." Genoa is the birthplace of the man who set off in the Middle Ages and landed in the Renaissance; the man who irrevocably changed the Old World by discovering the New; and the man who was ultimately broken by his success. Genoa used to be called "the Proud One." For centuries Genova, la Superba was the hub of maritime trade in the Mediterranean, and its harbor lay at the apex of major trade routes. But the city was unable to deal with the advent of the modern era. Sandwiched between craggy mountains and the ocean, it was left with no other option than to expand vertically. For centuries Genoans have constructed high-rise buildings, stacking them high on terraces up the steep mountainsides. Alternatively, they have burrowed deep into the ground, excavating beneath the historic ruins to build multistory parking garages.

Battling through the exhaust fumes in the streets' canyons, visitors inevitably land at one of the city's most chaotic plazas, the Piazza Dante. A steep and narrow alley leads off the main square, under the arch of the Porta Soprana, and directly into the history behind the discovery of America. With its fortified towers, the old city gate was built around 1100 to protect Genoa from its foes. Now it protects the old part of the city from the modern, offering a haven of peace and quiet amid the noise of traffic. At one time this flagstone path, Vico Dritto di Ponticello, was the address of a family named Colombo.

Wedged between a parking lot for mopeds and a bus stop stands a narrow two-story home, looking forlorn, like part of a period-piece movie set left behind. The bricks are crumbling, seemingly held together only by sprawling Virginia creepers. A corridor, barely three feet wide, leads into the unfurnished rooms. Parts of the floor have been torn up by archaeologists, and the supporting beams are now preserved under glass. A random array of sea charts covers the walls, and a wheel-mounted miniature cannon stands in the corner. Outside, leaning next to the door, is a large display case containing a copy of the lease contract for the property, dated January 18, 1455. The name of the leaseholder is Domenico Colombo, a wool weaver. At the time of purchase, Domenico had a three-year-old son christened Cristoforo.

It is said that Columbus grew up in this vine-covered house overlooking the ocean. From the Porta Soprana, the horizon is just visible as it melts into the haze, swallowing the ships at the dividing line between sky and water. If Cristoforo was like all other boys, he would have wondered what might lie beyond the horizon.

Cristoforo was the first child born to his parents, Domenico and Susanna. There followed a brother, Giovanni Pellegrino, but he probably died at an early age. His next brother, Bartolomeo, would later become Columbus's most loyal ally. He was a fighter and, unlike Cristoforo, a womanizer. Bartolomeo went far in life, ultimately being awarded the title of *adelantado,* or governor of the province of the islands of the West Indies. Giacomo, whom the Spaniards later called Diego, was the baby of the family, born seventeen years after Cristoforo, who doted on him, promoting and protecting him, such as during his second voyage into the New World. Yet Giacomo never turned into an able seaman or an adventurer. He was a little meeker than the others and ultimately joined the clergy. The Colombo family also had a daughter, Bianchinetta. Little is known of her, other than that she later married a cheesemonger who took over the house in the Vico Dritto.

The display case containing the lease agreement also contains a proclamation, Genoa's assertion of claim to the man who found the New World, albeit by order of Spain. It states that Columbus was unequivocally Italian, or rather Genoese. For centuries, however, Columbus experts from various countries have cast doubt on the assertion. Some argue that Columbus was from Spain. The provinces of Galicia, Extremadura, and Catalonia, for example, have long battled over the honor of claiming Columbus as their own. Others allege that he originally came from Majorca, born the illegitimate son of a prince. Corsica and Greece have maintained that Columbus was born there. Serious scholars—as well as patriotic enthusiasts—have even brought Poland, England, and France into the list of contenders. It was long assumed that Columbus was a devout Catholic. Most researchers now presume that he was Jewish. Columbus himself made every effort to conceal all traces of his origins, as can be seen in this boastful letter to the Castilian royal family: "I am not the first Admiral of my family. Let them call me, then, by what name they will, for after all, David, that wisest of kings, tended sheep and was later made king of Jerusalem, and I am the servant of Him Who raised David to that high estate."

Columbus went on to earn many names, but he was probably baptized Cristoforo Colombo. His son Fernando sometimes called him Colonus but usually referred to him, as we've seen, as Admiral. The Spaniards call him Cristóbal Colón, and Colón was of course the name that he bestowed on his direct descendants. The Portuguese use Cristovão Colom, but internationally Columbus has become generally accepted. Columbus himself preferred a modified version of his name, much like a nobleman who needs only a Christian name: Christoferens—meaning "Christ-bearer." That is how he usually signed documents (or, to make it even more complicated, Xpo Ferens, "Xpo" being the Greek and Spanish acronym for Christ; *ferens,* Latin for "messenger" or "bearer"). Columbus considered himself an emissary of Christ, the man who had brought Christ across the vast ocean to the heathens. In later life Columbus signed documents with a four-line *sigla,* a kind of monogram he had devised for himself. The highly complicated design continues to puzzle scientists and historians, who are still unable to decipher all of its meanings; that was probably Columbus's intention.

Further confusing the issue of Columbus's origins is that he seems to have had no real mother tongue. He rarely wrote in Italian or even used Italian expressions. Historians have only ever found two brief notes in the margins of books suggesting that he spoke any Italian at all. Linguists have carefully examined the logbook of his first voyage, the original of which has been lost, and his handwritten letters, analyzing his style, grammar, sentence structure, vocabulary, and handwriting. They have concluded that Columbus wrote clearly, quickly, and without elaboration. He didn't write like a poet, in other words, or a scientist or a highly educated man; he wrote like a merchant, a Spanish merchant at that. He tended to employ Castilian, punctuated by Portuguese, even when writing to acquaintances in Genoa or to his house bank, the Banco di San Giorgio, which was located there. He never made any references to poets from his homeland, never compared anything he saw with regions in Italy. And he virtually never mentioned his family or relatives in Italy.

Kirkpatrick Sale—author of the controversial book *The Conquest of Paradise,* published in 1990—wrote, "For the trail that Colón left behind is so confused and incomplete, from his birthdate and birthplace on, as to suggest more than mere carelessness about fact-and-fiction on his part.... The darkness there suggests rather that he was a man truly without a past that he could define, without a home, or roots, or family, without ever a sense, or love, of place. His early years are dark because, in a sense, they are empty." Sale believes Columbus to be the incarnation of aggression in Western civilization, the founding father to all the exploitation and genocide that followed in his wake. However valid his point of view, Sale wasn't quite accurate with regard to the family. Columbus did have roots and a native land. Admittedly, he wanted nothing to do with them, renouncing his origins with such stubborn consistency that not even his son Fernando could say exactly where his father was originally from. Shortly before his death in 1539, Fernando, a dedicated scholar and bibliophile, had sat down to write the biography of his father. Although he had amassed a vast collection of his father's writings, he found very little pertaining to his family and his childhood. The original edition of Fernando's biography has been lost; the version we have today is an Italian translation dating from the sixteenth century, the *Historie della vita e dei fatti di Cristoforo Colombo.* Nonetheless, it remains the authoritative source for Columbus historians. In it, Fernando described his travels through northern Italy in a vain attempt to locate lost relatives.

> *I have not been able to find how or where they [the relatives] lived, although the Admiral himself says in a letter that he and his ancestors always followed the sea. To inform myself better on this point, in passing through Cugureo [in Italy] I tried to learn what I could from two brothers of the name of Colombo,*

who were the richest men of that place and were said to be re-
lated to the Admiral in some way; but as the younger of the two
was more than a hundred years old, I could learn nothing. I do
not think that we in whose veins flows his blood should feel less
proud on that account, for I think better that all our glory
should come from him than that we should go about inquiring
if his father was a merchant or went hunting with falcons.

Because Columbus himself acted so mysteriously, speculation about his origins continues. Proponents of the Portuguese
theory argue that Cristovão Colom's mother tongue was obviously Portuguese, citing his extensive use of the language and the
fact that he bestowed Portuguese names on dozens of islands he
christened on his voyages. Moreover, they point out, were Columbus really the son of a humble wool weaver from Genoa,
how did he manage to marry the daughter of a Portuguese nobleman at a time when class distinction was everything?

What Fernando Colón failed to find does in fact exist: a paper
trail leading back to the Colombo family of Genoa and to a certain Cristoforo Colombo.

This trail begins behind the pale yellow facade of an old city
palace, the Archivio di Stato di Genova. Visitors, mostly students
and researchers, are permitted entry only by appointment, for it
is here that the city has collated all its documents since the year
1200. Storerooms spread out over five floors contain tons of documents, centuries of everyday life condensed by generations of
town clerks, scribes, and notaries. Among these thousands of forgotten and obsolete documents, archivists occasionally find papers that shed light on the case of Christopher Columbus. And
no one knows the trail of his early years better than Dr. Patrizia
Schiappacasse, the guardian of these documents.

Friendly but resolute, Dr. Schiappacasse emphasized that she
was an archivist. Archivists are not historians, she remarked, for
they don't draw conclusions; they don't interpret and they don't
analyze. They connect loose ends when they find conclusive

evidence in documents, and therefore think nothing of assertions based upon theory or even the laws of probability. The Columbus house on the Vico Dritto presents a case in point. Schiappacasse pointed out that while it's possible that this was the house referred to in the lease agreement, it is by no means as certain as the tourist guidebooks and the city council would lead one to believe. The lease agreement states only that the house was located on the Vico Dritto, "between the buildings of Giovanni Palarania and Antonio Bondo." At the time this was all that the signatories needed to know, for they knew the neighbors referred to in the lease. But today nobody knows who these two people were. Several small homes were built in the fifteenth century in this alley. Of that much Schiappacasse is sure. But as only one house has survived over the centuries, the city had a plaque erected in front of it. Since then everyone has simply assumed that this was actually Christopher Columbus's childhood home.

That's how it is when people twist the truth to suit their needs, Schiappacasse commented, permitting herself a smile. The archivist placed her version of the truth on the large reading table in one of the dark paneled halls of the Archivio di Stato. She carefully untied cords and removed the protective wax paper to reveal yellowing documents crumbling from age. It had taken over a century, she said, to collate the eighty documents that constitute the trail leading back to the Colombo family.

On February 21, 1429, a wool weaver named Giovanni Colombo from Quinto, near Genoa, went to a notary to set the seal on an apprenticeship contract for his son Domenico with a German wool weaver named Gerardo di Brabante d'Alemagna. Domenico was eleven at the time, old enough to leave his village and his parents. Gerardo taught him well, and eleven years later, on September 6, 1440, according to another document, Colombo had become a master wool weaver. According to this document, he had achieved a degree of prosperity, enabling him to take a lease on a house near Genoa's eastern city gate, the Porta dell'Olivella. This is the house where Christopher Columbus would later be born.

At first, fate was kind to Domenico Colombo. Sometime around 1445 he married Susanna da Fontanarossa, the daughter of a fellow guild member. As an established and respected citizen, Domenico became involved in politics, an extremely dangerous game in those days, for Genoa was caught up in an embittered struggle between two families, each vying for the position of doge. Barnaba Adorno was elected on January 4, 1447, but his power rested upon the support of six hundred mercenaries belonging to King Alfonso of Aragón. The prospect of being ruled by an occupying force so enraged the citizens of Genoa that merely three weeks later, the leader of the rival faction, Giano di Campo Fregoso, carried out a bloody but successful coup. "Columbus's father must have sided with Campo Fregoso," Schiappacasse said, citing as evidence a letter of appointment signed a mere week after the victory, in which Campo Fregoso named his "beloved Domenico Colombo" warder of the Porta dell'Olivella. This was an important post, given to only the most loyal followers. The wool weaver assumed command of several men and had control over who entered and left the city. The job also paid well. Schiappacasse's files revealed two payment orders for over twenty-one lire that Colombo had earned for three months of duty, "a tidy sum of money at the time," she noted. Sometime between September and October 31, 1451, the Colombos' first son was born. Domenico named him Cristoforo, and when the child was three years old, the family moved to Vico Dritto.

Many citizens of Genoa had become prosperous, the maritime city having flourished over the preceding decades due to its century-old links to the East and its harbor. The narrow hinterland afforded the city protection and the ocean gave the city everything it needed. Ship owners, merchants, and bankers controlled Genoa, and the ships belonging to the large clans imported every kind of luxury goods—spices, fine cloths, jewels, and perfume. Two hundred years previously, the Venetian explorer Marco Polo had penetrated into the Mongolian Empire, advancing to the very source of wealth. And while his tales of gold-covered palaces met with skepticism, some measure of that skepticism melted away when convoys from the Far East, transporting some of the treasures Polo had described, began to arrive at Black Sea ports where Genoese merchant ships were docked.

Genoa's great heroes were not noble knights but ships' captains and owners. The city operated much like an import-export company, governed by the logistics of money, capital, and a business nexus. Power was in the hands of a few large families who ruled over an empire of merchants, held together by the Genoese fleet. As Paolo Emilio Taviani, a Genoese patriot and an expert on Columbus, wrote some five hundred years later, "By the fifteenth century, Genoa had an economic regime that could well be defined as capitalistic, or, if one prefers, mercantile. It had already emerged from the Middle Ages. The young Christopher Columbus grew up in this mercantile world; the notarized acts in which he appears constitute unequivocal proof thereof. Purchases, sales, interests, percentages, commissions, profits: these are the terms of a language unknown to the Middle Ages." These were also the terms that shaped Columbus's mind-set decades later, when he was developing his grand plan. The discovery of America would primarily be a business venture, one that required repayment with interest. On the day he set forth into the unknown, Columbus might have spoken of God but he was thinking of percentages. That was Columbus's inheritance from the Genoese moneybags, and it explains why Columbus was perceived as having failed so utterly. Gold ruled Genoa. "The need for gold increased with the growth of commerce and the diffusion of coins," wrote Gianni Granzotto, an Italian scholar. "There were wars to be financed, ships to launch, moneys to invest. Gold created wealth, and was at the same time a reflection of the wealth that was spreading to new classes of citizens. At the beginning of the fifteenth century, things had gotten to the point throughout Europe where the demand for gold far exceeded the supply."

As Columbus grew older, the profitable order of things began to crumble. For one thing, business dealings with the East grew increasingly difficult. A new power had risen, blocking access. In 1453, when Columbus was presumably taking his first baby steps, the Ottoman Turks conquered Constantinople, the old Christian orthodox and imperial city of Byzantium, located on the Golden Horn, the entrance to the Black Sea. The fall of this outpost of Western civilization was traumatic for all of Christendom and devastating for the Genoese. The city sent four hundred soldiers to Constantinople as reinforcements, and the survivors told of their defeat at the hands of the enemies of the true faith. What business magnates feared most, though, were the Moors blocking their passage to the East and capturing their ships in the Dardanelles. As a result, the merchants were beginning to try their luck in the West, extending trade relations with Spain and Portugal, even daring to do business with England.

The Colombo family didn't suffer greatly from Constantinople's ignominious fall. They remained relatively well-off and continued to enjoy the support of the mighty Campo Fregoso clan. Domenico was well liked, at least within his trade guild, where he held minor honorary posts and was a member of the committee for apprenticeships. Cristoforo went to the guild school, where he was taught Latin, religion, geography, and mathematics. Fernando later wrote that his father studied at the university, but this seems highly unlikely and there is no evidence to support his contention:

> Let us speak of the sciences to which he most devoted himself.
> He learned his letters at a tender age and studied enough at the
> University of Pavia to understand the geographers, of whose
> teaching he was very fond; for this reason he also gave himself
> to the study of astronomy and geometry, since these sciences are
> so closely related that one depends upon the other. And because

Ptolemy, in the beginning of his Geography, *says that one can-not be a good geographer unless one knows how to draw, too, he learned drawing, in order to be able to show the position of countries and form geographic bodies, plane and round.*

At some point in his youth, Columbus learned to draw sketches, read maps, and follow the course of the stars, and he acquired basic navigational skills. As a seafaring city-state, Genoa boasted several excellent cartographers who produced nautical charts for ships' captains. Cartography was considered both an art and a science, and good cartographers were revered. Their knowledge could help to win wars or open new markets. Domenico also taught his son how to weave. Everything boded well for a peaceful, albeit tedious life.

In the early 1460s, however, the Columbuses' world began to fall apart, mirroring the crumbling power of the Campo Fregoso family. Civil war consumed the streets and alleys of Genoa. In 1464 the last of the Campo Fregoso clan fled to Corsica, foreshadowing the fall of the Colombo family. The dukes of Milan now reigned over their old rival Genoa. Forced to leave Genoa, the family moved to the neighboring town of Savona. There is evidence that the family was now starting to have money problems. Christopher experienced firsthand how wretched life on the edge of bankruptcy could be. In a document dated March 2, 1470, Domenico is referred to as a "cloth weaver and tavern keeper." It would suggest that his former trade wasn't generating enough income to feed the family. The notary's file also notes that Columbus's father owed back pay to an apprentice. The first documented mention of Domenico's eldest son, "cristoforus filius," was no happy occasion. Both father and son were forced to borrow money from a Genoese named Gerolamo del Porto. The document reveals the extent of the family's decline in status; Domenico's word was clearly no longer enough, and Christopher, just turned eighteen, was compelled to act as a guarantor for the loan. Only a few months later, the family was once again forced to borrow money. In the bond of debt, drawn up on October 31, 1470, Christopher is described as being "over 19 years of age." Historians' calculation of Columbus's year of birth is based upon this document, which also offers insight into Columbus's character, such as his propensity for self-aggrandizement. Rather than sign his name, he used the XFRS acronym. Domenico obviously never managed to pay off his debts, causing his son to be plagued by a guilty conscience for the rest of his life. Shortly before his own death thirty-six years later, Columbus remembered the man from Genoa who had loaned them twenty ducats. He repaid the debt in his last will and testament, and—obviously still mortified by the whole affair—stipulated that nobody inform the del Porto family where the money came from. This connection between Columbus's early years and his death proves almost beyond doubt that he was born in Genoa.

Short-term loans didn't help the Colombo family. Soon Susanna was forced to sell some of the property that had been part of her dowry, and they vacated the house near the Porta dell' Olivella. Schiappacasse quoted historians who have concluded that this was when Columbus may have begun sailing. "Maybe because the family needed money. For now documents show that he traded wares. And merchants on the coast nearly always sailed." Like most Genoese children, Columbus learned to sail at a tender age. Antonio Gallo, a notary and family friend, wrote that Christopher and his brother Bartolomeo had sailed *puberes deinde facti—* "since childhood." The feel of ships' planks creaking under his feet became so completely natural to Columbus that later he couldn't even remember when he first hauled a sheet. In the logbook of his first voyage in 1492, he commented, "I have followed the sea for twenty-three years." But he told his son Fernando that he had been sailing since the age of fourteen.

In a city as cramped as Genoa, open water must have seemed inviting to the young Columbus. His father had proved that working as a wool weaver didn't get one very far in a city ruled by bankers, merchants, and sailors. Columbus had two options:

destitution or the sea life. Historians like Taviani believe that it was during this dismal time spent in Savona that Columbus decided to try his luck on the water and that this explained why the only Caribbean island that Columbus named after an Italian city is now called Saona, near Hispaniola. Savona is probably the city where Columbus first signed on to a ship that did more than just travel up and down the coast. At the time several Ligurian families dominated the very lucrative trade with Chios, an island belonging to the Sporades, an archipelago in the Aegean. Chios is Europe's farthest outpost, and only a narrow strait separates it from Asia Minor, the empire of the Turks. With its colorful bazaars and the pervasive and intoxicating smell of essential oils, the island feels like the Orient. Rosemary, sage, and thyme grow there, but it is famous for producing the best quality mastic, *Pistacia lentiscus*. The farmers used to make small cuts in the bark of the mastic tree to bleed the resin that was then used to make medicine, perfumes, and candy. The smell of mastic was so engrained in Columbus's mind that later in Cuba he believed he recognized it because a tree had a similarly aromatic smell. The patrician families Centurione and Spinola sent their ships to Chios, and it was probably Paolo di Negri, a partner of the Centurione family, who first commissioned Columbus for the trips on which he learned basic seamanship. This contact with di Negri proved very helpful in his later life.

But not every one of his journeys served the cause of peaceful trade. According to Columbus's own account, he was soon thrust into his first naval conflict. In a letter he recounted a sortie made by order of King René of Anjou from Naples, who at the time was an ally of Genoa in the ongoing war against Aragón:

> *It happened to me that King René, whom God hath taken, sent me to Tuni to capture the galleass Fernandina. And in the vicinity of the island of San Pietro off Sardinia, another galley told me that the said galliot was with two other vessels and a carrack. That perturbed my crew and they insisted that we not*

continue the voyage but rather return to Marseilles for another
ship and more men. I saw that I could not force their will with-
out risking a mutiny, and so I complied with their demand. But
I changed the alignment of the compass, we sailed through the
night and at sunrise the next day, we found ourselves off the
Cape of Carthage, while all on board were convinced we were
actually going to Marseilles.

There is no mention of the outcome of this strange episode. While it is possible that Columbus did engage in battle on behalf of King René of Anjou, and he might well have manipulated the compass, some of the details lead one to suspect Columbus simply made up the entire episode. Not even a modern state-of-the-art yacht could have sailed to the Cape of Carthage in just one night, and it is highly unlikely that Columbus, twenty years old at the time, would have been put in charge of such a risky naval venture. In his classic 1942 Pulitzer Prize–winning biography of Columbus, *Admiral of the Ocean Sea*, Samuel Eliot Morison—historian and navy veteran—noted: "No young fellow of about twenty who had been carding and weaving wool most of his life could so quickly have risen to command. I suspect that Christopher was really a foremast hand on René's ship, and one of those who discovered the trick played on them when Cape Carthage hove into sight."

In 1476 Columbus signed on for a trip that, for the first time, would take him out of the Mediterranean and into the Atlantic, which sailors and cartographers referred to as "the Oceanic Sea" because they knew of no other. The Genoese merchants wanted to ship mastic from Chios to Lisbon and then on to England, a risky venture, as dangers lurked everywhere. Various countries on the Mediterranean coastline were at war with each other, inciting their privateer fleets to seize enemy vessels. The wrong flag on a ship's stern could mean almost certain doom; even the right flag was no guarantee of safe passage. Many a captain on a combat mission seized a merchant ship merely because it promised to

yield rich cargo. To counter these attacks, the Genoese put together a convoy, consisting of galleasses, a whaling boat, and a
cog, the *Bechalla,* on which Columbus is said to have served. The
convoy sailed past the Strait of Gibraltar, then set a course for
Cape Saint Vincent, located on the southwestern tip of Portugal,
and there some French buccaneer ships appeared on the horizon.
The pirates armed their cannons, opened fire, and the convoy
was forced to defend itself. That, at any rate, was how the story
got told in Genoa. In another version it was the greedy Genoese
who attacked, but their attempt to capture the enemy ships went
miserably awry when the enemy, four galleys sailing under the
Venetian flag, returned fire. This is how Columbus's son Fernando recounted the story:

> *Here they came to blows, fighting with great fury and approach-
> ing each other until the ships grappled and the men crossed from
> boat to boat, killing and wounding each other without mercy,
> using not only hand arms but also fire pots and other devices.
> After they had fought from morning to the hour of vespers, with
> many dead and wounded on both sides, fire spread from the Ad-
> miral's ship to a great Venetian galley. As the two ships were
> grappled tight with hooks and iron chains which sailors use for
> this purpose, and on both sides there was much confusion and
> fear of the flames, neither side could check the fire; it spread so
> swiftly that soon there was no remedy for those aboard save to
> leap in the water and die in this manner rather than suffer the
> torture of the fire. But the Admiral, being an excellent swimmer,
> and seeing land only a little more than two leagues away, seized
> an oar which fate offered him, and on which he could rest at
> times; and it so pleased God, who was preserving him for
> greater things, to give him the strength to reach the shore.*

The country that Columbus saw from the burning deck of
the *Bechalla* was the coast of Portugal. Fishermen from the village
of Lagos near Cape Saint Vincent pulled Columbus ashore, more
dead than alive. A number of historians have expressed doubts as

to the authenticity of Columbus's story, arguing that it sounded too much like a heroic epic. The fact that Bartolomeo also found his way to Portugal around the same time has led scholars to assume that the two brothers simply immigrated there. At any rate, Columbus believed it was Divine Providence that had brought him to Portugal. "God our Father miraculously sent me here so that I may serve your Highness," he later wrote the Spanish king. "He miraculously ordered me to come to Portugal and come ashore here."

It was August 13, 1476. Though a mere village, Lagos had already figured in the world of exploration. It was from there that the Portuguese prince Henry the Navigator had organized several expeditions along the African west coast, their mission being to find a sea route to India. Portugal was unquestionably the most important seafaring nation of the day. Every year there were more stories of captains driven far off course and sighting mysterious coastlines. Inhabitants of islands in the Atlantic reported finding strange flotsam on their beaches. And scholars were circulating maps that showed land masses off to the west. Columbus, now twenty-five, had arrived with no more than the clothes on his back. He couldn't even speak Portuguese. He could, however, sail and he could navigate; he was therefore the right man in the right place. To the man who sat on the beach at Lagos, there was no more logical step than making his way to the metropolis of the discoverers, the mecca of the astronomers and geographers, the Cape Canaveral of its day—Lisbon.

CHAPTER 3

The Secret Behind
the Great Enterprise

*I could do this by using a sphere shaped like the earth, but I
decided that it would be easier and make the point clearer if I
showed that route by means of a sea-chart. I therefore send His
Majesty a chart drawn by my own hand, upon which is laid
out the western coast from Ireland on the north to the end of
Guinea, and the islands which lie on that route, in front of
which, directly to the west, is shown the beginning of the
Indies, with the islands and places at which you are bound to
arrive, and how far from the Arctic Pole or the Equator you
ought to keep away, and how much space or how many leagues
intervene before you reach those places most fertile in all sorts
of spices, jewels, and precious stones. And do not marvel at my
calling "west" the regions where the spices grow, although they
are commonly called "east"; because whoever sails westward
will always find those lands in the west, while one who goes
overland to the east will always find the same lands in the east.*

—Excerpt from a letter written in 1474
by Paolo Toscanelli dal Pozzo

King João I of Portugal was a most fortunate sovereign. He had
already produced two male heirs when in 1394 he was blessed

with another son, Infante Dom Henrique. Being third in line to the throne, Prince Henry's chances of being crowned were slight, of course, but he was driven by a very different kind of passion, one that would ultimately make him a legend. He loved anything to do with seafaring, faraway lands, and adventure. In 1419 Henry was appointed governor of the Algarve, the outermost tip of the European mainland. This region encompassed Cape Saint Vincent and the neighboring village of Sagres, where Henry built a residence the likes of which had never been seen before.

Sagres was essentially a seafaring research center, a nautical think tank, complete with lecture halls and chapels. Set atop a steep cliff, the ramparts of his fortress still stand, as does the enormous stone compass rose, measuring more than 130 feet in diameter. At Sagres Henry gathered the most brilliant navigational minds of his day, an eclectic mix of cartographers, sea captains, geographers, and astronomers. Together they collected data, studied sea charts, exchanged ideas, and advised the prince as to where he should next send his ships. As early as 1418, the Infante gave orders to colonize Madeira and its neighboring island of Porto Santo. In 1427 his expeditionary vessels discovered nearly all of the nine islands of the Azores, some eight hundred nautical miles out in the Atlantic. Twenty-five years later, his ships reached the last of the Azores, the tiny island of Corvo—from there the distance to Labrador is merely a thousand miles.

Henry's main project involved Africa's western coast, and his largest obstacle was the fear of the unknown, dread of what lay beyond the twenty-eighth parallel, the legendary Cape Nun. Sailors were afraid they might burn to death in the southern sun, or drown in remote whirlpools, or be devoured by monsters rising up out of the seething waters. Nonetheless, the prince, who probably never sailed once in his life, urged his men farther on, and before long the captains of his caravels had explored the entire African coastline, all the way down to the bulge of what would later become Sierra Leone. In a papal bull issued in 1456, the pope, who often acted as a kind of referee for warring potentates, granted Portugal all newly discovered lands "from the Capes of Bojador and Nun, throughout all Guinea, and beyond that southern region as far as the Indies." This was the sea route that Henry had been searching for his entire life, but when he died four years later, his ships had not yet rounded Africa.

The riches of the new African colonies, however, were already making their way toward Lisbon. The king's ships would unload their precious cargo—consisting of gold, spices, and slaves—then quickly set sail again, their holds filled with horses and the little bells and trinkets that the African tribal chiefs had grown so fond of that they gladly traded them for gold. Portugal's capital drew sailors and navigators, merchants and bankers from around the known world. Everyone wanted to share in Lisbon's newfound wealth. The city also attracted cartographers, who sketched navigational charts, keeping the Portuguese sea captains abreast of all the latest information regarding recently discovered coastlines, capes, and islands. One such cartographer was Bartolomeo Colón, younger brother to Christopher. For several decades Lisbon had been home to a large community of expatriates from Genoa who by this point had amassed some wealth and developed contacts. When the Colón brothers arrived sometime in 1476, they received assistance and were soon able to set up their own mapmaking business. Drawing, designing, and copying navigational charts gave the brothers access to inside information. They drew up portolan charts of the Mediterranean, providing reliable and detailed sailing instructions. They copied maps of recently discovered lands, as well as maps that were based purely on rumors, hearsay, and vague evidence. When the Venetian cartographer Zuane Pizzigano, for example, drew his map of the world in 1424, he included a semimythical group of islands called Antillia in the region of the Caribbean. Similar maps referred to them as Brendan's Islands, named for the legendary Irish saint.

Soon copying maps was not enough for Columbus; he wanted to do more than record others' discoveries. By 1477, a year after his arrival in Portugal, he had signed on with a ship sailing out into the Atlantic.

Years later Columbus wrote a short, somewhat cryptic note in the margins of his copy of Enea Silvio Piccolomini's *Historia rerum,* revealing the destination of his journey as well as his interest in the various routes by which one might reach India and China. "Men of Cathay which is toward the Orient have come hither. We have seen many remarkable things, especially in Galway of Ireland, a man and a woman of extraordinary appearance in two boats adrift." Columbus believed these people of "extraordinary appearance" were Chinese; more likely they were from Finland or Lapland, their broad faces giving them a slightly Asian appearance that would have seemed exotic to the young sailor. Columbus's ideas and notions were already going far beyond the conventional. He was clearly in search of clues about lands lying beyond the oceans, perhaps already nurturing a concept he would later term "La Empresa de las Indias," or what historians like Paolo Emilio Taviani called the "Wonderful Adventure." A man from Genoa, keenly aware of the problems his native city faced because of the Ottoman Empire, would have understandably been obsessed by the thought of finding a new route to Asia. "His scheme had the potential to tie together and accomplish the dreams that European merchants, monarchs, missionaries, and mystics had held since the end of the Crusade," wrote historians William and Carla Rahn Phillips. "An established sea route to Asia would surely produce great riches, and it might also lead to an alliance with the Great Khan against the Muslims and an unprecedented opportunity to spread the Christian message."

It may not have been pure coincidence that took Columbus to Ireland on his first major voyage beyond the Mediterranean. At the time rumors surrounding Saint Brendan, after whom cartographers named their phantom islands, were abundant. Legend had it that in the dim and distant past, Brendan the Voyager, or Brendan the Navigator, sailed across the ocean and discovered a wonderful country far out in the West. Every child in Ireland knew the legend. Centuries later historians would know more. They would be able to ascertain that Saint Brendan was born in County Kerry, Ireland, sometime around the year 489; and that he became an abbot and founded several cloisters, such as the one in Clonfert, in County Galway, where he eventually died at the age of ninety. In addition to being a man of God, Brendan was also an accomplished sailor who felt at home on the treacherous waters of the Irish Sea; he probably sailed across to Wales and up to Scotland.

Those are the historical facts. From there the legends take the helm. At the age of seventy, Brendan received a visit from a monk who told him that he had sailed westward across the sea and found there a magnificent land. The idea became fixed in Brendan's mind that this might be the Promised Land itself; he became determined to find it before he died. Together with fourteen monks, he built a boat similar to the curraghs still being used by Irish fishermen today. They tanned ox hides in oak bark, stretching the leather across a framework made of sturdy ash. Then they sewed everything together using leather strips, smearing fat all over it as waterproofing. They wove a square sail and loaded provisions for forty days—symbolically enough—as well as ample amounts of ox hides and fat for repair. Finally, in early summer, they set sail. Forced to row for weeks on end because of becalmed seas, and with provisions running low, they caught sight of land—a cold and forbidding-looking island on which they saw a house and a dog but no people. The next island they came across was full of sheep, "large as oxen," so the legend went. The third island appeared to have no vegetation; while Brendan remained on board, the others clambered ashore and lit a fire. Suddenly, the whole island began to move and then to submerge. Panic-stricken, they rushed back to the boat. They had, it was said, landed on the back of a sleeping whale. The next island was teeming with seabirds screeching infernally.

Far out in the ocean, the monks spotted a towering, shimmering white crystal, and it was so large that Brendan was able to maneuver his curragh through one of the archways. Next the legend tells how they headed straight into some hellish place, with fire, smoke, and dreadful creatures. In a written version of the legend, the episode is described as follows:

> They came within view of an island that was very rugged and rocky, full of smiths' forges. They heard the noise of bellows blowing like thunder and the beating of sledges on the anvils and iron. All the dwellers on the island crowded down to the shore, bearing, each of them, a large mass of burning slag, which they flung, everyone in turn, after the servants of God. And then they returned to their forges, which they blew up into mighty flames, so that the whole island seemed one globe of fire. The sea on every side boiled up and foamed. All the day the brethren heard a loud wailing from the inhabitants thereof, and a noisome stench was perceptible at a great distance. Then Saint Brendan sought to animate the courage of the brethren, saying: "Soldiers of Christ, be strong in faith unfeigned and in the armor of the Spirit, for we are now on the confines of hell; watch, therefore, and act manfully."

Following a journey through an ocean of fog and darkness, they finally reached the coast and thought they had found the entrance to Paradise:

> When they had disembarked, they saw a land, extensive and thickly set with trees, laden with fruits. All the time they were traversing that land, during their stay in it, no night was there, but a light always shone, like the light of the sun in the meridian, and for the forty days they viewed the land in various directions, they could not find the limits thereof. One day, however, they came to a large river flowing towards the middle of the land, which they could not by any means cross over. Saint Brendan then said to the brethren: "We cannot cross over this river, and we must therefore remain ignorant of the size of this country."

As the monks stood helplessly by on the banks of the river, something miraculous happened, something that the devout Columbus would later interpret as his mission statement. In the legend the episode bears a prophetic note:

> While they were considering this matter, a young man of resplendent features and very handsome aspect came to them and said to Saint Brendan: "This is the land you have sought after for so long a time. But you could not hitherto find it, because Christ our Lord wished, first, to display to you His divers mysteries in this immense ocean. Return now to the land of your birth for the days of your earthly pilgrimage must draw to a close. After many years this land will be made manifest to those who come after you.... When the Most High Creator will have brought all nations under subjection, then will this land be made known to all His elect."

After seven years, so the legend goes, Brendan arrived back home in Ireland.

The legend of Saint Brendan, handed down by word of mouth for centuries, appeared in written form, in Latin, in the tenth century as the *Navigatio sancti Brendani abbatis* (The sea voyage of the abbot Saint Brendan). In the mid-1970s, an English adventurer and geographer named Tim Severin compared the medieval text of the *Navigatio* to modern sea charts. Having studied the ocean currents and wind systems in the North Atlantic, Severin came to the conclusion that it would have been possible to sail across the Atlantic to America in a boat made of ox hides. Severin decided to prove his theory by building a curragh and re-creating Brendan's mythical journey based on a certain route that lay far to the north where the wind and the current would push the boat from astern. He discovered that his craft's flexible construction, appropriately christened *Brendan,* could withstand much more than experts had expected. Nonetheless, given that the boat had no keel and therefore was incapable of tacking against the wind like modern sailboats, the *Brendan* could only bob along in the wind like driftwood.

On his journey across the ocean, Severin found possible explanations for some aspects of the Brendan legend. Whales, for example, approached much closer to the *Brendan* than to other ships, whose diesel motors and whistling echo sounders put them off. The island with the teeming birds could well have been the Faeroe Islands, which do indeed teem with tens of thousands of seabirds during nesting season. With their hot springs, steaming geysers, and volcanoes, they closely resembled the hellish place described by Brendan. The wind and currents carried Severin's curragh past huge icebergs just south of Greenland. An Irish monk who had never seen an iceberg could well have imagined it as a gigantic crystal pillar. Drifting with the wind, Severin passed through the dreaded "fog zones" located to the north of the Newfoundland banks, just as described in the *Navigatio*, until finally reaching the American mainland, so far north that at least during the summer months the sun never sets. Severin was not out to prove that Saint Brendan did sail to America. He only wanted to demonstrate that Brendan could have accomplished such a journey, particularly if armed with unshakable faith.

Many believe that Columbus was profoundly influenced by Brendan's legend. In 1992, on the occasion of the five hundredth anniversary of Columbus's landing in the New World, the city of Genoa donated a statue to Galway. It is a six-foot rectangular block of stone above which a stylized bird spreads its wings. The inscription, in Gaelic and English, reads: "On these shores around 1477 the Genoese sailor Cristoforo Colombo found sure signs of land beyond the Atlantic."

From Ireland, Columbus sailed farther north. It was now winter and it must have been torture on the North Atlantic. In a memorandum quoted by his son Fernando, Columbus wrote:

> *In the month of February, 1477, I sailed one hundred leagues beyond the island of Tile, whose southern part is in latitude 73 degrees N, and not 63 degrees as some affirm; nor does it lie upon the meridian where Ptolemy says the West begins, but much*

farther west. And to this island, which is as big as England, the English come with their wares, especially from Bristol. When I was there, the sea was not frozen, but the tides were so great that in some places they rose twenty-six fathoms, and fell as much in depth.

The legendary Tile, or Thule, probably refers to Iceland. Historians have argued about whether Columbus actually landed there or not. Records show that the winter of 1477 was indeed unusually mild in Europe and thus that Iceland's coasts might have remained ice-free, as Columbus wrote. But for many that is not sufficient proof, particularly given that Columbus made a major mistake in his calculations of the latitude (understandably, given the lack of precise navigational instruments). He also vastly exaggerated the tidal range, however, and it is highly unlikely that a sailor whose life depended on such vital nautical details could have made such a glaring miscalculation. It is also conceivable that he noted it down incorrectly, or that Fernando made a mistake while copying his father's notes, or that Fernando's translator, who was not a sailor, confused the details. So much can get distorted when information gets passed down through the centuries. In truth, nobody knows for certain whether Columbus really sailed to Iceland or merely boasted that he had.

But if Columbus *was* in Iceland in 1477, he would have been in the right place at the right time. For just as the Irish have their legend of Saint Brendan, so rumors abounded on Iceland about Erik the Red, his son Leif Eriksson, and his sidekick Bjarni Herjolfsson. The Vikings, so the legend says, discovered a continent far to the west on their voyages from Iceland and Greenland—a distant land with vineyards.

The Vinland Sagas open in Iceland sometime around the year 982. At the time this colony of the Norsemen was a wild place, even by the Vikings' standards. One of the men, Erik the Red, exceeded the bounds of acceptable Viking conduct. After committing several murders, Erik was banished from their island by the Norsemen. Erik had heard fascinating stories from another Viking about new lands. With high hopes it would bring him fame and fortune, Erik set out to find a land where he could rule and where nobody could banish him. One of the sagas says: "He equipped his ship for a voyage and told the people that it was his intention to go in search of that land which Gunnbiorn, son of Ulf the Crow, saw when he was driven out of his course, westward across the main. He told them that he would return again to his friends, if he should succeed in finding that country." Together with his son, Leif, Erik sailed off to the new land, founded a Viking colony, and named it Greenland. The name was an early form of spin-doctoring and little more than an attempt to lure new settlers, for while cattle could graze on the grass near the coastline, and although the climate was more hospitable than today, the rest of the island was buried under a thick layer of ice all year-round. Yet despite the inclement weather, the colony thrived and the settlers soon spread out to two villages along the coast.

At this time a Viking merchant named Bjarni Herjolfsson set sail from Norway, planning to visit his father in Iceland. When he got there, he discovered that his father had succumbed to temptation and followed Erik the Red to his green land. With only a vague idea of where this new island could be, Bjarni set off again. Dangerous at any time of the year, the journey was suicidal in winter. Sailing into a terrible storm, the winds lashed Bjarni's ship and finally hurled him onto a desolate shore, bearing no resemblance to the descriptions of Greenland. Angry, disappointed, and indifferent to his discovery, Bjarni turned around. What he saw was Labrador.

Eventually making his way to Greenland and reuniting with his father, Bjarni recounted the story of his battles with the sea, of his circuitous route and the desolate coast in the west. Fascinated by these campfire stories, Leif Eriksson decided that he would outdo his father, and he set sail to find this new land. Together with thirty-five men, among them a holy man from the south (what is now Germany) named Tyrkir, Eriksson sailed off and discovered an uninviting coast that he named Helluland, the "Land of the Flat Stones." Farther south the land grew more fertile and Eriksson named it Markland, "Land of Woods." Finally the ship reached a coast that seemed suitable for a Viking settlement, with rich pastures and rivers teeming with salmon. This became the legendary Vinland.

The New World was not as untouched as the Vikings assumed. There were already people living there, whom the Vikings called *skrælings*. The first encounter between the Europeans and the native inhabitants—probably Algonquin Indians—ended in a bloodbath. Yet the Vikings were loath to give up easily. They continued to sail to this new country, where they fought the *skrælings* and built settlements. One of the sagas says: "They headed into the fjord where they unloaded the ships and settled. They had brought all kinds of livestock and explored what products the area had to offer. Tall grass grew everywhere. They stayed all the winter that was very hard." But at some stage, this new country was no longer mentioned in the sagas. Did the Vikings give up, did the *skrælings* wipe them out, or was this whole story of discovery no more than a fairy tale?

For centuries nobody found any evidence proving that the Vikings had reached America five hundred years before Columbus. Experts analyzed the old Nordic legends word by word in an attempt to locate Helluland, Markland, and Vinland. According to the sagas, Vikings never sailed for longer than a few days, so these countries couldn't have been too far south. Among supporters of the Viking theory, the description of Helluland, "Land of the Flat Stones," seemed a match with Baffin Island, a desolate island far above the polar circle. Markland could have referred to what is now Labrador; around Cape Porcupine there are thirty miles of sandy beaches with a backdrop of spruce forests, just as described in the sagas.

Viking aficionados found the most promising clue to Vinland's existence in descriptions in *Grænlendinga*, or *The Greenland*

Saga. In 1960 these descriptions led a tall, white-haired Norwegian to Sacred Bay in Newfoundland. Helge Ingstad, adventurer and scientist, traveled with his archaeologist wife, Anne Stine, aboard a medical ship doing the rounds of the isolated fishing villages on the coast. One of the villages was L'Anse aux Meadows. Only three families lived in L'Anse aux Meadows in 1960, and while a nurse vaccinated the fishermen and their wives and children, Helge Ingstad took a look around. He asked one of the fishermen named George Decker whether he had ever noticed anything strange on the outskirts of the village. Decker led him to a group of overgrown mounds in Epaves Bay, not far from the village. Ingstad immediately saw that these low knolls formed a rectangle. He asked Decker whether the bay had been home to any whalers during the last century. "They must have been crazy if they settled here, where they can't even get close to land in their boats," replied Decker. "They would've had to wade through the bay and lug the whales on their backs." Ingstad gazed across the ocean and the bay. The Vikings used ships known as *knarrs*— short, open-cargo ships with a low draft. Being Norwegian himself, Ingstad knew that the Norsemen loved bays such as these. They usually built their houses in the protected end of a fjord, to which they could haul their *knarrs*. They also needed pasture for their livestock, as well as fresh water or a river. Epaves Bay provided an ideal location for the Vikings. Ingstad believed he had finally found Vinland.

Over the next seven years, Ingstad and Stine led an international team of archaeologists in excavating the site at Epaves Bay, unearthing one foundation after another until they had dug up the remains of an entire village with a forge, cooking pits, and community houses. They found conclusive evidence that Europeans had once lived there: iron nails, bronze rings, and a round spindle whorl. They saw notches in the wood beams made by iron axes that were unfamiliar to the Indians living there at the time. The researchers also had the charcoal remains found in the forge analyzed. They dated to between 860 and 1060.

One thing has puzzled scholars and researchers. In *The Greenland Saga*, Tyrkir the Southerner disappears one evening and later returns quite distraught, stammering, "I've found grapes." According to the saga, there were so many grapes that Eriksson's crew later "filled their long boat with grapes and a cargo of wood. And when the spring came they got ready and sailed away, and Leif gave the land a name after its qualities, and called it Vinland, or Wineland." The idea that grapes ever grew in L'Anse aux Meadows is absurd. Newfoundland is located too far north. It's quite possible that Tyrkir might have been referring to wild berries, and Leif Eriksson might have exaggerated a little and made grapes out of berries (after all, his father had dubbed his island Greenland on the basis of a few blades of grass). But another discovery made at L'Anse aux Meadows did provide evidence that these grapes could have existed and that the Vikings might have picked them up on their travels farther south. Among the remains of the excavation site, archaeologists found butternuts, which don't grow in Newfoundland and never have. There had to be some explanation for their existence. Butternuts come from New England. It is possible L'Anse aux Meadows was merely a base of operations for the Vikings, a staging place on their way south or on their way home to Greenland. During one of these voyages south, one of Erik's companions must have picked up the butternuts. There are still plenty of mysteries surrounding the settlement in L'Anse aux Meadows, though Ingstad and Stine's discovery at least proved that the sagas contain a kernel of truth and that the Vikings did actually land in America.

Soon after Ingstad and Stine's breakthrough, experts began arguing over whether Columbus might have heard about this settlement. Columbus would have been familiar with Saint Brendan's *Navigatio;* that the mythical islands on the old sea charts often bore the monk's name would indicate as much. Columbus may also have heard of the sagas. William Fitzhugh, former curator of a Viking exhibition at the Smithsonian Institution in Washington, said that if Columbus was in Iceland, "then he could have learned from Icelandic seamen that there is land in the west." The historian Felipe Fernández-Armesto maintained that this didn't make any difference. "What the Vikings achieved didn't change the history of the world. They traveled from one Godforsaken part of Europe to another desolate place in North America. That didn't change anything." Columbus, on the other hand, "linked the most heavily populated part of the Old World with the most densely populated part of the Caribbean and Middle America. That had enormous potential."

Neither of the legends could have served as models for Columbus's Great Enterprise. The sagas and the *Navigatio* tell of routes far in the north, of icy countries with wild inhabitants—and not of palaces with golden roofs in warmer climes such as Columbus was trying to find. There was no Great Khan, no China, no India, and, above all, no gold. There was only snow and death, possibly a few grapes. But the legends surrounding Brendan and Leif Eriksson could well have turned Columbus's thoughts farther west. Both stories suggested that the ocean was by no means a vast and desolate expanse enclosing a central landmass, the island of humanity consisting of Europe, Asia, and Africa, as ancient geographers believed. They seemed to prove that seamen could navigate the ocean and that lands lay beyond the horizon. Both legends regarded the Atlantic not as the end of the world, but as a transportation route that could be useful to navigators, if they could unveil its secrets. Columbus knew the secrets of the north, particularly if he had sailed via the Azores on his way to Ireland. This was the customary route due to the advantageous winds. He had to know that in this longitude, the wind usually blows from the west. He knew that no one should try sailing westward here; most of the ships at the time could tack against the wind much better than Saint Brendan's little ox-hide boat. Columbus knew that one had to sail back to Europe via the Azores if one was coming from the west.

At the very least, he knew how to get back home. Of course what Columbus couldn't have known at the time was that the Atlantic Ocean is an enormous carousel of global forces. However, he did have a sense that winds and currents off the Azores pushed ships from west to east. From there they drifted farther south, ending up between the Canary Islands and the equator, moving from east to west. Columbus's next commission would have enabled him to learn more about the outer edges of this area, the realm of the trade winds. The northeastern trade wind blew more powerfully and more consistently toward the west than sailors in the Mediterranean ever imagined. This is where Columbus saw his westward route. His guess must have seemed prophetic.

Upon his return to Lisbon from Iceland in 1478, Columbus met an old acquaintance, Paolo di Negri. While working as a shipping agent to the powerful Genoese businessman Lodisio Centurione, di Negri had been commissioned to purchase thirty tons of sugar on the island of Madeira. Columbus needed the money and wanted to feel a ship beneath his feet again, so when di Negri offered him the job, he happily accepted. But when Columbus sailed to Madeira, things went terribly wrong, and later all parties involved ended up before the arbitrators of the Chamber of Commerce in Genoa on August 25, 1479. This was the last time Columbus ever saw his native homeland.

———————

Archivist Patrizia Schiappacasse seemed even more cautious than usual when retrieving one particular document and placing it on the table at the Archivio di Stato. "This is one of my prize possessions." You can see why. This fading and crumbling document offers the best proof that the Columbus who appears in her older files as the young boy from Genoa is the same man who called Portugal his home in 1478. It offers one of the clues Columbus involuntarily left behind while preparing for his Great Enterprise. In the document the notary described Columbus as "Civis Janue," a citizen of Genoa, approximately twenty-seven years of age. It attests that he had worked in Lisbon for a year, that he was currently working as a commercial agent for Genoese families, and that he had to re-embark for Lisbon the following day. Columbus had been forced to appear before the Chamber of Commerce as a witness because di Negri had very likely used the sugar transaction in Madeira to line his own pockets. Although the Centurione family sent him 1,290 ducats, di Negri passed only 103 ducats on to Columbus to purchase the sugar. Arriving in Madeira's port of Funchal, Columbus had therefore only been able to make a deposit for part of the purchase. He negotiated with the merchants, but the money never came and the dealers in Madeira flatly refused to give Columbus the sugar in good faith; he was, after all, an Italian whom they hadn't done business with.

Columbus finally sailed back to Genoa with only a fraction of the load, causing embarrassment and difficulties for Centurione, who had presumably already resold the sugar, most of which was still in Madeira. Centurione had everyone involved in this botched business arraigned, which explains why testimony lay here in Genoa's city archives.

Today, apart from the northern coast, with its charm and beauty, the island of Madeira has fallen victim to the building boom of the last decades of the twentieth century. Hotels and resorts crowd the coast, and cruise liners congest the harbor. Some 250,000 people currently live on the island. High above the port of Funchal lies a small park with a tiny church, Santa Catarina, and a statue commemorating "Cristovão Colombo." The Admiral towers over the harbor, his left hand resting on the pommel of his sword, his calves swollen to the size of a football player's, his demeanor stern and hard. Naturally, he is gazing out into the distance (toward the west and open water).

Although Columbus spent a considerable amount of time on Madeira, probably while he was waiting for money to pay for the sugar to arrive, he left no traces. He lived on the tiny island of Porto Santo, which lies forty miles away and consists of a few hills, a couple of beaches, many craggy cliffs, and about five thousand inhabitants. In the seventeenth century, Porto Santo was home to pirates, who spent their days intercepting merchant ships en route to the West Indies.

Down in the main part of town stands a house said to have belonged to Columbus. Unfortunately the house dates back only to the seventeenth century, though this doesn't seem to deter the tourists. Next door is the Columbus museum, which contains some letters and documents, as well as an array of paintings. In some Columbus looks like the king of Sweden; in others he bears an uncanny resemblance to Oliver Cromwell. The natives in the paintings all look as if they're ecstatic to have finally been discovered. Artur Ferreira is the director of the museum and a true-blue patriot. Porto Santo belongs to Portugal, which is why Ferreira claimed Columbus as Portuguese. Columbus spent two and a half years in Porto Santo. "At the time Columbus didn't have a profession, but it was here that he saw all the sea charts and navigational documents," explained Ferreira. "And it was here that he first had his idea." This in turn explains why Porto Santo erupts in celebrations on September 23. They drink to the discoverer and eat Columbus cotton candy. One local politician dresses like Columbus. A replica of the *Santa María* sails into the harbor, where the discovery of America is being reenacted on the beach.

Further up on the westernmost tip of the island is the perfect vantage point. The landscape there is barren, the cliffs are brown, and the waves swirl about the headland known as Miradouro das Flores. West of here lies open water, at the other end of which lies America. Ferreira claimed that the idea of sailing westward came to Columbus while he was here. Here is where he would have brooded about the Chinese he thought he had seen in Ireland, about the charts he had copies of, the legends he had read and heard. Nonetheless, the main opportunity for his Great Enterprise was provided by a noblewoman who eventually became his wife. Centuries later historians remain puzzled as to how the son of a petty bourgeois who so yearned for greater things ended up marrying Doña Felipa Perestrello e Moniz.

Consuelo Varela has spent her life trying to put herself in Columbus's position, analyzing each of his moves and assessing the reactions of those around him. Varela believes that although Columbus wasn't all that interested in women, women found him irresistible. "He was probably a very attractive man, charming, and articulate. And he carried himself well in society. He certainly knew how to market himself, and he was a man with a mission. He was always to be found in places of power, and he probably also seemed like a man with a future."

There are somewhere around seventy portraits of Columbus hanging in museums and collections around the world. Some portray Columbus with a beard, some with a mustache, some clean-shaven; sometimes he is gaunt, sometimes fat; sometimes he looks grim and inhibited, sometimes relaxed, self-confident, and determined. None of them were painted during his lifetime, nor did the artists ever meet Columbus. Naturally, these portraits convey an artistic projection of the man, and over the centuries these projections have changed. The portrait that comes closest to matching written descriptions is Paolo Giovio's work, which dates from 1550. Giovio painted a haggard, elderly man wearing what looks like a frugal monk's habit. He has frizzy hair, a receding hairline, a large nose, and big eyes with heavy lids. Resembling neither tyrant nor hero, Columbus looks like a painfully serious man, a battle-worn veteran.

The Giovio portrait matches uncannily the detailed descriptions left by Columbus's son Fernando as well as by the chronicler Bartolomé de Las Casas. Las Casas also knew Columbus personally. His father and uncle had traveled to Hispaniola with Columbus on his second voyage and stayed on to set up a colony. They were later joined by twenty-six-year-old Bartolomé, who, like many young hidalgos, or sons of noblemen, wanted to strike it rich in the colonies. However, so moved was Bartolomé by the plight of the "Indians," as he called them, that he had himself ordained as the first priest of the New World.

Apart from Fernando's biography, Las Casas's book *Historia de las Indias,* written around 1550 but first published some three hundred years later, remains the most important literary source for information about Columbus, in part because it is so specific in its description:

> [Columbus was] more than middling tall with a long face giving him an air of authority. He had an aquiline nose, blue eyes and a light complexion, tending to turn red. His beard and hair were red when young but soon turned gray from his labors; he was affable and cheerful in speaking, and eloquent and boastful in his negotiations; he was serious in moderation, affable with strangers, and with members of his household gentle and pleasant, with modest gravity, and so could easily incite those who saw him to love him. He was sober and moderate in eating, drinking, clothing and footwear; it was commonly said that he spoke cheerfully in familiar conversation, or with indignation when he gave reproof or was angry with somebody: "May God take you, don't you agree to this and that?" In matters of the Christian religion, without doubt he was a Catholic and of great devotion; for in everything he did and said or sought to begin, he always interposed "In the name of the Holy Trinity I will do this." In whatever letter or other thing he wrote, he put at the head "Jesus and Mary be with us on the way." His oath was sometimes: "I swear by San Fernando." When gold or precious things were brought to him, he entered his cabin, knelt down, summoned the bystanders, and said: "Let us give thanks to Our Lord that he has thought us worthy to discover so many good things."

As Las Casas's description suggests, Columbus was quite devout and, in his youth, attractive. Columbus met Doña Felipa Perestrello e Moniz during Mass in the chapel of the holy convent in Lisbon not far from his cartographer's workshop. At the time the convent was a boarding school for daughters of the Portuguese aristocracy, but it also served as a kind of marriage market, with the public gallery attracting young men eager to be wed. Fernando, Columbus's illegitimate son from a mistress, briefly described how the two flirted and made advances: "As he behaved very honorably and was a man of handsome presence and who never turned from the path of honesty, a lady named Doña Felipa Moniz...had such converse and friendship with him that she became his wife."

Doña Felipa Perestrello e Moniz was already twenty-five when she met Columbus, virtually an old maid. The family might have had an old and highly respected name, but they hardly had enough money to pay for her dowry. However, meeting Felipa was a stroke of luck. He could hardly have found a more suitable wife. Felipa's late father, Bartolomeo Perestrello, the son of immigrants from Piacenza in Italy, had married into a very old noble family. Felipa's mother, Doña Isabel, had strong connections to the kind of social circle that Columbus's ambitions demanded. Bartolomeo had served as a sailor under Henry the Navigator and was involved in the colonization of Madeira and Porto Santo. As a reward, he had received the hereditary captaincy of Porto Santo, giving him virtual control over the island. When Bartolomeo died, Columbus's new mother-in-law, Doña Isabel, kept her late husband's sea charts and documents. Fernando later wrote, "His widow, who, observing the Admiral's great interest in geography, told him the said Perestrello, her husband, had been a notable seafarer; and she told him how he and two other captains had gone with license from the King of Portugal to discover new lands....Seeing that her stories of these voyages gave the Admiral much pleasure, she gave him the writings and sea-charts left by her husband. These things excited the Admiral still more." Soon after the wedding, which probably took place in 1479, Columbus and his wife moved from Lisbon to Porto Santo, where Columbus's first son was born around 1480. Christopher named the boy Diego after his favorite sibling Giacomo, alias Diego, the baby of the family from the Vico Dritto in Genoa. Over the next few years, the young family lived in Porto Santo and Madeira. And it was from here that Columbus continued his research.

The most important facet of his future enterprise must have caught his attention when he stepped outside his front door in the morning—the wind. The island lies nearly on the border of the trade-winds zone. At the time sailors knew that these prevailing winds blew mainly from the northeast off the African coast. Columbus probably sailed at least once along the African coast. But nobody had ever observed far out in the ocean that the winds blow in exactly the same direction. On Madeira trade winds are hardly noticeable because the steep cliffs deflect them, sometimes even turning them in a southwesterly direction. But on the smaller island of Porto Santo, the wind often blows out into the ocean. If you throw a piece of wood into the waters off Miradouro das Flores, it will eventually make its way into the Caribbean. And if you wait long enough, it will wash ashore once again, swept along by the current carrying it past the Azores. Columbus now knew what winds would carry him on his journey westward.

The question, of course, was what lay out there? Strange objects sometimes washed up on Portugal's beaches. Columbus had heard about them and later told his son Fernando, who wrote:

> A pilot of the Portuguese King, Martín Vicente by name, told him that on one occasion, finding himself four hundred and fifty leagues west of Cape St. Vincent, he fished out of the sea a piece of wood ingeniously carved, but not with iron. For this reason and because for many days the winds had blown from the west, he concluded this wood came from some islands to the west.
>
> Pedro Correa, who was married to a sister of the Admiral's wife, told him that on the island of Porto Santo he had seen another piece of wood brought by the same wind, carved as well as the aforementioned one, and that canes had also drifted in, so thick that one joint held nine decanters of wine.... Since such canes do not grow anywhere in our lands, he was sure that the wind had blown them from some neighboring islands or perhaps from India. Ptolemy ... writes that such canes are found in the eastern parts of the Indies.

Even stranger things were washed ashore, things that might have led Columbus to deduce that there must be inhabited land to the west. Fernando wrote, for example, "On the island of Flores, which is one of the Azores, the sea flung ashore two dead bodies with broad faces and different in appearance from the Christians."

Columbus had heard countless stories from sailors who had drifted off course and claimed to have seen land in the West. These stories were the source of inspiration for all the mystical and mythical islands, such as Saint Brendan or Hy-Brasil, that dotted the oceans in cartographers' sea charts. Antonio Leme, a sailor from Madeira, assured Columbus that once, when driven off course, he had sighted three islands far out in the ocean. Columbus knew that the English were not the only ones to set off in search of Hy-Brasil. Even the Portuguese king took these legends seriously and occasionally commissioned sailors to search for land. Most of the geographers of the day believed in the legend of Antillia, after which the Antilles were later named. In the year 714, so the story went, seven bishops fled to sea from Portugal with their band of followers, hoping to escape the terror of the invading Moors. They discovered Antillia and built seven cities there, burning their ships so as not to succumb to the temptation of returning home. It was said that a caravel belonging to Henry the Navigator once reached Antillia but had been forced to flee because the captain feared he would be taken prisoner. Henry the Navigator did send out a captain and a pilot in 1452, Diego de Teive and Pedro de Velasco, on a mission to find Antillia. Instead, they discovered Flores, an island in the Azores. Columbus also studied the works of the ancient geographers. Aristotle, for example, claimed that it was possible to sail from Spain to India "in only a few days." Strabo, who lived during the reign of Augustus, wrote in his seventeen-volume *Geographica* that discoverers had once dared to venture out. "Those who have returned from an attempt to circumnavigate the earth do not say that they have been prevented from continuing their voyage by any opposing continent, for the sea remained perfectly open, but through want of resolution and the scarcity of provision." Columbus also read the prophecies of the Roman philosopher and poet Seneca. In a text taken from *Medea,* one of his tragedies, Seneca wrote:

> an age will come,
> after many years when the Ocean
> will loose the chains of things,
> and a huge land lie revealed;
> when Tiphys will disclose new worlds
> and Thule no more be the ultimate.

This prophecy must have pleased Columbus, for it was his desire to become a latter-day Tiphys, the helmsman of the Argonauts.

Columbus collated all known facts; the references to the corpses washed ashore, the opinions of the ancient geographers, the sea charts, and his knowledge of the ocean winds. Adding one detail after another, he assembled his dream, painting an image in his mind. Columbus's enemies, however, later claimed his painting was a copy, not an original. In 1535, twenty-nine years after Columbus's death, a rumor began to spread. Columbus, it was whispered, had probably met a mysterious pilot during his time on Madeira and Porto Santo, and this pilot had shown Columbus the way. It seems like no coincidence that this rumor was circulating at the very moment that the Spanish crown was engaged in a lengthy legal action against Columbus's heirs, the Pleitos de Colón. The crown's lawyers were attempting to belittle Columbus's merits, so as to be released from paying his heirs the promised percentage of the immense wealth in the New World. And it was around this time, about 1535, that Gonzalo Fernández de Oviedo, an old acquaintance of Columbus's, spread the rumor about the mysterious pilot. Oviedo, a Spanish nobleman, initially met Columbus when the former was still a teenager and a page at the Spanish court, first in Granada and then in Barcelona. Fascinated by the adventures of the great captain, the young nobleman traveled to the New World as a chronicler, enthusiastically noting down everything he saw. He described plants, animals, as well as the natives, whom he considered depraved liars and lazy swine, who would rather die than do an honest day's work. Apart from learning about the vegetation and the inhabitants in the "West Indies," Oviedo, over time, also learned to hate Columbus, and his testimony proved most unpleasant for Columbus's heirs, as Oviedo was considered to be somewhat of an authority. Oviedo also spread his malicious rumors in his writings:

> Some say that a caravel that was sailing from Spain to England was subjected to such mighty and violent tempests and foul winds that she was forced to run westward for so many days that she picked up one or more of the islands of these regions and Indies; and the pilot went ashore and saw naked people. And when the winds moderated which had driven him thither against his will, he took on water and wood to return to his first course. They also say that the better part of the cargo, which this vessel carried, consisted of provisions and things to eat and wines whereof they were able to sustain life on so long a voyage. Moreover, it is said that this pilot was a very intimate friend of Christopher Columbus, and that he understood somewhat of the latitudes and marked the land which he found, and in great secrecy shared it with Columbus, whom he asked to make a chart and indicate on it the land which he had seen. It is said that Columbus received him in his house as a friend and sought to cure him, as he too landed very weak; but that he died like the rest, and thus Columbus was informed of the land and navigation of those regions, and he alone knew the secret. Some say that this master or pilot was Andalusian, others have him Portuguese, others Basque; some say that Columbus was then in the island of Madeira and others in the Cape Verde Islands, and that the aforesaid caravel came to harbor, and in this way Columbus learned of the land. Whether this was so or not, nobody can truly affirm. As for me I hold it to be false.

This final sentence is deviously hypocritical. The gossip was made public and Columbus's mysterious pilot even given a name—Alonso Sánchez de Carvajal, a Spaniard either from the Andalusian city of Palos de la Frontera or from the neighboring Huelva. Over the centuries, however, all trace of him has been lost.

While the experts still debate the authenticity of this story, several facts speak against this version of events. Only rarely do trade winds blow across the Atlantic at storm strength for weeks at a time. Furthermore, no sailor, however proficient, would ever be able to maneuver a caravel on his own, let alone across the ocean; there had to have been a crew. And all of these men must have seen the islands on the other side of the Atlantic. It seems highly unlikely that Columbus would have been the only one to know about this sensation. Moreover, Columbus already knew a man who could show him the way. And he already possessed a copy of this man's sea chart.

In the fifteenth century, the university town of Florence was a mecca for Christian scholars and a center for geographers. The Christian image of the earth, based on the Bible, hadn't changed much over the previous centuries. Most people still believed that the three continents of Europe, Asia, and Africa, with Jerusalem as the epicenter, swam on the Northern Hemisphere, surrounded by an impenetrable ocean. The Southern Hemisphere, on the other hand, was a death zone, swelteringly hot and hostile.

Then scholars rediscovered the pre-Christian authors of antiquity, among them the Greek text of Claudius Ptolemy's second-century *Geography,* which was translated into Latin in 1410. Ptolemy not only described the Spice Islands in Asia; he also claimed that Africa extended far south beyond the equator. From this text the Florentines were able to deduce that the south might be habitable. Like Strabo, Ptolemy believed that the ocean was navigable. He also estimated the size of Europe, Asia, and Africa. If one divided the earth into 360 lines of longitude, he estimated that the land-mass would comprise half of that, meaning 180 degrees.

To Florentine thinkers, Ptolemy's rediscovered texts neatly corresponded with the fantastic accounts published in *The Travels of Marco Polo* just a century before. Apart from being more color-ful, Polo described the Spice Islands in much the same way as

Ptolemy. He also portrayed India's province of Cathay, China, and the island of Cipango, Japan. But Polo described Asia as extending thirty lines of longitude farther east than Ptolemy, which led many Florentine scholars to consider him a liar and a braggart who had overstated the size of Asia simply for the purpose of self-aggrandizement.

The most distinguished scholar of the day was the physician and mathematician Paolo Toscanelli dal Pozzo. Toscanelli's ideas and research brought him into close contact with—among others—the German astronomer Johann Müller, also called Regiomontanus. (One of Müller's students, Martin Behaim, later constructed the world's first terrestrial globe that positioned Asia directly opposite the European west coast. What had long mystified historians was that Behaim finished his globe in 1492, before Columbus returned from America. Behaim and Columbus had probably both used Toscanelli.) Toscanelli lived a quiet and scholarly life before the Turks captured Constantinople. Like the Genoese merchants, the Florentines now feared for their trade with Asia, and Toscanelli's family also traded in spices. "It cannot be ruled out," wrote the historian Paolo Emilio Taviani, "yes, it is even probable that the events taking place in the world prompted Toscanelli to set aside the examination of the stars and mathematics to further promote geographic research." Unlike Columbus on the remote island of Porto Santo, when he began researching alternative routes to the east, Toscanelli had access to the best libraries and was able to question travelers and diplomats from faraway countries. And soon he began to believe Marco Polo, combining his descriptions with all the other information and, above all, with the conception of the world as put forth by Ptolemy. In 1474, at the age of seventy-seven, Toscanelli recapitulated all his acquired knowledge in a letter to an old friend, Fernão Martins, the canon of the cathedral in Lisbon. The king of Portugal wanted to know whether Toscanelli considered other routes to Asia to be feasible and asked his confidant Martins to intervene. In his letter to Martins, Toscanelli not only claimed that Asia lay in the west, directly opposite Portugal, but he also included a chart with a grid showing longitude and latitude. On the right, Toscanelli drew the European and African coastlines, and on the left, Cathay and Cipango; in the middle lay Antillia and other smaller islands. Toscanelli also included a legend, explaining everything a sailor needed to know:

> The straight lines drawn lengthwise on this map show the distance from east to west; the transverse lines indicate distance from north to south. I have also drawn on the map various places in India to which one could go in case of a storm or contrary winds, or some other mishap.... From the city of Lisbon due west there are twenty-six spaces marked on the map, each of which contains two hundred and fifty miles, as far as the very great and noble city of Quinsay. This city is about one hundred miles in circumference.... That city lies in the province of Mangi, near the province of Cathay, in which the king resides the greater part of the time. And from the island of Antillia, which you call the Island of the Seven Cities, to the very noble island of Cipango, there are ten spaces, which make 2,500 miles, that is, two hundred and twenty-five leagues. This land is most rich in gold, pearls, and precious stones, and the temples and royal palaces are covered with solid gold. But because the way is not known, all these things are hidden and covered, though one can travel thither with all security.

At the court in Lisbon, Toscanelli's letter and map were treated like top-secret information and kept under wraps. It remains unclear how Columbus found out about the letter and the map, but it seems possible that his mother-in-law's old contacts might have helped. It is also possible that she heard rumors and benefited from the good reputation of her dead husband. At any rate, by the year 1480, Columbus was in possession of both prized items, the directions and a copy of the map, which he then copied once more. This must have given him cause for joy, for the famed Toscanelli corroborated what he, Columbus, had long suspected. In 1481 Columbus made contact with Toscanelli. He wanted to find out whether the Florentine scholar had more information he might use. The scholar replied:

> *Paolo the Physician, to Christopher Columbus, Greetings.*
>
> *I perceive your grand and noble desire to sail from west to east by the route indicated on the map I sent you, a route which would appear still more plainly on a sphere. I am pleased to see that I have been well understood, and that the voyage has become not only possible but certain, fraught with inestimable honor and gain, and most lofty fame among Christians. But you cannot grasp all that it means without actual experience, or without such accurate and copious information as I have had from eminent learned men who have come from those places to the Roman court and from merchants who have traded a long time in those parts and speak with great authority on such matters.*

Ptolemy had already overestimated the size of the world's known regions by 50 percent, thus halving the rest of the undiscovered world. Marco Polo—and with him Toscanelli—had magnified this mistake. In his letter to Columbus, Toscanelli calculated a distance of only five thousand miles from the Canary Islands to Quinsay in China. Columbus believed the ocean was even narrower than that and considered Toscanelli's distances exaggerated. He conducted his own research, studying the works of astronomers, such as the Arab Alfraganus or Marinus of Tyre. Columbus read what he wanted into these texts and then began to calculate. His two variables were as follows: If the globe had 360 degrees of longitude, how many would the known world measure? Secondly, how many miles made one degree?

In truth, Columbus was engaging in creative math. He strained, stretched, compressed, and tweaked the numbers of degrees and miles until the results suited him. Centuries later scientists reconstructed his calculations, but the figures were just as complicated as they were false. Columbus claimed the distance between the Canary Islands and Quinsay was not five thousand miles, as Toscanelli stated, but only thirty-five hundred miles. He estimated that if a caravel could sail one hundred miles a day on the trade winds—and it could manage that easily—then he would be in China within five weeks. The actual distance measures some twelve thousand miles. A caravel would need four months, and by then Columbus and his crew would have long since died of thirst.

But Columbus believed he knew all he had to know: that the earth was round, so one could sail westward, arriving in the east. From Europe's farthest outpost to the islands off India was a trip of only a few weeks. On no account could one sail westward directly from Portugal, because the favorable winds blew in the south, off Porto Santo. Sailing back, Columbus ventured a guess that one had to sail on the latitude of the Azores, for there the winds blew from the west. Those were his key navigational elements. Columbus's great enterprise was complete, and in 1484—possibly with the help of his mother-in-law, who might have pulled a few strings—he approached the Portuguese monarch.

King João II was open-minded and receptive to new ideas, believing that the future of his nation lay on the ocean and that new discoveries could only enhance his power and wealth. In an attempt to continue what his great-uncle Henry the Navigator had started, King João sent Portuguese caravels farther south along the African coast. He hoped that they would reach the end of the continent, turn toward the northeast, and then have a clear run to the Orient. However, none of the captains commissioned by the king followed Toscanelli's directions and map. The Portuguese believed they already had an option on the route to India and therefore did not need a second one. In 1488 Bartolomeu Dias discovered and sailed around the Cape of Good Hope, and twelve years later Vasco da Gama even ventured as far as Calicut, on India's southwestern coast.

Then again, there was no reason to investigate other routes. After all, King João had the ships, the financial means, and the manpower. Theoretically, the Portuguese monarch would have been the ideal partner for Columbus.

However, something went dreadfully wrong during their meeting. Perhaps the king was put off by Columbus's self-

confident manner. He certainly must have noted the disparity between Columbus's practical experience and his lofty ambitions.
Perhaps Columbus made excessive demands, similar to those he
later made in Spain, where he not only requested money and
ships but also titles, chartered rights, and, as we've seen, a percentage of the revenue. A scribe from the court in Lisbon later
provided the following account of the meeting:

> The king, as he observed this Cristovão Colom to be a big talker
> and boastful in setting forth his accomplishments, and full of
> fancy and imagination with his Isle Cypango than certain
> whereof he spoke, gave him small credit. However, by strength
> of his importunity it was ordered that he confer with D. Diogo
> Ortiz bishop of Ceuta and Master Rodrigo and Master José, to
> whom the king had committed these matters of cosmography
> and discovery.

Master Rodrigo was the king's physician and confessor, José Vizinho a mathematician, and Ortiz a Portuguese theologian. The
three men belonged to the Junta dos Mathemáticos, a sort of scientific advisory council whose primary function was developing
navigational instruments for use on the king's merchant vessels.
Rodrigo, in fact, was responsible for streamlining the astrolabe,
an instrument that measured the position of the stars. Vizinho
worked on mathematical tables that navigators could use to assess their latitude. As expert navigators, the men of the *junta* were
appointed with the task of examining Columbus's plan. They
came to the conclusion that Columbus's plan was little more than
"vapor." The experts doubted that any sailor could reach the Indian islands in the way that Columbus had imagined, and they rejected his plan. Theirs was the only sensible decision, based on
the knowledge available at the time. Yet it was also the wrong decision, for it later cost Portugal an empire.

Over the next centuries, scholars have shaken their heads at
the stupidity of the Portuguese commissioners, as well as that of
their Spanish colleagues who later also rejected Columbus. They

maintained that these self-styled experts must have thought the earth was flat and that Columbus had been a pioneer of the modern age. In actuality, the geographers at the court of King João knew as well as Columbus that the earth was a sphere. This fact was already being taught at most universities. They also knew full well that one could sail westward and arrive in the east, at least theoretically. As Samuel Eliot Morison later wrote: "Since there was no doubt of the world being a sphere, almost everyone admitted that Columbus' theory was valid; his originality lay in proposing to do something about it. A concept of sailing west to China in 1480 was much like that of flying in 1900—theoretically sound, but impractical with existing means."

Unlike Columbus, the commission members could calculate. They were unwilling to make the earth smaller than it was, which is why they surmised that every man on board would have died of hunger or thirst long before the ships reached India. The experts estimated a halfway realistic distance between Europe and India. Columbus didn't. To Columbus's credit, he did later write in the log of his first voyage that he presumed there were islands like Antillia located between Europe and India, just as Toscanelli had said. It could have been part of his ultimate goal to find and occupy new islands in the ocean, which would explain why he later took possession of these islands for the Spanish crown. After all, if he actually thought that he had landed in India, he would have had to assume that these lands belonged to the Great Khan.

Unbeknownst to Columbus and the members of the *junta,* there were not merely a few islands located between Europe and Asia, but an entire continent. Just as Columbus had wanted the right thing for the wrong reasons, the men of the *junta* made the wrong decision for the right reasons. Rejected and ridiculed, Columbus saw no future for himself in Portugal. He had unsuccessfully tried to gain acceptance for eight years, and now it was time for something else. There were other reasons that made it prudent for Columbus to leave the country. He had apparently run up considerable debts in Portugal, more than he could possibly settle. According to Las Casas, Columbus left the country "secretly." Several years later King João II sent him a letter in which he not only offered Columbus safe passage, but wanted to reopen discussions on the Great Enterprise. "And because, perchance, to you there may be some concern regarding our justice due to some things to which you may be obligated, we guarantee you that during your arrival, stay and return, you will not be arrested, held, accused, tried or considered responsible for anything civil or penal, of any kind."

The letter arrived too late. When it finally reached him, Columbus was in Spain, trying to assemble all the elements that he needed. An alliance of the willing was already working toward making his impossible plan a reality.

CHAPTER 4

Monks and Slave Traders

In 1485, probably during the summer, a ship departed Lisbon heading south. On board were two passengers for whom this must have been a most dreary journey, Columbus and his young son Diego. They had embarked secretly for they were on the run. Having lost everything they owned in Portugal, they carried with them only a few documents and charts. They were also grieving. Aged only thirty, Doña Felipa had died of unknown causes shortly before their departure, leaving Columbus in charge of Diego, who was four or five years old at the time. Columbus never mentioned his wife's name again. The past meant nothing to him; the future was everything. He was already thirty-three years old and had spent eight years in Portugal—years that had ended in ignominy and left him with little more than his ideas. And those ideas had been dismissed as nonsense by the world's best geographers and navigators.

The ship passed Cape Saint Vincent and headed up the Río Tinto to one of Spain's first ports near the border with Portugal, Palos de la Frontera, in Andalusia. Palos had seen better days. Until 1481 the Spaniards had used both Palos and the nearby port of Huelva as a place to unload shiploads of slaves from Africa.

Then, in an attempt to avert the danger of a possible war with Spain, which was competing for possession of the colonial territories along the African coast, the Portuguese successfully sought a papal decree sanctioning their monopoly over the slave trade. Spain was forced to relinquish its slave trade, resulting in the decline of ports like Palos. To Columbus, accustomed to the relative glamour and bustle of Lisbon, ending up in the sleepy town of Palos must have seemed like banishment. He could not have known how important this provincial backwater would one day prove to his Great Undertaking.

Shortly before the ship carrying him and his son anchored in the Río Tinto, Columbus would have seen a white bell tower high on a hill belonging to the Franciscan monastery La Rábida. The monastery was a well-known meeting place for sailors, a place where they could exchange news, hear the latest rumors about pirates and battles, and peruse the nautical books and charts in the library of the cloister. It was here that they prayed before an alabaster statue of the Virgin of Miracles, leaving gifts of thanks when they returned safely from dangerous voyages.

Columbus went ashore in Palos and headed to Huelva, where relatives of his deceased wife happened to live. A local physician later wrote "that the said Admiral Don Cristóbal Colón with his son Don Diego came on foot to La Rábida, a monastery of friars in this town, and asked the porter to give him bread and a drink of water for that little boy who was his son." The porter invited the travelers in. Later that evening Columbus met Fray Antonio de Marchena, who, as the historian Paolo Emilio Taviani noted, "would become the spiritual advisor, the guardian angel of the future discoverer." In a letter to the Spanish court, Columbus later claimed, "I never found support from anyone, save father Friar Antonio de Marchena, beyond that of eternal God."

Marchena was a passionate astronomer and cosmographer, but knew more about the stars in the heavens than about the oceans below the cliffs of La Rábida. With Columbus he was face-to-face with a man who purported to know what lay beyond the horizon. Columbus was generally mistrustful, always fearing that somebody would steal his ideas. Nonetheless, he trusted Marchena enough to show him his greatest treasures, the charts and the Toscanelli letter. Marchena began to believe in Columbus's idea, and, as the custodian of the Franciscan subprovince of Seville, he was not without influence. But he was still an insignificant nobody compared to the guardian of the monastery, Fray Juan Pérez. Pérez knew Queen Isabella of Castile, for whom at one time he had been confessor. Porto Santo might have been the place where Columbus assembled his ideas, but La Rábida—working with both Marchena and later Pérez—was where he drew up a plan of action.

———————

Huelva today is a hellish place. The air has been made sulfurous by the refineries, cement works, power stations, and automobile pollution. Nonetheless, the white monastery with its small bell tower still stands. Adjacent to it is a large parking lot for tourist buses, and in this lot stands a tall column, a monument to the discoverers of America. Indeed, the monks have turned their mountain retreat into a kind of Columbus theme park. A small-scale train trundles over the site, its windows milky-gray from all the pollution. The gate at which the Genoese sailor once knocked still exists, but now it features a wrought-iron doorknob shaped like a ship. Where the porter once sat is the ticket booth. In a pond down by the river are replicas of the *Santa María*, the *Niña*, and the *Pinta*. These replicas have steel masts and synthetic fairleads. Plastic turtles float in the water while unclothed plastic Indians stand on the edge of the pond with plastic fish hanging from their fishing rods.

The monastery opens for only a few hours each day. Calm returns to La Rábida when the tourist buses finally depart. The doors of the sparsely furnished refectory, where Columbus and his son Diego sat and ate, open onto a colonnaded courtyard, where Marchena and Columbus would once have strolled. The entrance to the church—with its tiny side chapel and the statue of the Virgin—lies at the far end.

———

Marchena and Columbus soon established the fundamentals of the voyage. A large fleet was not necessary; three or four seaworthy, maneuverable ships would suffice, as well as the proper equipment and an experienced crew of maybe 90 to 120 men. Such an expedition, they knew, could only be financed by the crown or by Spain's nobility. The Franciscan friar knew exactly whom they should approach. Don Enrique de Guzmán was the wealthiest businessman in the country and also the Duke of Medina-Sidonia. Though initially he expressed some interest in Columbus's plan, Don Enrique eventually decided against getting involved. Marchena and Columbus then approached Don Luis de la Cerda, the Duke of Medina-Celi, who maintained a large fleet of merchant vessels and could easily have underwritten such an adventure. Columbus explained his idea and his concept of the shape of the world (although he would certainly not have revealed the key element, namely, his understanding of the ways the Atlantic winds worked). Having convinced the duke that this expedition could be a profitable business venture, Columbus was offered use of his ships. Then the duke was beset by doubts: was a private individual, even a member of the nobility, permitted to finance such a risky venture on his own? Should he not ask for permission from the crown? The duke was uncertain enough that he inquired at the court whether he might be permitted to give Columbus use of his ships.

Alas, this turned out to be a bad idea, one that would cost Columbus more than six years of his life. Bartolomé de Las Casas later wrote:

> He began to sustain a terrible, continued, painful and prolonged battle; a material one of weapons would not have been so sharp

and horrendous as that which he had to endure from informing so many people of no understanding, although they presumed to know all about it, and replying patiently to many people who did not know him nor had any respect for his person, receiving insulting speeches which afflicted his soul. It was the worst imaginable time to ask the King and Queen for anything, for they faced a host of other problems.

The marriage of Queen Isabella of Castile and King Ferdinand of Aragón in 1469 had united the confederation of independent realms, creating one nation. But Spain remained an enormous construction site, with a population of 5.5 million people who spoke various languages (only later would Castilian be established as the official language). Civil wars had torn the country apart, and in an effort to keep their power-hungry nobility under control, Isabella and Ferdinand had traveled up and down the Spanish provinces, accompanied by a train of followers, from Córdoba to Seville, from Madrid to Barcelona.

At the same time, the monarchs were engaged in a religious war with their fiercest enemy, the Moors, who had occupied the Spanish heartland since the eighth century, when Muslim troops had attacked from Morocco. The Moors had named their new empire to the north of Gibraltar "Al-Andalus." Spain blossomed under their control. They transformed cities like Seville and Córdoba into magnificent metropolises, cultivated the arts and sciences, and extended religious freedom to Christians and Jews alike. The borderlands, however, were constantly ravaged by war. A coalition of Christian kings had driven the Moors from central Spain and pushed them south. One by one, the Muslim cities fell until, by the time of Isabella and Ferdinand, there were only a few strongholds remaining, including Granada and its hilltop fortress, the Alhambra. The Christian knights were followed by the Inquisitors, Dominicans who were also known as the pope's bloodhounds. Muslims fled and Jews were forced to convert for fear of being burned at the stake. Despite being baptized, many Jews led a shadowy existence, for many of the *conversos,* as they were known, continued to practice their faith in secret.

Ferdinand and Isabella had one aim, which was to live up to their epithet Los Reyes Católicos, "the Catholic Sovereigns." Their goal was one nation, one people—and the means to accomplish that was to institute one religion. When Columbus and Marchena approached them, Ferdinand and Isabella were already close to achieving their goal. They had brought an end to the constant disputes with Portugal by ceding the trade along the African coast. It had been a sacrifice, but it meant they could focus their attention on the most important battlefront, the crusade against the heathens who still controlled Granada and the port of Málaga on the Mediterranean. The campaign cost the monarchs vast amounts of money and consumed all their energies. Thus was the fate of Granada and the Moors inextricably linked to that of Christopher Columbus—as well as those of the persecuted Jews.

In early 1486 Columbus and Marchena traveled to Córdoba, where they hoped to meet the king and queen. The monarchs, however, had left for Madrid just prior to the New Year, and the hopeful applicants missed them by a matter of mere days. Columbus decided to wait until April, when they returned. Ferdinand showed no interest at all in Columbus's plan. In addition to being pious and puritanical, Isabella was a power broker, more farsighted than her husband. She received Columbus in early May 1486. After listening to his plan, she remained undecided whether she would grant permission to the Duke of Medina-Celi. After all, were Columbus correct, the duke would gain control over the sea route to India; to preclude such an eventuality, the crown should finance the voyage. But if this foreigner turned out to be no more than a dreamer, and Spanish sailors and Spanish ships were sent out on a mission of folly, she would be ridiculed. Why should she support an idea that the Portuguese had already dismissed?

Isabella's indecision led the queen to ask one of her courtiers, Father Fernando de Talavera, to assemble a commission of experts.

Columbus understood what this meant; he had been through it once before in Portugal. The Talavera commission first convened around Christmas. Talavera had appointed astronomers, cartographers, and lawyers, all of them scholars; in other words, these were Spain's scientific elite—sure of their opinions and self-regarding. Before them was an obscure foreigner, a braggart, a sailor who had not yet accomplished anything of real merit, a nameless cartographer, and a man who purported to be learned but who had not even written a book. Columbus's chances of being taken seriously were slight. A few years later, Francisco López de Gómara, a chronicler, wrote that since Columbus was "a foreigner and was poorly dressed, and with no greater support than that of a friar, he was not believed or listened to by anyone.... He felt a great torment of the spirit," added Gomara.

In the months and even years that followed, the commission met many times, and the scene repeated itself over and over again. Columbus presented his plan, and the scholars expressed their doubts about his calculations. The estimates that Talavera's experts came up with corresponded with those of their Portuguese colleagues. Three thousand five hundred and fifty miles to China? They juggled figures and quoted such authorities as Aristotle, the Bible, and Ptolemy to prove the notion ridiculous. Columbus continued to make no mention of his secret route to the west, revealing nothing about the winds he had observed on his travels to Iceland, Ireland, and to the south; he also kept Toscanelli's letter hidden. Columbus probably did not help his case. He is known to have been a terrible diplomat, both obstinate and dogmatic, and very likely he told the experts exactly what he thought of them and their calculations. Decades later Columbus's son Fernando continued the tradition of ridiculing the scholars:

> The members of this committee were not so well informed as the business required. Nor did the Admiral wish to reveal all the details of his plan, fearing lest it be stolen from him in Castile as

it had been in Portugal.... The Admiral gave suitable replies to
all these objections, but the more effective his arguments, the less
these men understood on account of their ignorance; for when
a man poorly trained in mathematics reaches an advanced age,
he is no longer capable of apprehending the truth because of the
erroneous notions previously imprinted on his mind.

Fernando may have overstated matters, for Columbus's arguments did cause some of the jury members, possibly even Talavera himself, to reconsider. Although the members were torn and unable to make any recommendation to the queen, they didn't reject his plan outright.

While he waited, Columbus received a stipend of 3,000 *maravedís* every three months from Isabella. This wasn't enough to keep body and soul together, and as Las Casas noted, Columbus resorted to drawing sea charts to make ends meet. There was little he could do, aside from wait and occasionally meet with Talavera's experts.

Córdoba must have been a lonely place for a petitioner and widower. Nonetheless, over the centuries a number of Genoese had ended up in Córdoba, settling mainly around the Puerta del Hierro on the right bank of the river Guadalquivir. One day, not far from there, Columbus came upon an apothecary that had become a meeting place for Genoese expatriates and Spanish men of letters. Here he met Diego de Arana, a young man from a family of wine merchants who invited Columbus home. Years before the Arana family had taken in a distant cousin, who had been orphaned as a child. Beatriz Enríquez de Arana was twenty-one years old when she met Columbus. She could read and write—a remarkable achievement at the time—but she still hadn't found a husband; her lack of dowry was an enormous problem. The widower whom Beatriz's cousin brought home might have been going gray, but he was also someone who lived on the fringes of society. He could also be, as we've seen, extremely charming if he chose. He knew the queen and a host of influential men; and he was refined and mixed easily in the best society. The orphan from the countryside and the immigrant from Italy began an affair. This was not outrageous in an age when even bishops kept mistresses, and at any rate the Arana family learned of their affair, for its consequences soon became visible. In 1488 Beatriz de Arana gave birth to a son whom Columbus named Fernando and who would later become his father's most important biographer.

Unlike his half-brother Diego, Fernando was to remain illegitimate. Columbus never married Beatriz. She was, after all, the orphaned daughter of a farmer and, pretty and young as she was, he couldn't possibly have presented her at court. Beatriz had nothing to offer a Colón, as Columbus now called himself in Spain, especially one for whom titles and wealth were critically important. Although she supported him through the difficult years in Spain, he refused to marry her. Even after he had made his great discovery, earning the titles of viceroy and Admiral of the Ocean Sea, Columbus never gave her more than an annual income of 10,000 *maravedís*. Only on his deathbed would he try to make amends. In his last will and testament, drawn up in 1506, he decreed that provisions be made for her: "Beatriz Enríquez, mother of Don Fernando my son, is put in a way to live honorably as a person to whom I am in so great debt, and thus for discharge of my conscience, because it weigheth much on my mind." Traces of Beatriz de Arana would be found centuries later in Córdoba's city archives. She never married, but she did survive Columbus.

———————

Over the centuries history has transformed Columbus into a name, just as his name has become history, delineating a moment of before and after, East and West, then and now. And while the name appears prominently in nearly every history book and textbook—in addition to serving as the name of an entire country and several cities—the man remains inaccessible, unreal, inhuman. The Columbuses supplied over the years by his biographers have varied enormously. Samuel Eliot Morison saw Columbus above all as a man of action and a remarkably gifted sailor, and celebrated him on those terms. Taviani, the patriotic Genoese historian, viewed him as a flawed genius and visionary whose life was a "wonderful adventure." Kirkpatrick Sale, as we've seen, regarded Columbus as little more than a mass murderer, his 1492 landing an extinction-level event.

On one corner of a cobbled square in the historic part of Seville stands a house belonging to Consuelo Varela and Juan Gil, and if there is one place in the world where Columbus remains alive today, this is it. The house is four stories tall but so cramped inside as to make movement difficult. Somewhere around fifty thousand books are stacked in piles reaching up to the ceiling; heaps of documents seem to cover the remaining space. Together, Varela and Gil have logged some eighty years of work on Columbus, tracking down the explorer and trying to find out what he thought, who influenced him, who helped him, what drove him. They know him better than anyone else alive.

Gil began his career as a lecturer, engaged in research into myths and legends and how they made their way from the Old World to the New—a somewhat abstract topic but one that led him straight to Columbus. Much of what had been previously presented as fact about the explorer was, after all, myth. Some of the legends had a dogged way of surviving, like the one that had Queen Isabella pawning her jewelry to pay for Columbus's first journey or the claim that it was Columbus who discovered that the earth was round and convinced the Spanish this was so. When Gil first met Varela, she was a student looking for a dissertation topic. She could have had no idea that her husband-to-be would recommend a topic that would keep her busy for the rest of her life. Nobody had compiled all of Columbus's writings, he had told her. Why didn't she rummage through a few of the archives in search of his letters, instructions, reports, and other written traces? (He neglected to mention that some of the archives would be in places like Mexico.) Varela persevered and *Textos y documentos completos* was her first book.

Conveniently, the couple's home is located a few minutes away from the Archivo General de Indias. Housed in a sixteenth-century, two-story structure are some forty million documents, the oldest dating back to 1492. Some have yet to be sorted and analyzed, and indeed have laid unread for centuries. These include the files from the Spanish colonial administration, the Casa de la Contratación, which include freight lists, payrolls, tax rolls, administrative inquiries, death certificates, birth certificates, and account logs. The Spaniards were fanatics when it came to bureaucracy. Anything undertaken by one of His or Her Majesty's subjects had to be recorded, copied out, countersigned, and filed away. Little went undocumented. Most material relating to the Age of Discovery ultimately found its way to Seville, turning the Archivo General into a treasure trove, literally. There are files containing reports of sunken gold bullion shipments and statements from survivors. Although research can often take years, the Archivo General has attracted droves of treasure hunters. Professional gold diggers may not be as welcome there as those whose motivations are more pure, but when the treasure hunters uncover clues leading to a shipwreck, the historians will ultimately benefit. Several years ago the files from Seville enabled Mel Fisher to locate the Spanish galleon *Nuestra Señora de Atocha,* which sank off the U.S. coast in 1622. Her shipment was worth $400 million.

Historians tend to have a different concept of what constitutes treasure. Varela and Gil can become quite restless and edgy when their thoughts turn to what might still be lying, undiscovered, on the shelves both here in Seville and in the country's second largest archive, which is located in Simancas. They have already found Columbus's crew list from the fourth voyage and many other details contained in expense accounts and letters. They reveal to what degree Columbus was plagued by red tape, such as when, for example, he tried to purchase tax-free provisions for his crew in Seville; or how he complained when he fell ill; or his outrage when he believed he had been cheated. Columbus was a prolific writer, and to date Varela and Gil have uncovered ninety-nine letters, notes, and directives. These are in addition to Columbus's will and the logbook of his first voyage to the New World (though it only exists as a transcript done by Bartolomé de Las Casas). There is also what has become known as the *Book of Privileges,* which Columbus compiled shortly before his death, to support his claims to the rights and titles that the crown was attempting to deny him, and the *Book of Prophecies,* an eclectic collection of writings, apocalyptic and mysterious in nature, in which the aging Columbus positions himself as God's envoy.

"Famous people are subject to interpretations," said Varela, "and these interpretations become unassailable truths through repetition over the course of time. If one questions them, one risks being considered crazy." Varela has questioned all of the theories, studied all works on Columbus—academic and general—and often wondered where their authors acquired their information. She and Gil have scoured the archives and come as close as they can to visualizing Columbus the man, so far as he is discernible today.

Varela is not overly fond of the man who has defined and affected her life. "Sometimes, I really hate him," she put it. In her view, Columbus was a liar and so mistrustful of others because he assumed they were as untruthful as he. "He thought everybody was against him, and he had a very tactical approach to the truth." For example, on his second voyage, he forced his crew to swear that Cuba was not an island but part of the mainland, though no one could have known one way or the other. Anything that didn't fit into his image of the world was suppressed. Columbus was also moneygrubbing and stingy. On his first voyage, for example, he offered a prize of 10,000 *maravedis* to the first man to spy land on the horizon. When one of his sailors claimed the prize, Columbus counterclaimed that he himself had seen a light on the horizon the previous night—which is not likely. Moreover, Columbus never spent even one *maravedí* on creature comforts— a house, furniture, carpets, or gifts. "Columbus wasn't able to savor anything," commented Varela. "He never needed anything for himself, unless of course, he wanted to impress others. He pursued his goals but he couldn't even appreciate it when he achieved success. He didn't need other people." Varela believes that Columbus was an egotist who kept only his own interests at heart. "Me, me, me—that was his motto. He couldn't make other people happy and he never even considered it." He was always traveling, constantly on the run, haunted by the idea that his time was running out. "Columbus was restless and had no home. He couldn't keep hold of anything or anybody—and he didn't want to. He switched friends whenever it seemed necessary. Columbus only took, he never gave," said Varela, "and he behaved despicably toward Beatriz Enríquez, and also toward Diego Méndez, who saved his life on the fourth voyage—never a word of thanks or any acknowledgment. Nothing."

Columbus's strengths were his weaknesses and his weaknesses, his strengths. He ignored everything but his goal, yet that single-mindedness was what he needed to succeed. He was restless; yet someone at peace with himself would never have been so driven. He was inconsiderate and ruthless, pushing his friends away when they could no longer be of service and surrounding himself only with those who might advance his cause. He was hard on other people, yet equally hard on himself, disciplined enough to endure the endless years of struggle and the stresses and strains of the voyages. He thirsted for fame, for status, for gold and power, and this pushed him beyond the horizon. Above all, Columbus's intense egotism stemmed from an unwavering belief that he was a tool of fate, an envoy of God. In the dawning of this new age, he was certain that he of all men had been chosen to bear the one faith across the seas to new lands. That was why he changed his name to Christoferens—the "bearer of Christ." In the *Book of Prophecies*, he wrote: "Our Lord opened to my understanding (I could sense his hand upon me), so that it became clear to me that it was feasible to navigate from here to the Indies; and he unlocked within me the determination to execute the idea.... Who doubts that this illumination was from the Holy Spirit? I attest that [the Spirit], with marvelous rays of light, consoled me through the holy and sacred Scriptures...encouraging me to proceed, and, continually, without ceasing for a moment, they inflame me with a sense of great urgency."

While killing time in Córdoba, chasing after the monarchs and squabbling with Talavera's commission, Columbus must have been alarmed to learn that the Portuguese were making progress. The Portuguese king had commissioned two adventurers, Fernão Dulmo and João Estreito, to sail westward rather than south along Africa's coast. It was possible that they had already found the legendary island of Antillia previously mentioned by Toscanelli. It was possible that they had found the sea route to India. Nonetheless, Dulmo and Estreito set sail from the Azores, and Columbus knew perfectly well that he had neglected to mention to the Portuguese king that, in his humble opinion, one had to sail south before setting a westerly course. Columbus was right, of course, and the Portuguese expedition was doomed to failure. At the latitude of the Azores, the wind blows constantly from west to east, and even with seaworthy caravels, Dulmo and Estreito had no chance of succeeding.

Nonetheless, a short time later the Portuguese did manage a breakthrough on Prince Henry's favorite route. In December 1488 Bartolomeu Dias returned to Lisbon from a long voyage, bearing sensational news. In 1487 Dias had managed to sail south, finally reaching and rounding the southerly tip of Africa. He named it the Cape of Good Hope; from there he had seen open waters to the east and the north. Columbus knew that it would not be long before the Portuguese sailed even farther around the cape and then headed north. Some historians believe that Columbus took advantage of the Portuguese monarch's offer of safe passage and was standing on the pier when his toughest competitor sailed home. A marginal note in one of his books reveals that

Columbus at least concerned himself with Dias. The Portuguese captain, he wrote, had discovered by astrolabe that the Cape of Good Hope lay forty-five degrees from the equator. In actual fact, both Dias and Columbus were off by more than six hundred miles. But the distance on this route, along the coast of Africa, was irrelevant. Columbus sensed that the Portuguese ships were close to discovering the route to India, since he, like many geographers, believed that Africa's east coast and the coast of India were fronted by the same ocean.

In the meantime, as he was not making much headway, Columbus turned his focus to convincing the commission and the queen that it was now or never. If the Spanish didn't do it, the Portuguese would. If the scholars kept brushing him off with their book learning, he would have to beat them at their own game.

———————————

One of the greatest treasures housed in Seville's cathedral is the Biblioteca Colombina, which consists of hundreds of well-thumbed and slightly singed books that Fernando Colón inherited from his father and later bequeathed to the cathedral. Hidden behind an inconspicuous door in the cathedral's outer wall, the Columbus library resembles a maximum-security wing. The books sit in long wooden showcases, in which temperature and humidity are constantly monitored. Though anyone bearing a recommendation or letter of introduction can look at the books, they do so under the watchful eye of a warden.

These are some of the texts that have enabled historians like Varela and Gil to put themselves inside Columbus's head. Whenever he read, Columbus always kept a quill and ink handy to write comments in the margins. These notes sometimes consist of only a word or two; sometimes, however, they take up every inch of the margin. Some three thousand of these notes exist—Columbus read a great deal during his long and miserable period of waiting in Spain—and what they reveal is that he was systematically scouring for ammunition in his battle against the Talavera commission. He read the latest edition of Pliny's *Natural History*, printed in 1489, and a 1477 edition of the *Historia rerum ubique gestarum* by Enea Silvio Piccolomini, who later became Pope Pius II. One of his favorite books seems to have been *Imago mundi* by Pierre d'Ailly. Sometime around 1410, the Cardinal of Cambrai in France had compiled a comprehensive almanac of the world's geography. Columbus marked and commented upon nearly every statement in which d'Ailly posited that the earth was smaller than it really was, such as, "It is evident that this sea is navigable in a few days if the wind be fair, whence it follows that the sea is not so great that it can cover three-quarters of the globe, as certain people figure it." Naturally this would have seemed a useful quotation to Columbus, especially as it came from a cardinal. He would use this argument when facing the experts on Talavera's commission.

Other notations reveal what it was he was searching for on the other side of the ocean. Columbus's edition of Marco Polo's accounts of his travels to China contains no marginal notes, no exclamation marks or squiggles, even when Polo recounted the story of the Great Khan—until Polo wrote of a marble palace in Ciandu with "camere auro ornate" (ornate golden rooms). Columbus recopied the sentence in the margin. And where Polo elaborates upon the wealth of the Great Khan—"He has a very large palace entirely roofed with fine gold"—Columbus noted, "aurum, argentums, lapides preciosas" (gold, silver, gemstones). Columbus was also interested in nautical details, such as those contained in Polo's account (in chapter 23) of a city by the sea where large ships lay anchored in the bays and the people possessed vast quantities of pearls. Columbus marked this passage and also underlined the part where Polo described the ruler as wearing a golden chain set with pearls. He also made a note of Polo's description of the Chinese province of Tibet, where the people possessed an abundance of gold they called "de payollo" but—at least according to Polo—preferred to pay in pieces of coral. Columbus wrote in the margin, "aurum de paiolo" and "coralum pro moneta."

———————

In the summer of 1489, Isabella of Castile received Columbus yet again. He had obviously found favor with her by this point, so much so that some historians have speculated that the two had an affair, pointing out that Isabella's marriage to Ferdinand of Aragón had been no love match. Apart from the evidence of several meetings between Columbus and Isabella, however, there is nothing to substantiate rumors of a romantic attachment. It was probably in Jaén that Isabella informed Columbus of the verdict of the Talavera commission. Neither Pliny nor Marco Polo nor Pierre d'Ailly was able to help him, for the scholars had rejected Columbus's plan. They had many arguments for doing so: that the ocean was infinitely too large and probably not navigable; that a voyage to India would take three years; that even if he did make it to the other side of the globe, he would never be able to return because he would have to sail back uphill; that it was unlikely that there was anything new to discover so many hundreds of years after the creation of the earth.

Evidently, Isabella was not convinced that her scholars were entirely correct in their decision. Instead of sending Columbus away, she deferred, citing the war against the Moors and the battle for Granada. Fernando later wrote:

> So, having spent much time and money on this project, their Highnesses replied to the Admiral that they were preoccupied with other wars and conquests, especially the War of Granada, which they were then bringing to conclusion, and so could not give their attention to a new enterprise, but that presently they would have a better opportunity to consider the Admiral's offer. Actually, the Sovereigns did not take seriously the large promises made to them by the Admiral.

Columbus had only one chance left: Bartolomeo. By the end of the 1480s, Columbus's brother had also left Lisbon, and while

Christopher was endeavoring to drum up Spanish support, Bartolomeo had set sail for London to offer his brother's plan to the English. Marauding pirates raided his ship, and he arrived in London penniless and in poor health. He took some time to recover, earning a little money by selling sea charts, until finally he was received by King Henry VII. Bartolomeo was evidently not as gifted a speaker as his brother. With limited English and probably no skill in Latin, he must have seemed like a backwoodsman to the English. Nonetheless, Bartolomeo focused on what he knew best, namely, drawing, and submitted to them his brother's plan with the help of a world map. His map wasn't as detailed as Toscanelli's sketch and essentially showed the world as Ptolemy had imagined it—with a huge Asian continent stretching so far east that it stretched back near Europe. Maps or no, the English rejected the plan. Bartolomeo rolled up his charts and in 1490 made his way to Paris to visit the next monarch on his list, Charles VIII.

Centuries later a researcher stumbled across Bartolomeo's trail. In 1925 Charles de la Roncière examined a very old and mysterious-looking vellum chart in the Bibliothèque nationale in Paris. Although the cartographer had forgotten to sign it, he had left behind something resembling a signature. Individual elements of the map were annotated with explanations, very brief passages from the text of d'Ailly's *Imago mundi*. And they were exact copies of the marginal notes Columbus had made in his copy of the book. Bartolomeo's chart obviously made an impression at the French court, although not in the way that the Genoese had hoped. Anne de Beaujeu, older sister to the king, gave Bartolomeo an appanage and permitted him to live at the court in Fontainebleau. Bartolomeo must have thought that France was the right country to help them with their plans and sent cautiously optimistic letters to his brother in Spain. Although the king showed little interest in the plan, Anne de Beaujeu did possess some influence.

By 1491 Columbus decided he was tired of waiting and had lost all hope that Queen Isabella would help him. He had by now wasted six years. France looked to be his last best chance. He would turn forty this year and was uncertain how long it would take him and Bartolomeo to convince the French king. Columbus traveled to La Rábida to say farewell to his son Diego, who was still living with Fray Marchena. When he arrived at the monastery, he was met by Abbot Juan Pérez, the queen's former confessor. Pérez became fascinated by Columbus's plan. He knew nothing about navigation and the shape of the earth, but he did know a physician in Palos, a scholar of some renown named Fernández. The three of them spent days poring over books and charts. The monk and the physician cross-examined Columbus in much the way the experts from the Talavera commission had done so, training and preparing him for his last meeting with Isabella. Pérez and Fernández looked for weaknesses in his reasoning and helped him to find better arguments to convince the queen. When Pérez finally decided that Columbus was ready, he brought his influence to bear and wrote to Isabella, requesting an audience. The reply arrived two weeks later—naturally, Isabella's old confessor would be welcome at the court. As there were no horses at the monastery, Pérez borrowed a mule. The animal was paid for by a devout friend from the neighboring village of Palos. Pérez's benefactor was Martín Alonso Pinzón, a sea captain. His small caravel was often anchored down by the river, and Columbus would have been able to see it from the monastery. She was called the *Pinta*.

Father Pérez met the queen at an army encampment at Santa Fe. The monk had arrived at an opportune moment. Determined to drive the Moors from their final stronghold, Isabella had laid siege to Granada, and victory over her enemies was in sight. She was therefore in an excellent frame of mind. Father Pérez didn't have to plead long to get Columbus one last hearing. The queen went so far as to have 20,000 *maravedís* sent to Columbus, so that he could purchase respectable clothes and a mule for the journey to Santa Fe.

Columbus arrived at the encampment in late summer. Another royal commission was hastily mobilized to consider his plan. This time the experts returned a more positive verdict, and it seemed as if the queen would finally be disposed to grant him a commission and provide him with ships. Negotiations began, and after all the years he had spent waiting in Portugal and Spain, Columbus seemed close to achieving his goal. Anybody else would have jubilantly signed the contract immediately and prepared to set sail. But not Columbus. He broke off negotiations.

Without a penny to his name, Columbus made demands to which Queen Isabella could not agree. Regardless of the outcome of his voyage, for example, he insisted on a hereditary title of nobility. In addition, he claimed the title of Admiral of the Ocean Sea for himself and his heirs and demanded to be appointed governor of all discovered lands as well as viceroy with full powers. He also requested 10 percent of all wealth derived from the discovered lands until the end of all days for himself and his heirs. Those were his terms. The fawning courtiers were aghast at the demand for 10 percent of all of India's riches. What Columbus was demanding was more than a principality. It was a kingdom. Columbus's son Fernando later acknowledged as much:

> For even if the scheme were sound, the reward he demanded seemed enormous; and if it proved a failure, it would later seem a piece of folly to have given what he asked. . . . Let me say here that I greatly admire the wisdom, courage, and foresight of the Admiral, who, though so unlucky in his affairs and so desirous of remaining in that kingdom, and reduced at the time to a state in which he should have been content with anything, yet demanded great titles and rewards as if he foresaw the fortunate outcome of his enterprise.

Why Isabella didn't throw him out immediately remains unclear. Possibly she was too preoccupied, for on January 2, 1492, the Moors finally capitulated, surrendering Granada. Columbus was among those who walked through the gates of the fortress in victory. Shortly afterward Isabella summoned Columbus and informed him that the crown would not yield to his demands. It seemed like the end for Columbus. He had finally gone too far. The day before he had been a viceroy in the making, and now all he had was the mule he'd ridden in on. Beaten and rejected, he "set out for Córdoba to prepare his journey to France," wrote Fernando. Columbus only got as far as the bridge to the village Pinos-Puente, some seven miles from Santa Fe, before fortune caught up with him again. An envoy from the queen appeared, bearing the message that Columbus's demands could be met after all. The man who made this miracle possible was Luis de Santángel, manager of the king's household accounts. And as Fernando later recounted, Santángel had gone out on a limb for Columbus:

> On the same day that the Admiral departed from Santa Fé, ... Luis Santángel ... presented himself before the Queen and with words that his keen desire to persuade her suggested, told her he was surprised that her Highness, who had always shown a resolute spirit in matters of great weight and consequence, should lack it now for an enterprise that offered so little risk yet could prove of so great service to God and the exaltation of His Church, not to speak of the very great increase and glory of her realms and kingdoms. The enterprise, moreover, was of such nature that if any other ruler should perform what the Admiral offered to do, it would clearly be a great injury to her estate.

Had Santángel really spoken to the queen in this tone, he would have been risking his neck. Furthermore, the whole affair was none of his business; he worked for King Ferdinand, not for Isabella. And yet Santángel not only pressured the queen; he also offered to finance the expedition. Experts later estimated that it cost 2 million *maravedís* to equip three ships for Columbus. Santángel offered to raise more than 1 million without burdening the queen's budget. After all, he was also treasurer of what was known as Santa Hermandad, a civilian militia. The fact that Santa Hermandad was hopelessly bankrupt after many long years of war did not seem to have concerned Santángel. He planned to take out a loan in the name of the militia, and there were plenty of wealthy businessmen who would gladly lend him the money.

The so-called miracle of Santa Fe has long fascinated historians. Samuel Eliot Morison wrote that Santángel's arguments worked because his "reasoning was irresistible. So little risk for so vast a gain!" Columbus had spent years describing the anticipated profits of the voyage in the most glorious terms. It must have been clear to the queen that Castile was able to equip three caravels for such a journey. But what drove Santángel to risk so much? The Santa Hermandad, for which he was only treasurer, had nothing to do with voyages of discovery. A theory exists that had once seemed absurd but has since gained some acceptance among even serious Columbus experts. The theory consists of two parts: First, that Columbus's forefathers were Jewish; and, second, that Queen Isabella was determined to drive all Jews from Spain after the Moors were expelled, and thus that the Spanish Jews were desperately searching for countries that would offer them refuge. The key figure in this theory is Santángel. The man who brought about the realization of Columbus's Great Enterprise was a *converso*. Some of Santángel's relatives had even been victims of auto-da-fé.

In the 1970s Simon Wiesenthal began searching for traces of Jewish roots in Santángel's and Columbus's families. Wiesenthal, who died in 2005, had by then earned an international reputation for his work as a Nazi hunter who had found and exposed more than one thousand people for their part in the Holocaust. Though the level of his participation remains disputed, Wiesenthal claimed to have helped track down Adolf Eichmann in Argentina; Eichmann was abducted by Israeli agents and executed in 1962. Through his work in archives in Europe, Wiesenthal discovered there was plenty of evidence to support the theory that Columbus descended from baptized Jews, a theory that had sprung up shortly after Columbus's death. In northern Italy, for example, a number of Jewish families bear the name Colombo, as do Christian families. Columbus's mother's maiden name was Susanna da Fontanarossa; her father's name was Jacobo. In those days these were considered Jewish names (though many Christians were also baptized under those names). Researching Columbus's writings, Wiesenthal learned that the man was unusually familiar with the Jewish mind-set and the Old Testament. For example, in one of Columbus's books in the Biblioteca Colombina, Wiesenthal found a marginal note in which Columbus had converted the year 1481 to the Jewish calendar and come up with the year 5241. An odd thing for a Catholic to have done. Moreover, in a letter Columbus attested, "I am the servant of Him who raised David to that high estate." By "high estate," Columbus meant the rank of sovereign.

"It could well be that Columbus was of Jewish descent," argued Juan Gil. Just like Wiesenthal, he noticed that Columbus seemed more inspired by the stories in the Old Testament than by those in the New Testament. For example, Columbus once claimed that he also voyaged to find the legendary gold mines of King Solomon in the land of Ophir. Solomon was said to have used the treasures from these mines to build the temple in Jerusalem. Columbus wrote that he wanted to use gold from exactly the same mine to rebuild the temple. On February 3, 1500, Columbus reported that he had rediscovered those mines on the island of Hispaniola, suggesting that Hispaniola (as mentioned earlier, today shared by Haiti and the Dominican Republic) was none other than the legendary Ophir. Said Gil, "The idea of the temple, particularly the idea of rebuilding the temple, is by no means Christian. It is definitely an ancient Jewish guiding concept."

Time and again in his letters, Columbus drew comparisons between contemporary events and scenes from the Bible, mostly from the Old Testament. Abraham, Isaac, and Sarah were his particular heroes and heroine. Two details about his first voyage to the New World seem particularly telling. Columbus had whetted the appetite of the Catholic sovereigns for an expedition by arguing that its true purpose was to extend the realm of faith and to convert heathens. Yet he did not take a single priest along on his voyage. Instead he chose a *converso* interpreter named Luis de Torres. One reason might have been that Torres spoke various Arabic dialects. Arabic was then a universal language, and it was hoped that it would prove useful for communicating with the Indians. There were a number of Arabic translators living in Castile more accomplished than Torres, but none who spoke Hebrew. Secondly, when Columbus planned to set sail on his first voyage on August 3, 1492, he saw to it that everyone on his crew remained aboard the ships on the evening of August 2. Four months previously, on March 31, 1492, Spain's sovereigns had signed the Edict of Expulsion. Following the defeat of the Moors and the fall of Granada, any Jew who refused to be baptized was ordered into exile.

> In these our kingdoms there were some wicked Christians who Judaized and apostatized from our holy Catholic faith, the great cause of which was interaction between the Jews and these Christians. . . . We order all Jews and Jewesses of whatever age they may be, who live, reside, and exist in our said kingdoms that by the end of the month of July next of the present year, they depart from all of these our said realms along with their sons and daughters, menservants and maidservants, and they shall not dare to return to those places under pain that if they do not comply with this command, they incur the penalty of death and the confiscation of all their possessions.

The end-of-July deadline meant that the Jews were forced to sell their possessions rapidly and at ludicrously low prices. Whole convoys of refugees assembled at the ports. Fleeing Jews paid any price to get on ships that would take them out of the country. Many of them died when their unseaworthy vessels sank. The deadline for expulsion was extended to August 2. On August 2, 1492, at the stroke of midnight, Columbus's ships were ready to put to sea.

In Wiesenthal's mind, the evidence was substantial enough, but he believed it irrelevant whether or not Columbus had Jewish predecessors. More to the point was the *converso* Santángel and his concern for the suffering of the 300,000 *conversos* fleeing the henchmen of the Great Inquisitor Tomás de Torquemada. Many, including the Santángel family, were wealthy. They controlled banks and trading houses, which only fueled the public envy and incited denunciations. The devout men of the Inquisition were only too glad to be given reports of baptized Jews who were secretly adhering to their old faith. *Conversos* were tortured and murdered, their possessions seized. Wiesenthal believed that Columbus's plans "raised hopes among the persecuted and the potential victims of future persecutions...offering Jews the prospect of reaching an emigration country, a possibility of escaping the pressures of the Church."

In addition, Wiesenthal cited the ancient Jewish legend of the lost tribes of Israel, who were dispersed in all directions and had founded a Jewish empire somewhere in the world. "If a bridge existed between Columbus and the Jews and *Conversos*, then it was this opportunity to discover Jewish lands," noted Wiesenthal. Whatever the truth behind the theory, it remains a fact that Santángel intervened in a decisive moment and with motives that remain mysterious. When Columbus returned from his great voyage of discovery, the first person he wrote with the news was not the queen but Luis de Santángel.

———

Columbus and the crown spent months negotiating the finer details of their contract. Juan de Coloma, secretary to the king and author of the Edict of Expulsion, acted on the crown's behalf. Father Juan Pérez from La Rábida represented Columbus. The Franciscan monk fought hard on every item, wresting concessions from Coloma and ultimately gaining all that Columbus had asked.

Pérez had a good hand, explained Consuelo Varela. The king and queen were holding court as victors and "were so happy during that time that they would have agreed to nearly anything," as she explained. By choosing to address him as "Don Cristóbal Colón" in the Capitulations—as the contract between the queen and Columbus was termed—the degree to which he had prevailed was clear. "Don" is a form of address used only for nobility. Columbus had come far, and the contract promised to take him even further.

First, Your Highnesses, as the lords you are of the Ocean Seas, appoint Don Cristóbal Colón, from now on as your admiral on all those islands and mainland discovered or acquired by his command and expertise in the Ocean Seas during his lifetime and, after his death, by his heirs and successors one after the other in perpetuity, with all the rights and privileges belonging to that office.

Your Highnesses also appoint the said Don Cristóbal Colón their Viceroy and Governor-General in all those islands and any mainland and islands that he may discover and acquire in the seas. For the governance of each and every one of them, he will nominate three persons for each office, and Your Highnesses may take and choose the one most beneficial to your service, and thus the lands that our Lord permits him to find and acquire will be best governed to the service of Your Highnesses.

You wish him to have and take for himself one-tenth of all and any merchandise, whether pearls, precious stones, gold, silver, spices, and any other things and merchandise of whatever kind, name, or sort it may be, that is bought, exchanged, found, acquired, and obtained within the limits of the admiralty that Your Highnesses from now on bestow on Don Cristóbal Colón, deducting all the relevant expenses incurred, so that, of what remains clear and free, he may take and keep one-tenth for himself and do with it as he pleases, reserving the other nine-tenths for Your Highnesses.

Should any lawsuits arise on account of the merchandise that he brings back from the islands and mainland acquired or discovered, or over merchandise taken in exchange from other merchants there in the place where this commerce and trade is held and done, and if taking cognizance of such suits belongs to him by virtue of the privileges pertaining to his office of admiral, may it please Your Highnesses that he or his deputy, and no other judge, shall be authorized to take cognizance of and give judgment on it from now on.

On all vessels outfitted for trade and business, each time, whenever, and as often as they are outfitted, Don Cristóbal Colón, if he wishes, may contribute and pay one-eighth of all that is spent on the outfitting and likewise he may have and take one-eighth of the profits that result from such outfitting.

These are authorized and dispatched with the replies from Your Highnesses at the end of each article.

These rights are guaranteed in the city of Santa Fe de la Vega de Granada on the seventeenth day of April in the year one thousand four hundred and ninety-two after the birth of Our Savior Jesus Christ.

[signed] Juan de Coloma, Secretary of Aragón

Oddly, there is no mention of India, the land Columbus intended to find, and, equally oddly, there is no mention of the heathens Columbus intended to convert to Christianity. The Capitulations were purely and simply a contract for a joint venture, setting out the percentage of Columbus's entitlement to whatever wealth he discovered. Whatever motives Santángel might have had, Columbus and the queen were focused upon the money. While the queen had given him a Letter of Credence to the Great Khan, relevant to his mission to reach India, the Capitulations fail to mention this. The voyage of discovery was a business venture, and business was its main purpose. On that score, it does seem odd that Columbus was expected to pay an eighth of the expedition's costs. All that Columbus possessed was a slew of bad debts incurred in Portugal and a mule that had been given to him.

Centuries later Consuelo Varela would "follow the money trail," as she put it. In the archives of the notaries in Seville, she found the last will and testament of a Florentine merchant named Gianotto Berardi, whom the Spaniards called Juanoto. Shortly before his death, Berardi wrote that Don Cristóbal Colón still owed him a fortune. Over the years Varela has found other documents here and there, and in the end she was able to piece together exactly how the discovery of America was financed. It is not a pretty story.

Columbus and Father Pérez were not the only ones present during the negotiations leading up to the signing of the Capitulations. Two other men had also traveled from Seville to Santa Fe: Berardi and his assistant, a young Italian named Amerigo Vespucci, the man for whom a whole continent would later be named because of a cartographer's error. At the time Vespucci was a mere errand boy. Berardi, on the other hand, was the local representative of the great Medici family of Florence, whose family business was organized along the lines of a multinational, with branches in every major city of the known world. Company directors dealt with all kinds of goods by order of and for the accounts of the Medicis, and very occasionally these local bosses were allowed to engage in business transactions on their own. There were three Medici representatives on the Iberian Peninsula: Bartolomeo Marchioni on the Atlantic in Lisbon, Cesare Barchi in Valencia, and Berardi in Seville. All three were involved in trading slaves from Africa's western coast. Spain had of course ceded the slave monopoly to Portugal, so it was Marchioni's job to procure the goods in Lisbon. Once the slaves arrived there, they were brought to Seville, where Berardi would sell them. The slaves he couldn't sell were brought to Valencia, where Barchi then shipped them to Italy.

While neither Fernando Colón nor Bartolomé de Las Casas ever mentioned the slave traders in their accounts, Columbus must have been acquainted with these men. He had probably established contact with his compatriots during the years he had

spent biding his time in Castile. And there may have been a Florentine connection from the time he spent with the Genoese expatriate community in Lisbon. Berardi and Columbus founded
something similar to a joint company, with the slave trader providing the financial means and Columbus providing the plan.
Santángel borrowed 1.14 million *maravedís,* and Berardi the slave
trader put up around half a million *maravedís*—far more than the
eighth that Columbus was contracted to pay. The nature of their
agreement could possibly explain Columbus's strange behavior
later, when he sailed from one Caribbean island to the next. He
took possession of these new lands in a manner that seems
matter-of-fact, as if they were there for the picking, rather than
the possessions of so powerful and fearful a man as the Great
Khan. He lost no time enslaving the gentle natives, noting that
they were best suited as servants on account of being so docile.

This, then, was the unholy trinity that was to be achieved by
Columbus's expedition: land for Viceroy Columbus, gold for the
king and queen back home, and slaves for Berardi. To the slave
trader, all this must have seemed like an excellent business propo-
sition. He staked all the money he had by investing it in the first
and second voyages. Shortly after Columbus's first discovery, Berardi drew up a long-term business plan, which he presented to
the queen in a letter. He proposed that the ships sail three times
a year, like a shuttle service for slaves.

Before long Berardi had concentrated all his efforts on doing
business with the Indian islands, neglecting everything else. He
invested every last *maravedí* he had in Columbus's enterprise. Before returning from his second voyage of discovery, Columbus
ordered the capture of five hundred slaves. Were they for Berardi?
We don't know. Berardi went bankrupt and all traces of his company have disappeared from the files. The business partners had
not counted on mortality. Most of the Indios taken as slaves were
unable to endure the hardship of months at sea and died below
deck. This was a disaster for Berardi, who died in desperate straits
in late 1495. He was succeeded by Vespucci, who liquidated the
old company.

In 1492, however, Berardi was still solvent, and together with Santángel's 1.14 million, his contribution meant that Columbus was close to achieving his budget of 2 million. The crown's administrators solved the problem of where the rest might be found. The small town of Palos de la Frontera owed the queen a penalty for a misdemeanor (probably smuggling or piracy). Isabella's magistrates drew up a royal command in which the citizens of Palos were ordered to provide Columbus with two caravels, fully equipped and manned, for the duration of one year. Columbus was already familiar with the small harbor town near La Rábida. Martín Alonso Pinzón from Palos had paid for the mule that carried Father Pérez to Santa Fe. The queen's command sealed Pinzón's fate.

———————

The village of Palos de la Frontera hasn't been a port for years. The waters of the Río Tinto retreated and silted up long ago, leaving the piers high and dry. Although the port basin has been filled up, one can still guess where it once lay in Columbus's time. Today it is a gigantic gravel parking lot. On the edge stands a well from which Columbus's crew filled their water barrels. No more than a trickle of water comes from it now; it runs across the parking lot and disappears among the reeds. The largest house on the main street, which had once belonged to the Pinzón brothers, was recently gutted. Now only the walls are left standing. A sign hangs on one of walls: "In this house lived the famous mariners from Palos: Martín Alonso, Vicente Yáñez, and Francisco Martín Pinzón, who set sail from here and discovered America." Not one word of Columbus. He isn't even mentioned on the column in front of the pink-colored village church, though it was in this church that the crew prayed before setting sail. The names of the sailors who sailed off in 1492 are inscribed on the column. Except that of Columbus.

On May 23, 1492, the village elders were called together in Saint George's Church to hear a scribe read a royal decree. In the background stood a gray-haired stranger, the friend of the Franciscan monk from La Rábida. This was how the people of Palos learned that they would have to hand over two of their ships for a long voyage, and without any compensation, not one *maravedí*. Many of the old sailors believed it would be a voyage without return. The decree made no mention of their destination, only that it would go "toward certain regions of the Ocean Sea" where Columbus would "perform certain things for our service." The men gathered in the church probably had an uneasy sense of foreboding. They had doubtless heard rumors about a Colón and his belief one could sail to India. It wasn't clear who had chosen the ships for this suicide mission, but the choice must have been limited. Palos only numbered a few hundred citizens.

One caravel already lay anchored in the harbor—the *Pinta*. A second caravel, the *Niña,* belonged to a man named Juan Niño, from the neighboring village of Moguer. But Columbus wanted more. He demanded use of a third ship. The men of Palos stood firm, however. The royal command had spoken of two ships, not three. Nonetheless, a ship from Galicia in the north was anchored just beyond the harbor, and this was all they would offer. Although the *Gallega* was not a speedy caravel but a potbellied freight ship, a *nao,* Columbus had to take what he was offered. He persuaded the owner, Juan de la Cosa, to charter out the ship. Cosa even agreed to accompany Columbus, along with ten of his men. This was a stroke of luck, for Cosa would later become one of Columbus's stalwarts during the Great Enterprise. Only the name of the ship didn't suit Columbus. He rechristened the *nao* the *Santa María. Santa María, Niña,* and *Pinta*—the small fleet lay ready.

CHAPTER 5

Tierra, Tierra!

This great and wonderful field is far beyond our merit, and can correspond only to the magnificence of the Christian Faith, and to the piety and religion of our Sovereigns. It is not the accomplishment of a human intellect, but is truly the gift of the Divine Mind. It is not unusual indeed with God to listen to the entreaties of his servants who love his precepts, even when they seem to be asking impossibilities, as appears to have been his dealing with us, who have been permitted to perform what the powers of men had never before so much as bordered upon. For whatever may have been hinted in former times of the existence of these islands, either in writing or in discourse, it is certain that it was only obscure conjecture, and that no one ever asserted that he had seen them; and accordingly their existence appeared merely fabulous. Let then our King and Queen, their Nobles, and all their happy realms, and indeed all the nations of Christendom, return thanks to our Savior the Lord Jesus Christ, because he has magnified us with so great a bounty and victory: let solemn procession and other holy offices be celebrated. Glory be henceforth to Christ on the earth, as there is glory in the Heavens, for he is advancing forth to bring salvation to the perishing souls of the

*Heathen. Let us too rejoice, both on account of the exaltation
of our Faith, and to the increase of our temporal advantages,
in which not only Spain but all Christendom will participate.*

—last passage of a letter Columbus wrote to Queen Isabella
after returning from the New World

Columbus spent the summer of 1492 on the Andalusian coast.
This was an anxious time for him, and once again it was Father
Antonio de Marchena who stood by him. Although Columbus
now had his three ships, he needed sailors to man them. He had
Cosa and his ten men. Diego de Arana, cousin to Columbus's
mistress Beatriz, agreed to serve as marshal of the fleet, making
him responsible for weapons and discipline, as well as for Columbus's safety—not a job to be given to a stranger. Columbus still
needed between eighty and a hundred men—tough, experienced
sailors rather than novices. After the reading of the royal decree
in the church of Saint George's, however, the able-bodied of
Palos stonewalled. Nobody wanted to go; everyone was afraid of
entrusting his life to a stranger with bizarre ideas. Only one old
jack-tar was prepared to help Columbus. Pedro Vázquez told the
men a tale about a sea of grass out west toward the Azores that
he had seen in his younger days. His ship had sailed through this
mysterious grass but been forced to turn back, probably for lack
of drinking water. He had sensed that land was not far away. The
men of Palos ignored him. They could not have known about the
Sargasso Sea.

Father Marchena pulled a few strings and spoke to his old friend
Martín Alonso Pinzón. The Pinzón brothers—Martín Alonso, Vicente Yáñez, and Francisco Martín—occupied their family's seat
in the center of Palos; if they acceded, others would follow.
"Nearly all of the citizens of Palos stood under their influence for
they were the wealthiest people in the town," noted Bartolomé de
Las Casas. Although Martín Alonso was Marchena's friend, it
didn't necessarily endear him to Columbus. The oldest of the
Pinzón brothers couldn't abide the man from Genoa. "Pinzón

considered Columbus a parvenu who had come from nothing, who had little experience but who possessed an extraordinary measure of energy, power and new ideas," wrote the Italian historian Gianni Granzotto. "Columbus considered Pinzón an excellent sailor, nothing more." Pinzón, then in his early fifties, was someone who gave orders rather than received them. It is quite possible that he had his own plans and ideas, and that they didn't involve Columbus. In the Complaint, or Pleitos de Colón, in which Columbus's heirs made their case for what they felt was owed them by the original agreement between Columbus and Queen Isabella (a case that dragged on for decades in the court), witnesses stated that Pinzón himself had wanted to discover new lands in the West. They based their statement on a journey Martín Alonso was said to have undertaken to Rome shortly before Columbus arrived in Palos. In Rome a cosmographer at the Vatican library had told Martín Alonso of legends surrounding undiscovered islands in the ocean. While it is a documented fact that Pinzón journeyed to Rome to sell a shipload of sardines, it is also entirely possible that Toscanelli's ideas had already reached Rome.

Although it took considerable effort, Marchena finally convinced Pinzón to command the *Pinta*. Moreover, Martín Alonso's younger brother Vicente Yáñez, aged thirty at the time, agreed to captain the *Niña*. Those who knew Vicente considered him one of the best navigators in the country. Later he would become famous as the man who discovered Brazil. Unlike his brother, Vicente was loyal. Martín Alonso would later betray Columbus, but Vicente and his *Niña* would ultimately save the Admiral and indeed salvage the entire expedition. Columbus himself commandeered the flagship *Santa María*. Once the Pinzóns were on board, others followed suit. On June 23, 1492, Columbus officially began to hire a crew of men he felt he could trust.

For centuries—four, to be more precise—nobody knew exactly how many men had sailed with Columbus. Their names had sunk into oblivion, partly because historians simply weren't interested. Important men made history; minor players were of no consequence. In 1911, on her way to Italy, a petite and genteel American lady named Alice Bache Gould stopped off in Seville. Gould was the eldest daughter of a wealthy New England family. One of her ancestors had fought at the side of George Washington; another was the president of Harvard. Gould had spent several years in Argentina, where she learned Spanish, and was one of the few women during that time to pursue a university career, studying mathematics and teaching at the Massachusetts Institute of Technology and the University of Chicago. In Seville she found her way to the Archivo General de Indias and began looking through some documents. By sheer luck, she came upon a receipt bearing the name Pedro de Lepe, a sailor on the *Santa María*. Although it was only a small scrap of paper, Gould was more than intrigued. At that moment she felt she had found the task that would occupy her for the rest of her life. Among the dusty files, documents, decrees, and receipts, she wanted to find traces of the men who had discovered America. She set about scrutinizing page after page in the Seville archives, as well as in the Archivo General of Simancas, and indeed in any Spanish village that had not yet destroyed its old files.

Samuel Eliot Morison described Gould as a "distinguished, gray-haired lady, dressed usually in black bombazine with a vintage hat, striding resolutely into the Archive of the Indies to find some document for me that the archivist insisted did not exist." She rummaged through piles of papers that soldiers had used as bedding for their horses during the Napoleonic wars. She salvaged birth certificates from the village of Moguer near Palos. Thrifty clerks had given the old documents to the local jail for the inmates to use as toilet paper. Luckily they had stacked the older documents in the middle of the courtyard and piled the more recent ones around them so that the birth certificates from the fifteenth century were still relatively complete. Gould shut herself away in the prison every day to sift through some of the most valuable toilet paper in history.

Year after year Gould discovered one name after another. She learned who sailed on what ship, who was paid, and who was cheated out of his wages. It took decades but she finally arrived at numbers she believed were accurate: forty had sailed on the *Santa María*, twenty-six on the *Pinta*, and twenty on the *Niña*. Eighty-six sailors, plus Columbus, were placed beyond a doubt. An additional thirty-one men may have accompanied the Admiral, although that cannot be proved.

Through her research, Gould disproved a number of legends, some cherished by historians, such as that the crew had consisted of released criminals with nothing to lose. Experts had long known that the queen had accorded Columbus the power to pardon convicts. Anyone who was prepared to sail with him might escape death and even become a free man—should he survive the journey. However, Columbus only made use of this privilege in four cases: A court of law had sentenced the sailor Bartolomé de Torres—no relation to the converted interpreter Luis de Torres—to death for murder. Three of his friends tried to rescue him but were captured and joined Torres in his cell; they were also condemned to share his fate, until that is, Columbus arrived and commissioned them. All the other members of the crew had spotless records. Gould also disproved the legend that several Englishmen and Irishmen had been on board. In truth, Columbus sailed with only four non-Spaniards: three Italians and one Portuguese. Everyone else came from Palos, Moguer, and other parts of Andalusia. And nearly all of them were experienced sailors.

Gould found records pertaining to the boatswain, Juan Quintero from the *Pinta*, who accompanied Columbus on all four voyages. There was also mention of a comptroller who reported to the queen—a certain Rodrigo Sánchez, whose job it was to make sure Columbus didn't stash away any gold—a goldsmith, and a physician aboard each ship. What was even more interesting was who did *not* accompany Columbus. Gould couldn't find a single priest among the crew to baptize the natives, as we've already noted. There was also no scientist aboard to examine the fauna and flora; Columbus later admitted that that had been a mistake.

Furthermore, there were no soldiers among the crew. The ships' cannons would serve as the only defense. Gould also came across the name of the man whom Columbus cheated out of the 10,000 *maravedís* by claiming he had spotted land first: Juan Rodríguez Bermejo.

In all, Alice Gould spent more than forty years uncovering the trail of all these men and compiling a dossier, done in alphabetical order, on each of them—from Juan Martínez de Acoque to Pedro Yzquierdo. The forgotten discoverers of America were her life. On a summer's day in 1953, the little old lady with the strange hats was discovered lying dead on the old fortress bridge leading to the Simancas archive. She was eighty-five years old.

Half an hour before dawn on Friday, August 3, 1492, Columbus gave the order to weigh anchors. It was a calm day and the sails hung limp, but the ebbing tide carried the *Santa María*, the *Pinta*, and the *Niña* down the Río Tinto in a ghostly procession. Some of the sailors rowed, and the ships glided past La Rábida, where, high on the hill, the monks chanted their Mass: *Iam lucis orto sidere* (now that daylight fills the sky) and *nunc et in perpetuum* (now and forever). Columbus doffed his hat and made the sign of the cross; the sailors knelt in prayer, for they knew that if this tall, gray-haired stranger on the deck of the *Santa María* had erred and the Ocean Sea were wider than he had estimated, none of them would ever return to hear the bells of La Rábida.

At eight that morning, the ships floated across the sandbar and out into open waters, where the winds blew stronger. Columbus set a new course—"sur cuarta del sudoeste" (south by southwest), toward the Canary Islands. Although Tenerife was still in the hands of resisting and warlike natives called the Guanches, and Las Palmas was just then being conquered by the Spaniards, La Gomera already belonged to the Spanish crown, the Guanches having been enslaved. Columbus planned to take on water, firewood, and meat in San Sebastián, the port of La Gomera. What was even more critical was that the Canaries lay at the edge of the trade-wind belt and approximately on the same latitude that Paolo Toscanelli dal Pozzo had positioned the empire of the Great Khan. Were the Florentine scholar correct, Columbus would only have to steer westward from La Gomera to reach the Indies.

Yet another reason Columbus was forced to put into port on the island was to allow his carpenters to work on the ships. In the notoriously rough seas between Palos and the Canaries, the *Pinta's* outboard rudder jumped its gudgeons, and although Martín Alonso Pinzón had made makeshift repairs, the rudder remained a handicap and it was only a question of time before the sea would make short shrift of any vulnerabilities. Columbus also wanted to alter the rigging of the *Niña* into a square rig. Unlike the other two ships, the *Niña* originally sailed with a lateen rig, triangular sails that stood lengthwise across the deck. Although this enabled her to sail closer to the wind than the other ships, Columbus's assumption was that his fleet would soon encounter following winds that would propel his ships westward. Also, there was always the danger of a mast breaking or hitting a sailor when the wind threw the lateen sails from one side to the other.

Columbus regretted his choice of flagship soon after setting out. The chunky *Santa María* rolled like a barrel in the rough Atlantic swell. She had dull sailing qualities; the two caravels sailed rings around her, which meant that the Pinzón brothers on the *Niña* and the *Pinta* were constantly having to wait for Columbus to catch up. Although the two smaller vessels always returned to the flagship whenever Columbus fired a cannon, it must have been an embarrassment to him. "The ship was not suitable for the business of discovery," he later wrote. It must have annoyed him, for he knew that if he remained on the *Santa María,* he would never be the first one to catch sight of the Indies.

The sailors cooked on deck, probably in a fire pit they had built with stones and sand. They slept below deck, wherever they could find any space between the baskets and coiled ropes, the barrels, ballast stones, and the rats. And when they had to relieve themselves, they headed for the railing. Nowadays, of course, things are a little more comfortable. The *Santa María de Colombo,* a modern replica of Columbus's flagship, for example, features two heads and is powered by a 455-horsepower diesel engine. This makes it hard to tell what life was like for Columbus and his crew when they were caught in the doldrums. Like its namesake, the *Santa María de Colombo* is a bulky vessel, a little over 72 feet long and 23 feet wide, weighing 102 tons, with 615 square feet of sails, and a draft of 9 feet. Robert Wijntje, a Dutchman living in Madeira, used 1,050 cubic feet of pine and mahogany wood to build this replica. Wijntje had always been fascinated by Columbus and built this replica over the course of a year with the help of seven carpenters, completing the project in July 1998. Over the years the replica has become a tourist ship. A ride costs around $30 and gives landlubbers a chance to feel a little like Columbus, even though he would not have provided benches for the seasick, nor a bar serving shots of vodka. Wijntje read everything he could find as preparation, but of course nobody really knows what Columbus's ships looked like. "Only one thing is certain," said Consuelo Varela. "They didn't look anything like any of the replicas, for none of them sail properly. The slightest swell makes them uncontrollable and they make no headway." The real caravels were speedy. The fleet's average day's run was 139 nautical miles, according to Columbus's logbook. On average, the ships sailed 5.8 knots an hour, and their top speeds would have been twice that. Even modern yachts can't go much faster.

While the shipbuilding experts at Texas A&M used the information gleaned from the wreck off Nombre de Dios to produce a construction plan for a caravel, like the *Niña,* the *Pinta,* or the *Vizcaína,* it remains unclear what a *nao* looked like. We only know that it was bulky and slow. Columbus's favorite ship was the little *Niña.* "If she had not been very staunch and well found, I should have been afraid of being lost," wrote Columbus after a storm in 1493. Of the *Niña* Samuel Eliot Morison enthused, "There's a vessel to sing about!"—calling her "one of the greatest little ships in the world's history." Columbus relied heavily on the *Niña* not only during his first voyage, but also on his second, where he took her on an exploring expedition to what is now Cuba. The *Niña* was the only ship in the fleet to survive a hurricane, bringing Columbus and dozens of his sailors safely back home; and on the third voyage Columbus used her as an advance guard. The smallest of the ships in the first fleet, she was the only one of whom experts can make a half-decent estimate as to size. One of the sailors said she was "about 60 tons"—about the same size as the *Vizcaína*.

However, Spanish tons, or *toneladas*, have nothing to do with the weight of the ship or its displacement, such as we use it for modern vessels. Sixty *toneladas* simply meant that the *Niña's* hold contained enough storage space for sixty standard wine casks. Iberian shipbuilders constructed most of their ships according to the "1-2-3 formula." "1" stood for the width of the ship; the keel was double—"2"—the length; and the hull three—"3"—times as long. Were the caravels constructed in the same way, Morison estimated, the *Niña* would have been approximately 70 feet long and 25 feet wide, with a draft of around 6.5 feet. The *Pinta* would have been a little longer, and the *Santa María* possibly measured 78 feet.

The *Niña* and the *Pinta* probably had a raised quarterdeck astern, smaller than the one on the *Santa María,* judging from what period depictions there are, for example, on coins. They probably had three masts, two for the square-rigged sails and one smaller mast for a lateen rig located at the stern. None of the vessels were warships and probably carried very little artillery—a few bombards would have been mounted on gun carriages on deck. Their stone cannonballs could sink enemy ships—if the cannons worked, that is. The small breech-loading swivel guns called falconets were mounted on the bulwarks. They fired a kind of lead shot that could cause a terrible bloodbath at a short distance. The sailors steered the ships with tillers affixed at the stern.

And in calm winds, such as they had had on the Río Tinto, the sailors could row with long oars made of ash. Although they made only agonizingly slow progress, it was better than being driven toward the cliffs by the currents.

They must have felt they had been cursed. The small fleet would have made good headway were it not for the *Pinta's* rudder. The Canaries were already in sight when it jumped its gudgeons yet again and had to be secured. And now, although they had barely begun their voyage, the ship began to leak and Martín Pinzón's men were forced to pump to avoid sinking. Losing patience, Columbus ordered Pinzón to take the *Pinta* to Las Palmas on Grand Canary Island, where he could undertake repairs.

In the meantime the Admiral headed for La Gomera with the *Santa María* and the *Niña*. The island was governed by the widow Doña Beatriz de Peraza y Bobadilla, acting as guardian regent on behalf of her young son Guillen. Columbus knew that Doña Beatriz had a ship at her disposal, a vessel of forty tons and therefore smaller than the *Niña,* but Columbus hoped to inveigle her into parting with her vessel, leaving her the crippled *Pinta* instead.

He arrived in San Sebastián on the evening of August 12, but Doña Beatriz had left, along with her ship. Columbus waited for nine days, during which time his crew altered the rigging on the *Niña*. When Beatriz still hadn't returned after nine days, he sailed back to Grand Canary, where Pinzón had completed repairs on the *Pinta*. Columbus had already wasted two weeks when he arrived in La Gomera on September 2, but there he finally met Doña Beatriz. She was younger than Columbus, not yet thirty years old, with a tempestuous and capricious nature. Columbus fell in love with her immediately. At least so the legend goes. Michele de Cuneo, an Italian who sailed with Columbus on his second voyage, spoke to the men who had been on La Gomera with the Admiral and later wrote about the adventure. Morison maintained that "we have it on good authority" that he fell in love with her. Even Columbus biographer Paolo Emilio Taviani would like to believe the love story. But would Columbus really have risked an affair with the ruler of the island in the fortress of San Sebastián? On the one hand, Doña Beatriz would not have had much diversion on this outpost of the Spanish empire, and she might well have been interested. On the other hand, Columbus had other things on his mind than whispering sweet nothings. Furthermore, Diego de Arana was on board the *Santa María,* and he was cousin to Columbus's mistress at home in Córdoba. Would Columbus have risked affronting the man whose job it was to guarantee his safety? And we should not forget that it was Sunday evening when Columbus sailed into Doña Beatriz's port. He ordered his fleet to set sail again the following Thursday morning. That would have given them only three days in San Sebastián; scant time for romance to blossom. The question remains whether this was a historical quickie or one of those Columbus legends lovingly preserved by biographers in desperate need to ascribe some human qualities to a man who seems so very cold.

On September 9, 1492, two days after putting to sea from La Gomera, Columbus reported in his logbook, "It was calm all Friday and Saturday until three o'clock in the morning." Then the trade winds began to fill the sails, albeit gently at first. He had taken in too many provisions and too much water, and the overloaded ships lay heavy and deep. For five days the ships drifted listlessly in the long Atlantic swell, still within view of the Canary Islands. Only on the morning of September 10 did the Old World disappear behind the horizon.

At first the voyage was uneventful, and the sailors settled into a quiet life on board. They had little work to do and could spend most of their time daydreaming. They soon began to convince themselves that they could see signs of land. As early as September 14, Columbus wrote in his log, "The crew of the caravel *Niña* said that they had seen a tern and a tropic-bird, neither of which go more than twenty-five leagues from land." On September 16, they saw grass floating on the water—"much weed, which was very fine and had grown on rocks; it came from the west." Rather than land, they soon reached the sea of grass—the Sargasso Sea—as had been described by Pedro Vázquez in the village square at Palos. And the old man had been right; the ships were able to push aside the grass and sail through without slowing down noticeably.

On September 18, Martín Pinzón reported that he had seen "a great flock of birds flying westward and hoped to sight land that night; this was his reason for not holding back. To the north there appeared a great bank of clouds, which is a sign that land is near." Later, navigators calculated that by this point the fleet could not even have sailed half the distance. The next piece of land was the Azores, more than eight hundred miles away. Columbus believed he was sailing between the islands that Toscanelli had drawn into his map of the Atlantic, but he was unwilling to explore them. He wanted, he wrote, to "press on to the Indies, and the weather is favorable." The two caravels surged ahead. Everyone wanted to be the first to spot land. During a lull in the wind, Columbus even had his sailors lower a plumb line to measure depth. But it hit nothing; little wonder, given that the line was only thirteen hundred feet long. When his men went swimming in the waters of the Atlantic, they had no idea there was nearly three miles of water below them.

On September 25, the *Pinta* drew alongside the flagship, on which Columbus and Pinzón were discussing a chart that the Admiral had sent to Pinzón's caravel and on which, according to Bartolomé de Las Casas, "as it would appear, the Admiral had certain islands depicted in that sea. Martín Alonso said that the ships were in the position on which the islands were placed, and the Admiral replied that so it appeared to him: but it might be that they had not fallen in with them, owing to the currents." They had now been at sea for nearly three weeks, longer than any vessel they knew of. After three weeks in the close quarters of the ships, three weeks of uncertainty, the men had grown edgy and irritable. In the evening Pinzón shouted that he had sighted land.

"When the Admiral heard this positively declared," Las Casas wrote, "he says that he gave thanks to the Lord on his knees, while Martín Alonso said the Gloria in excelsis with his people. The Admiral's crew did the same. Those of the *Niña* all went up the mast and into the rigging, and declared that it was land. It so seemed to the Admiral, and that it was distant 25 leagues."

Twenty-five leagues are quite a distance for a sailing ship, requiring as long as five hours to cover. The night came and the next morning dawned, and when it was light, the land had disappeared like a fata morgana. Columbus noted, "That what had been supposed to be land was not, but sky."

The sea became calm; the days passed. Morale was sinking and the men became rebellious. Columbus was afraid of a mutiny. Fernando recounted:

> The men feared they unknowingly had passed between some islands; for they thought the great multitude of birds they had seen were birds of passage bound from one island to another. The Admiral's people wished to turn off in one or another direction to look for those lands, but he refused because he feared to lose the fair wind that was carrying him due west along what he believed to be the best and most certain route to the Indies. Besides, he reflected that he would lose respect and credit for his voyage if he beat aimlessly about from place to place looking for lands whose position he had claimed to know most accurately. Because of this refusal, the men were on the point of mutiny, grumbling and plotting against him.

On October 6, Martín Alonso Pinzón put in a protest. According to his calculations, they had already sailed too far west to reach the island of Cipango, Japan. Pinzón pressed Columbus to sail farther south. Pinzón was right, though he could not have known this. At that point the fleet lay just north of Haiti. Had they stayed on Columbus's course, they would have reached the Gulf Stream off Florida. They might have reached the mainland, but it is also possible that the mighty current would have swept them northeast, back to Spain. Columbus, however, was unaware of the Gulf

Stream and unaware of Florida. He remained obstinate, and the fleet sailed farther west.

On October 7, the crew again spotted a shadow on the horizon to the west, where land would appear were the Admiral right. Fernando wrote:

> But since it was indistinct, none wished to claim having made the discovery, not for fear of being shamed if proved wrong but for fear of losing the 10,000 maravedís promised by the Catholic Sovereigns to the first person sighting land. In order to prevent men from crying "land, land!" at every moment and causing unjustified feelings of joy, the Admiral had ordered that one who claimed to have seen land and did not make good his claim in the space of three days would lose the reward even if afterwards he should actually see it. Being warned of this, none of the people on the Admiral's ship dared cry out "land, land!" but the Niña, which was a better sailer and so ranged ahead, fired a gun and broke out flags as a sign that she had sighted land.
>
> But the farther they sailed the more their spirits fell, until at last that illusion of land faded clean away. God, however, was pleased to offer them some small comfort; for they saw many large flocks of birds, more varied in kind than those they had seen before, and others of small land birds which were flying from the west to the southwest in search of food. . . . The Admiral changed course from west to southwest . . . in imitation of the Portuguese, who made most of their discoveries by attending to the flights of birds.

They had previously sighted flocks of birds. One wonders if he had decided to heed Pinzón's demand after all and veered off his westward course because he was uncertain.

"That man could navigate by the seat of his pants," declared Wolfram zu Mondfeld, a specialist on caravels who works at the Museum of Technology in Berlin. There one can find showcases filled with all the instruments Columbus might have used, such as an astrolabe, an instrument developed to detect the distance of the stars above the horizon; or a Jacob's rod, devised to help locate position by means of the stars. There is also a quadrant, a measuring device for angles. The quadrant functioned with the use of a piece of lead that dangled back and forth from a string connected to a scale. Quadrants worked well on land but were difficult to handle on a ship rolling in choppy seas. Finally, the most important instrument of all: the compass. Though not as accurate as today's compasses, which work with a needle and a scale of degrees, the old compasses used a magnetized needle set on a pivoting base, similar to a drink coaster, with a rough scale of thirty-two points. Under the most northerly mark, the instrument makers had stuck a magnet.

The compass was probably located on the *Santa María's* quarterdeck, where Columbus would have watched how the compass rose turned on its bearing with the ship's movements, from west to northwest and back again, for days and weeks. The general course was to the west with a slight turn to the south. There are paintings that depict Columbus as a great navigator, using not only a compass but also sophisticated equipment to measure the degrees and the stars as he navigated his way to the New World. But the question remains whether Columbus really navigated using them, and how he located his exact position, and, moreover, how he was able to relocate the same islands and harbors on his second voyage.

Columbus's route was virtually perfect. The British circumnavigator Jimmy Cornell is one of the world's most eminent authorities in navigational matters. In his definitive compendium of coordinates, currents, track angles, and distances, *World Cruising Routes,* he wrote about what is known as the Coconut Milk Run from the Canaries to the Caribbean. For decades experts have been debating how Columbus did it. Some argue that he was a "latitude sailor," meaning that he followed a north-south axis until he reached the latitude of his destination, at which point he would turn east or west by measuring the height of the polestar above the horizon by means of a quadrant or astrolabe. Depending on whether the polestar rose or fell, he would steer farther north or south. Theoretically, this method is exact to within sixty miles, based upon measurements from an astrolabe from Columbus's time. But as a theory it has its weak points. Nowhere in his log does Columbus indicate that he used the polestar to adhere to the twenty-eighth latitude. And in actual fact, Columbus was a lousy celestial navigator. On several occasions later on, probably while he was sailing through the islands, he used his hardwood quadrant and consistently miscalculated by hundreds of nautical miles.

Most historians believe that Columbus used dead reckoning. Every half hour a ship's boy would carefully turn the *ampoletta,* a glass sand-clock, and an officer would sound a gong. Then Columbus would estimate the speed of the ship, look at the compass rose, and note the distance traveled per hour and the course. His log was full of such notes. However, they were contradictory. Bartolomé de Las Casas concluded that he must have had two logbooks—one he kept secret, in which he noted the true distances traveled, and a second in which he wrote shorter distances, to allay the fears of his crew. Las Casas reported that on Sunday, September 9, the "Admiral made 19 leagues, and he arranged to reckon less than the number run, because if the voyage was of long duration, the people would not be so terrified and disheartened." The "false-log theory" seemed another one of those legends surrounding Columbus. Several years ago, however, nautical experts were able to prove that he did probably use two different calculations, one based upon the Iberian league, which was 3.2 miles long, and the other on the Italian league, which was approximately 2.7 miles.

From the distance traveled and the course taken, Columbus would have been able to calculate his exact position day by day. Dead reckoning was not as accurate as sailing by latitude would have been, for Columbus not only had to estimate his speed but current and drift. Everything depended on accurate estimations. Dead reckoning might be more an art than a science; it would seem Columbus was an artist.

———————————

The change of course toward the south, which Pinzón had more or less coerced Columbus into taking, did not improve matters. The fleet was becalmed, sails hanging limply. After three days, on October 10, the crews' grumbling grew so loud that many now believe they were close to mutiny. "Here the people could endure no longer," wrote Las Casas. "They complained of the length of the voyage." Columbus tried everything—reassuring them, beseeching them, threatening them with the queen's wrath, cajoling them about the wealth they would lose by giving up. At some point during this crucial moment, the captains of the other two ships, Vicente Yáñez and Martín Alonso Pinzón, came aboard the *Santa María* for an emergency meeting. Had they already sailed past Japan? What if the distances measured were wrong and they went on and on until the water casks were empty and they all died? Years later this emergency meeting was a major focus of the Pleitos de Colón court case. Some witnesses swore that Columbus had wavered and that Pinzón had been the one to speak the famous words "Adelante, adelante" (forward, forward). Witnesses for the Colón family, however, testified that the Pinzóns had wanted to give up and return to Spain, and that it had been Columbus who had uttered those memorable words.

Regardless of who said what when, the captains came to an agreement. They would sail on for another three days; if no land came in sight by then, they would turn back. The next day the trade winds blew at storm strength. Both caravels and even the sluggish *Santa María* shot across the waves at 7.5 knots. And once again the men on the faster caravels were the first to spot signs of land. This time there was tangible evidence. Columbus wrote in his logbook, "Those on the caravel Pinta saw a reed and a stick and they took another small stick formed as it appeared with iron, and a piece of a reed and other grass which grows on land, and a small board. Those on the caravel Niña also saw other indications of land and a little branch full of dog roses." The signs were cause for relief and rejoicing, as well as tension. At ten in the evening, Columbus stood on the quarterdeck and spied—he said later—a faint light directly ahead. A fire, possibly. Land, certainly. But then the light disappeared.

Navigational experts have calculated that at this point the ships would have been thirty-five miles offshore, too far away to sight land. Not even a modern lighthouse on a flat island could emit a beam that powerful. Either Columbus had imagined what he wanted to see, or he simply lied. More than the princely sum of 10,000 *maravedís* was at stake; it was also a matter of honor. The *Santa María* was too slow to overtake the two caravels. Columbus needed to come up with something to claim the reward and the honor.

The ships raced through the night of Friday, October 12, 1492, hitting a top speed of nine knots. The *Pinta* was in the lead. It was still relatively light, for the full moon was just on the wane. At around two in the morning, Juan Rodríguez Bermejo saw something shimmering far out ahead in the moonlight—two light streaks with a dark band between them. The light streak was the surf and the dark band was a reef. Behind it were white cliffs. "Tierra!" shouted Bermejo, and again "Tierra!" Martín Alonso Pinzón looked across the bow and quickly realized that this time there was no doubt. He ordered a cannon fired.

Columbus kept his nerve. Ahead lay the Indies, the object of his dreams, his whole life's goal. It was vital not to make a mistake. At the speed they were going, the ships could reach the shore within an hour. Columbus ordered all sails lowered. The fleet tacked slowly up and down the coast, maintaining a safe distance from land. It would have been too dangerous, perhaps deadly, to have landed on a strange coast at night and under full sails. The crew waited until morning. Fernando later re-created what they saw across the turquoise-green waters when the sun finally rose:

> *At daybreak they saw an island about fifteen leagues in length, very level, full of green trees and abounding in springs, with a large lagoon in the middle, and inhabited by a multitude of people who hastened to the shore, astounded and marveling at the sight of the ships, which they took for animals. These people could hardly wait to see what sort of things the ships were. The Christians were no less eager to know what manner of people they had to do with. Their wishes were soon satisfied, for as soon as they had cast anchor the Admiral went ashore with an armed boat, displaying the royal standard. The captains of the other two ships did the same in their boats with the banner of the expedition, on which was depicted a green cross with an F on one side, and crowns in honor of Ferdinand and Isabella on the other.*
>
> *After all had rendered thanks to Our Lord, kneeling on the ground and kissing it with tears of joy for His great favor to them, the Admiral arose and gave this island the name San Salvador. Then, in the presence of the many natives assembled there, he took possession of it in the name of the Catholic Sovereigns with appropriate ceremony and words.*

Columbus described the "Indians," as he called them in his logbook entry of that day:

> *That they might feel great friendship for us and because I knew they were a people who would better be freed and converted to our Holy Faith by love than by force, I gave them some red caps and some glass beads which they placed around their necks, and many other things of small value with which they were greatly pleased, and were so friendly to us that it was wonderful.*
>
> *They afterward came swimming to the two ships where we were, and bringing us parrots and cotton thread wound in balls and spears and many other things, and they traded them with*

us for other things, which we gave them, such as small glass beads and hawk's bells. Finally they took everything and willingly gave what things they had. Further, it appeared to me that they were a very poor people, in everything. They all go naked as their mothers gave them birth, and the women also, although I only saw one of the latter who was very young, and all those whom I saw were young men, none more than thirty years of age. They were very well built with very handsome bodies, and very good faces. Their hair was almost as coarse as horses' tails. Some paint themselves blackish, and they are of the color of the inhabitants of the Canaries, neither black nor white, and some paint themselves white, some red, some whatever color they find.... They do not carry arms nor know what they are, because I showed them swords and they took them by the edge and ignorantly cut themselves. They have no iron: their spears are sticks without iron, and some of them have a fish's tooth at the end.

They are all generally of good height, of pleasing appearance and well built. They must be good servants and intelligent, as I see that they very quickly say all that is said to them.

This all must have been very confounding to Columbus, particularly if he truly believed he had landed in the Indies or at least in Japan. Where was the fabulously wealthy civilization Marco Polo had described—the armies, fleets, palaces, and well-dressed noblemen? Instead, he had found naked people with friendly faces, who could not understand Spanish and couldn't even converse with Luis de Torres, who spoke Arabic and Hebrew. They lived off fish, corn, and roots. They wove cotton and made pottery, but they were unfamiliar with iron, had few weapons, and their chiefs, the caciques, lived in ramshackle huts. Their navy consisted of boats that they called *canoas.* "They came to the ship with canoes," Columbus wrote, "which are made from the trunk of a tree, like a long boat and all in one piece, and very wonderfully fashioned for the country, and large enough so that 40 or 45 men came in some of them. They rowed with a paddle, like a baker's peel, and go wonderfully well."

The next day the Spaniards explored the island the Indians called Guanahani. The sailors rowed their boats along the shore-line, while Columbus took his soundings like a general would his future battleground.

> *A great reef of rocks...encircles all that island and the water is deep within and forms a port for as many ships as there are in Christendom: and the entrance to it is very tortuous. And I went this morning in order to see all this, that I might be able to give an account of everything to your Highnesses and also to see where I might be able to build a fortress, and I saw a piece of land formed like an island, although it is not one,...but which could be made an island in two days. Although I do not believe it to be necessary, because these people are very simple in matters of arms, all can be taken, and carried to Castile or held captive on the island itself, because with 50 men all can be sub-jugated and made to do everything which is desired.*

Columbus also saw that several of the Indians bore scars. And with hands and feet, they indicated that they were constantly under attack from their enemies, who abducted their men. Inter-esting as this might have been, Columbus was even more inter-ested in the pieces of gold that some natives wore suspended from holes in their noses. Asked about the metal, the Indians pointed south, making gestures that led Columbus to believe "there was a King who had large vessels of gold and who had a great deal of it."

Columbus soon had enough of the island. Though it seemed like a place from some forgotten golden era, it wasn't his goal. Be-fore he set sail again, he had six natives taken and brought to the ship; he needed them as interpreters and scouts for what lay ahead. The men made signs, indicating that there were many is-lands "and so many that could not be numbered" and told the Spaniards the names of these places.

On Sunday, October 14, Columbus weighed anchor and headed for an island to which his captives guided him. The Indians already knew what these strange bearded creatures were searching for. "The natives told me that the people there wore very large golden bracelets on the legs and arms. I quite believe that everything they said was a hoax in order to flee. Nevertheless my intention was, not to pass by any island of which I did not take possession, although having taken one, it could not be said that all were taken." One of the natives fled shortly before the fleet arrived at an island that Columbus christened Santa María de la Concepción. The man threw himself overboard and disappeared. Once again the Spaniards gave away glass beads and small round bells used in falconry. These bells were particularly favored by the natives, and soon they approached and began shouting, "Chuq, chuq," which was how they referred to the hawk's bells. The next island Columbus landed on was La Fernandina, as he called it, and he stopped because "according to what I can understand, in it or near it there are mines of gold."

Virtually every entry in Columbus's logbook involves gold. He went from island to island in search of it, without success. "There may be many things which I do not know, because I did not wish to stop, in order to discover and search many islands to find gold," he noted. The Indians kept pointing him from one island to the next, trying to convince him that he would find gold there. To Columbus, each island looked like the next: verdant trees, fragrant flowers, colorful fish, friendly natives, but no gold. While his men filled their water casks in La Fernandina, Columbus wandered about this Garden of Eden: "I walked among those trees, which was a more beautiful thing to see than any other I had ever seen: seeing so much verdure in such condition as it is in the month of May in Andalusia, and the trees were all as different from ours as day from night and also the fruits and grasses and the stones and all the things."

Columbus continued to note that all the islanders they came upon were open, good-natured, and unsuspecting. He also wrote that they were remarkably clean and had strange customs. He went on to describe the "cotton nets" in which they slept and that they called *"hamacas,"* the ancestor, of course, to "hammock." But the kind of wealth he was looking for seemed nowhere to be found. The natives—later called Taínos—on La Fernandina and on the next island, which Columbus christened La Isabela, possessed no more than a few small pieces of jewelry. Then Columbus heard of "another very large island which I believe must be Cipango, according to the indications which those Indians I am taking with me, give me, and which they call Colba. They say that on this island there are many large ships and many skilled seamen." Sometimes Columbus found it difficult to understand the Taínos. He thought they said "Colba." Did they say "Cuba"?

———————

In 1986 the National Geographic Society in Washington invited media representatives from around the world to the nation's capital to announce a sensational discovery made after five years of research. "We believe that after five centuries, we have unraveled one of the greatest geographical mysteries of all time," said Joseph Judge, who was a senior editor at *National Geographic* magazine. "We believe we have shown that this matter is finally solved. Most of the history books are wrong." "This matter" referred to the landfall controversy, the question of where Columbus and the Pinzón brothers first set foot on land in the New World. What were the islands that the discoverer named San Salvador, La Fernandina, Santa María de la Concepción, and La Isabela? Judge believed he could answer this question.

Columbus undoubtedly drew up sea charts of the discovered islands. After all, he had earned his living as a cartographer in Lisbon. One of the witnesses in the Pleitos case confirmed that Columbus had worked on charts while he was on the *Santa María* and that these charts showed where his fleet arrived in the New World. But apart from one sketch of Haiti's northern coast—on which experts believe they recognize his handwriting—Columbus's charts have all disappeared. There are clues about other charts. In 1929 scientists examining the archives of the Topkapi

Palace in Istanbul found a world map that had been drawn in 1513 by the Ottoman admiral and cartographer Piri Reis (formerly Hadji Muhammad). Historian and continental drift theorist Charles H. Hapgood analyzed the map inch by inch. It showed, among others, the Caribbean islands of the Antilles. Some of the points of reference were wrong, and others were quite precise. The map also featured a reference:

> These coasts are named the shores of Antillia. It is reported thus, that a Genoese infidel, his name was Colombo, be it he who discovered these places.... The above-mentioned Colombo went to the Bey [king] of Spain, who gave him two ships, saw that they were well equipped, and said: "O Colombo, if it happens as you say, let us make you kapudan [admiral] to that country." Having said which he sent the said Colombo to the Western Sea. The late Gazi Kemal had a Spanish slave. The above-mentioned slave said to Kemal Reis, he had been three times to that land with Colombo.

There follows a long description of Columbus's voyages, and the final passage in Piri Reis's reference is "The names which mark the places on the said islands and coasts were given by Colombo, that these places may be known by them. And also Colombo was a great astronomer. The coasts and island on this map are taken from Colombo's map." The question, of course, is which map? Historians presume that Piri Reis's uncle and informer, Gazi Kemal, took one of Columbus's former sailors captive during a raid and made him his servant. This former member of Columbus's crew may have had one of the maps. Kemal's nephew Piri Reis copied sections of the map. This suggested, of course, that the "lost map of Columbus" might exist somewhere in Istanbul or, more specifically, in Gallipoli, which is where Reis drew up his charts.

The charts are not the only items lost shortly after 1492. Columbus's logbook, which he had been keeping for Queen Isabella and had sent to her shortly after his return, disappeared, perhaps in the abysmal depths of the Spanish archives. The only extant version, as mentioned, is the rather rough copy we have from Bartolomé de Las Casas. This is clearly an edited version; many of the passages are written in the third person. Moreover, unfortunately Las Casas seemed to have known nothing about navigation. And by the time he had copied passages from the original logbook (summarizing others), Columbus had already been dead for years. Las Casas's version teems with errors, so much so that some of the islands and bays are barely identifiable.

For centuries historians, archaeologists, and navigators have focused their search on the first island, the one Columbus named San Salvador and that the Indians referred to as Guanahani. Some ten of the twenty-five islands from the archipelagos of the Bahamas, Turks, and Caicos were involved when the experts from the National Geographic Society began their research. The Plana Cays was an early favorite, then Rum Cay, Grand Turk, East Caicos, Egg Island, and at some point Conception. In the end, they settled on two islands for their landfall theory, and both belonged to the Bahamas: Watling Island, which was renamed San Salvador in 1926, and Samana Cay.

In the eighteenth century, King Carlos III of Spain (1716–1788) sent an expert named Juan Bautista Muñoz on the trail of Columbus. With the limited means available at the time, Muñoz reconstructed Columbus's route across the Atlantic and came to the conclusion that Watling Island must have been the original San Salvador. A hundred years later Captain Gustavus V. Fox, undersecretary of the U.S. Navy during Abraham Lincoln's presidency, reread the material and came to a completely different conclusion, namely that Samana Cay was Columbus's San Salvador (alias Guanahani). That was the state of affairs until the National Geographic Society endeavored to answer the question once and for all. To do that, the society assembled an impressive team of historians, archaeologists, sailors, and cartographers.

To start things off, an expert in ancient Spanish documents retranslated those passages in Las Casas's logbook referring to the islands and the routes Columbus had taken from one to another. Then an experienced Atlantic sailor fed the data relating to currents and drifts into a navigational computer; he calculated Columbus's transit crossing from the day his fleet weighed anchor off La Gomera. They discovered that all previous calculations of Columbus's route had not adjusted for leeway or current. As Joseph Judge wrote in *National Geographic,* they had assumed that Columbus had sailed "in effect, a railroad track from Gomera to south of Watling Island." The computations made by the National Geographic experts came up with the exact coordinates of the location where Juan Rodríguez Bermejo had first seen land. The position was ten miles east-northeast off Samana Cay. They commissioned a computer company to translate sea charts of the Bahamas into software programs through which they could run all the routes Columbus had taken or might have taken after his first encounter with the Taínos on the beaches of San Salvador. The results revealed what is called the "Cape Verde fix," a position between the islands referred to in two logbook entries, a position that Columbus must have passed. From this Cape Verde fix, the experts backtracked Columbus's route—and landed in Samana Cay.

Judge then sent his team of experts to the Bahamas. In Samana Cay they found what they believed they had been searching for, which is why at his press conference, Judge announced, "Our expeditions to the island convinced us that it is a remarkable match for the features Columbus cites—namely, it is very green; it is very flat; it is encircled by the reef with openings on the south side that permit access to good anchorages; it has many waters, some eighty lakes, ponds, and water holes; and it has good candidates for each of the three distinctive pieces of geography in the log notes—a 'laguna en medio' (a lagoon in the middle), a port area, and a piece of land made like an island that is not one." Therefore, according to Judge, Columbus had made landfall in Samana Cay.

By no means was this the end of the story. A year after Judge's announcement, an oceanographer and a computer scientist from the Woods Hole Oceanographic Institute reevaluated the navigational data from Columbus's first voyage and challenged the previous estimates of wind and water currents. The Woods Hole experts placed Columbus some fifteen miles off Watling Island on the morning of October 12, 1492. Watling Island versus Samana Cay, and one computer versus another. The result was a tie.

William F. Keegan of the Florida Museum of Natural History had long believed the mystery would not be solved purely on the basis of the data found in the logbook. He claimed that additional information was necessary. He went to the Bahamas in search of it. The natives of San Salvador had told Columbus of an island called Saomete that he later named La Isabela. In his log he wrote that "it is there, according to the men I have with me, that the king lives who wears so much gold. Tomorrow I intend to go so far inland as to find this village and see and speak with this king, who, according to their signs, rules all the islands in this neighborhood and wears much gold on his clothes and person." Keegan believed that the remains of this village would still be there five hundred years later. Were it possible to make an archaeological confirmation of La Isabela, then one could trace Columbus's route back to the first landfall. Keegan's favorite choice for La Isabela was Acklins Island. Between 1983 and 1987, he and a team of assistants excavated large portions of the island. On the lee shore of Acklins, they found the remains of an Indian settlement with cooking pits, pottery, and midden deposits (piles of refuse). Keegan estimated that the settlement must have been around six times larger than the average Indian village. He also found that around a quarter of the pottery shards were fired from a kind of clay that did not exist on the island but came from Cuba. He concluded that the Indians must have imported pottery from Cuba, and that this was a sign of wealth. Keegan was certain he had found the old capital of the Taínos natives. Acklins Island was La Isabela, he concluded.

As a result of these findings, Keegan retraced Columbus's route by going backward. In his log Columbus wrote that the caravels approached La Isabela from the northwest. The only landmass in that direction is Long Island, some twenty-five miles away. This led Keegan to suggest that Long Island must have been Columbus's third stop, La Fernandina, where his crew filled their water casks. Keegan and his assistants unearthed the remains of thirty-one small settlements on Long Island, and behind one of the former villages, they found a freshwater pond, matching one of Columbus's "laguna en medio." Columbus had sailed twenty miles to reach La Fernandina. Some twenty miles from Long Island lies the island of Rum Cay, which, according to Keegan, was Columbus's Santa María de la Concepción. Out in the Atlantic beyond Rum Cay there is only one island: Watling Island, which is twelve miles long and around five miles wide, and which matches Columbus's description of the island's topography. In the middle of the island lies a very large lake and beside it are many other ponds ("muchas aguas"). But Watling Island is hilly, and that is where it differs from the log, as well as Fernando's description that the island was "flat." The highest hill on Watling Island rises some 165 feet. That wouldn't seem flat to a sailor, though it might have to a Genoese, or to someone who had spent years living in the mountainous regions of Andalusia.

The digging began anew, and while Keegan organized excavations on other islands, an American anthropologist found strange artifacts on Watling Island—a brass belt buckle; a copper coin, probably from around the 1470s; and, perhaps most importantly, very old green and yellow glass beads. They were discovered in a bay called Long Bay. If Watling Island really were San Salvador, then Long Bay must have been the bay where—according to descriptions in the log—the *Santa María,* the *Pinta,* and the *Niña* cast their anchors. Long Bay would be a logical choice as an anchorage ground; it offered protection from the northeast trade winds, and nowhere else could large ships have anchored so close to shore due to the reefs. It would have been a good navigator's first port of call.

Even Consuelo Varela believes that Watling Island "must be" San Salvador. Although one could also find everything described in the documents on Samana Cay, Watling Island seems the perfect match. If only it weren't for the word "flat," which comes up twice in the log (in another passage in his log, he noted that "all islands are flat"). Yet some of the islands definitely have hills. Varela talked of a discovery she had made and the reason why Columbus discovered the New World. Several years ago she went for a walk along the beach on Watling Island and gazed far into the distance toward Europe. This is a popular spot for divers and yachtsmen, especially those with low-drafted ships. The waters around the islands are turquoise green because they are so shallow. However, they are also treacherous—full of reefs and coral heads that have slit open many a ship's hull. Columbus was a good navigator, but he had also been lucky that he had chosen to approach San Salvador from the east in the early morning hours. The sun would have been behind him, and it would have been the only time he could have reliably seen the shoals beneath. During her walk on the beach, Consuelo Varela found a glass ball floating on the waves. It was one of those small glass floats used by fishermen to keep their nets afloat. In weather-beaten script, the owner's hometown appeared: La Coruña, Spain. Like Columbus, it had drifted westward with the currents and the trade winds.

At the time of their "discovery," the "Indians" had no name by which they referred to themselves. Later they were called the Taínos, a term for Indians who spoke Arawak. The Taínos from the Bahamas were called the Lucayas. Mainly fishermen and gatherers, and perhaps the most peace-loving people living on the entire continent, there would probably have been about fifty thousand of them, living in villages consisting of ten to twelve huts. The Taínos' ancestors had come to the Bahamas from the Antilles and from South America some eight hundred years before Columbus arrived. Farther south lived their less tranquil relatives, the Caribs, probably cannibals who occasionally raided the

Bahamas and took the natives captive. The Lucayas should have been far more afraid of these white people who were suddenly holding strange rituals on their beaches, rituals in which wafting banners on sticks played a key role.

———————

Last night at midnight I raised anchor from Cabo del Isleo on the north side of the island of Isabela, where I had lain, and set sail for the island of Colba, which these people tell me is very large and has much trade. They say that it contains gold and spices and large ships and merchandise and have told me by signs that I should steer west-southwest to find it, and I think this is right, for if I am to believe the indications of all these Indians and those I have on board—I do not know their language—this is the island of Cipango of which such marvelous tales are told, and which in the globes that I have seen and on the painted map of the world appears to lie in this region.

Columbus made this entry into his log in late October 1492, reiterating Toscanelli's worldview that had Europe and Africa on one side, then the ocean, then many small islands and between them one larger island—Cipango, or Japan—to the west, and beyond that the Asian mainland. The Florentine scholar had noted that one could as easily display this information on a sea chart as on a globe.

On the morning of October 28, Columbus's small fleet arrived at the mouth of a river in Cuba. "It was covered in trees right down to the river and these were lovely and green and different from ours, and each bore its own fruit or flowers. There were many birds, large and small, which sung sweetly." Columbus immediately had himself ferried to shore but found no natives, who had obviously fled in terror. There were only two huts, but no temples with golden roofs. The next day Columbus sailed farther west toward a bay that would later be called Puerto Gibara. Here his captured interpreters finally provided him with evidence that he was on the right path toward finding the Great

Khan of China. The captive Lucayas dispelled the fears of the Indians in Puerto Gibara of the white men and their winged monsters. In reply to the usual question of gold—*nucay,* as they called it—they nodded their heads vigorously. Yes, there was much of that here. "Cubanacan," they said, which Columbus misunderstood as "El Gran Can."

The natives were referring to the heartland, where there was gold; he took it to mean that the Great Khan possessed the gold. Columbus immediately revised his opinion and decided that this was Cipango. He now believed he had reached the Chinese mainland, for that was where—according to Marco Polo, of course—the Great Khan resided. "It is certain that this is the mainland and that I am before Zayto and Guinsey," he wrote.

Luis de Torres the interpreter and another sailor were sent on a diplomatic mission to find the court of the Great Khan. Columbus gave them strings of glass beads, so that they could buy something to eat, and a letter of credentials from the Spanish crown to prove their identity. While the two Spaniards marched off, Columbus had the *Santa María* careened and her hull cleaned.

De Torres returned empty-handed. All he had found where the city of the Great Khan should have been was a small village with fifty palm-roofed huts. No gold, no Khan. However, they did report on a strange ritual they had observed. In the villages they had encountered "women and men, with a firebrand in the hand, and herbs to drink the smoke thereof as they are accustomed." The natives called these rolled leaves "tobaccos." Following Torres's return, Columbus began to grow nervous. He still believed he was in China, and he needed the gold. His sailors received orders to collect plants he considered valuable: mastic, cinnamon, and Chinese rhubarb (although all these plants turned out to be something entirely different). And because he felt obliged to return to Spain with tangible evidence, he kidnapped five men, seven women, and three children. Martín Alonso Pinzón, in the meantime, had had enough of beautiful bays and green trees, and on November 21 he defected from the fleet in the *Pinta* and "without the will and command" of the Admiral, as was noted in

Columbus's log. This was obviously not the first time these two had clashed. "He has done and said many other things to me." One of the Indians aboard the *Pinta* had apparently told Pinzón about an island to the west called Babeque, where there was so much gold that people simply picked it up on the beach. While the *Pinta* sailed directly toward Babeque—the island that would later be called Great Inagua—Columbus and Pinzón's younger brother Vicente Yáñez continued to make their way along the coast of Cuba. Everywhere they went, every bay they saw, offered the same view.

On December 5, Columbus set a course to Babeque. He knew that he would have to proffer more than just the spices and a handful of Indians to the Spanish court if he wanted to undertake a second voyage. While waiting for more favorable winds, Columbus spied another island farther south. The Indians on board called it Bohio; it was the land of their ancestors and there was gold there. They all seemed very afraid, however, for behind Bohio lay Caritaba, the land where the "Canibas"—the cannibals—lived. Columbus thought they were merely being superstitious. All he understood was "Great Khan": "The inhabitants of all these islands live in great fear of the people of Caniba. And so I repeat as I have said at other times that Caniba is no other than the people of the Great Khan who must be very near here and have ships and come to capture these people, and as the captives do not return they believe they have eaten them." Columbus rechristened the island of Bohio as La Española, or Hispaniola—future home to Haiti and the Dominican Republic.

By that point Martín Alonso Pinzón had been on his gold-digging tour for nearly two weeks. Columbus knew that if Pinzón found gold and he himself returned empty-handed, the *Pinta*'s captain would trump him at court. The voyage had become less a matter of general success but of his reputation. Despite initial misgivings, Columbus had a good feeling about the island of Hispaniola. In one of the first bays where the depleted fleet cast its anchors, his men captured a young woman, breathtakingly beautiful and naked. Even more striking was that "this woman wore a small piece of gold in her nose, which was an indication that there was gold in that island." He ordered her to be clothed and returned to her home, bearing gifts of glass beads and hawk's bells. This would prove to be one of Columbus's happiest and most inspired ideas.

The woman he captured turned out to be the daughter of a cacique, and the next day the chief invited the foreign delegation to a feast with more than a thousand of the villagers. Word of Columbus's good deed spread quickly, and the *Santa María* and the *Niña* sailed from bay to bay in triumphal procession. At daybreak on December 22, Guacanagarí, the cacique who ruled over the northwestern part of the island, sent an invitation to Columbus by messenger, bearing a gift of a belt and a massive buckle made of solid gold.

On Christmas Eve Columbus and the younger Pinzón set sail, but the winds had died down during the night. The ships drifted in the calm waters of the bay, and at eleven o'clock at night Columbus fell asleep. No doubt the celebrations of the previous days had taken their toll. Soon everyone had fallen asleep, except for the ship's boy, who was steering, despite the fact that Columbus had expressly forbidden the helm be put in the hands of the ship's boys. The youth stood at the helm, but his view was impaired because the tiller stood at the stern. By the time he heard the slight swoosh of groundswell, it was already too late. The helm jerked in his hand, there was a grating noise, and the boy screamed. The flagship had slid onto a coral reef.

Columbus was the first on deck and ordered a kedge anchor to be cast into deeper water to pull the *Santa María* off the sandbank. The heavy mainmast was cut away to lighten the load, but although the swell was gentle, each wave drove the bulky *nao* further and further aground. It soon became clear that the *Santa María* was past saving. The seams broke apart and water quickly filled the bilge. Behind the sandbank the Spaniards saw a large bay and in the background a prominent-looking village (later Cap

Haitien). Both belonged to the realm of the great cacique Guacanagarí. The next day Columbus sent Diego de Arana and a lieutenant ashore to ask for assistance from the cacique. Columbus wrote:

> The village was about a league and a half beyond the said bank, and they say that he wept when he heard of the disaster and sent all his people from the village with many large canoes to unload the ship. And he in person with his brothers and relatives showed great assiduity both in the matter of unloading the ship and guarding what was thrown on land that everything might be in security.
>
> They are an affectionate people and free from avarice and agreeable in everything and I certify to your Highnesses that in all the world I do not believe there is a better people or a better country.

Now Columbus had only the little *Niña* on which to transport both the Spaniards and their captives. This was impossible. The ship would never have reached Spain. But if the *Niña* didn't make it, it would have been as if the discovery had never taken place. Nobody would know about it—nobody, that is, except Martín Alonso Pinzón. Columbus invited Guacanagarí aboard the *Niña* and told him of his plan to leave several men, mainly those from the *Santa María*, back in the bay. He himself would return to Spain on the *Niña*, and come back with several ships to rescue his stranded crew. The cacique permitted the Spaniards to build a fort. Guacanagarí was constantly at war with his neighbors and could use reinforcements, particularly if those reinforcements had the kind of weapons against which the Caribs would be defenseless. Guacanagarí regarded Columbus as a powerful new ally. Las Casas wrote:

> The Admiral told the Cacique by signs that the Sovereigns of Castile would order the Caribes destroyed. The Admiral ordered a lombard and a musket to be fired and seeing the effect of their force and what they penetrated, the Cacique marveled greatly.

And when his people heard the shots they all fell to the ground. They brought the Admiral a large mask, which had great pieces of gold in the ears and eyes and in other places.

Columbus ordered the Santa María *cannibalized, and from her planks and beams the ship's carpenters built a fort near the beach. Columbus named this first Spanish settlement in the New World La Navidad.*

Enough volunteers agreed to stay behind. They must have thought the naked women on the beach would be easy prey. They were also tempted by the promise of gold. Guacanagarí had told them there was plenty of gold in the riverbeds in the mountains. The men believed they would all be rich by the time Columbus returned. In fact, however, not one of them would survive, not even the man whom Columbus left in command of the fort, Diego de Arana, the man who had introduced him to his mistress and became one of his best friends.

Guacanagarí and Columbus organized a huge send-off, and so that word would spread of the white man's incredible power, the *Niña* fired a cannon shot on the sad remains of the *Santa María*.

Two days later, at the crack of dawn, the men on the now-heaving *Niña* weighed anchor and set sail for home. They soon sighted sails on the horizon—Martín Alonso Pinzón had returned after three weeks. He climbed aboard the *Niña* and commenced with a lengthy explanation for his absence. He told Columbus that he had unfortunately broken adrift and had then searched in vain for gold on Babeque. But farther to the west, on Hispaniola, one of his search parties had discovered gold, a lot of gold. It was now safely stored in the *Pinta*'s hold. Las Casas later wrote that Pinzón had acted in an arrogant manner, saying that he was driven by "pride" and that Columbus had "concealed his thoughts and accepted these excuses in order not to imperil the whole enterprise." On the off chance that Pinzón was telling the truth, the *Niña* sailed toward the bay where a river flowed into the sea. When Columbus's men began to scoop fresh water into their casks, little grains of gold got caught in the barrel's hoops. Columbus set the sails. He finally had the proof he needed to keep his promise. He had found nearly everything he had set out to discover: lands, gold, people. And the Great Khan could not be far away, especially since his men apparently came here to hunt natives. The *Pinta* and the *Niña* sailed home.

Just as he had on the outward journey, Columbus chose exactly the right route. At first he sailed north for a number of days; there was no point in tacking against the trade winds. Then he chose a more northwesterly course as they came within range of the trade-wind zone. The wind died down but finally returned at the end of January. And now the winds blew from the west. Columbus stayed on a northeasterly route, and this time he probably took advantage of the height of the North Star to find his way. But his calculations were merely rough estimates because, as Las Casas recounted, "he could not take the latitude with the astrolabe or quadrant, because the waves would not permit it." After four days Columbus reckoned that the North Star was just as high above the horizon as at Cape Saint Vincent and Palos de la Frontera. That meant both ships must now be on the same latitude as their home port. The helmsmen changed to an easterly course at daybreak and now steered in the general direction of Europe, a tailwind pushing them. The carousel of the Atlantic was working, just as it had for tens of thousands of years. But for mankind it was working for the very first time.

On February 12, the two boats encountered stormy seas. They were sailing right into the middle of one of the worst hurricanes of the year. Soon everyone on board feared for their life; Columbus prayed and gave thanks that his little *Niña* was "so very staunch and well found." He had all sails flattened, and with the wind from astern, the caravel flew across the waves, driven only by the force of the wind on the bare masts. "The sea became terrible and the waves crossed each other which racked the ships."

The next day the waves were "terrible." The crew drew lots to choose one man who would fulfill a vow to go on a pilgrimage, should they all survive. Las Casas wrote: "The first to put in his hand was the Admiral and he took out the pea marked with the sign of the cross." Soon, however, Columbus realized that one pilgrim was not going to placate the Almighty. Everyone made a vow: Should they ever reach land again, they would all go in their shirts in procession to pray in a church. The waves broke across the *Niña*'s bow. Columbus and Vicente Yáñez Pinzón took turns on deck. Suddenly the *Pinta* disappeared in the storm. Columbus wrote his last will and testament. Las Casas described the scene:

> So that, if he were to perish in that storm, the Monarchs would have news of his voyage, he took a piece of parchment and wrote on it everything he could about everything he had found, beseeching whomsoever might find it to take it to the Monarchs. He wrapped the parchment tightly in a waxed cloth and called for a large wooden barrel and put it in the barrel without anyone knowing what it was, for they all thought it was some act of devotion, and then ordered it to be thrown into the sea.

On February 15, the crew sighted the Azores. Then the wind turned and it took days before they reached the island of Santa Maria. Finally, they cast anchor. They had survived.

The Azores belonged to Portugal. Fulfilling their vow, the first group of sailors, dressed only in their shirts, set off for the church to give thanks to God and to the Virgin Mary. Columbus stayed on board with three sailors and the Indians he intended to present at court. But when the first group of pilgrims went on land, the local Portuguese official had the men arrested and imprisoned. He then rowed out to the *Niña* to arrest Columbus on charges of having violated a contract between Portugal and Spain. He claimed that the lands discovered by Columbus belonged to Portugal. Although this contract did in fact exist, Columbus hadn't violated it. He had stayed on the legal side of an imaginary border the pope had drawn up in a bull issued in 1456. This bull had drawn a line around the known and unknown world in an attempt to keep the two nations apart. It must have been a comic scene on that wet and windy day: imprisoned sailors in penitential shirts, a scrupulous bureaucrat in a rowing boat, Columbus frantic with outrage. Columbus tried to lure the official on board the *Niña,* but the Portuguese refused, suspecting that the Admiral wanted to hold him hostage. Columbus threatened to bombard the village with the ship's cannons if his sailors were not released immediately. Suddenly the wind picked up and a squall caused the anchor cables on the *Niña* to break; the ship began to drift. With what few deckhands he had left, Columbus struggled to get the ship back under control. By the time he did and had made it back to Santa Maria, the Portuguese official had already questioned his Spanish prisoners, and, realizing that they had not after all breached the papal decree, he set them free.

No sooner had the *Niña* set sail for the open seas again, this time with her complete crew, than the hurricane struck again. The storm drove them directly toward Lisbon, where, because the *Niña* was heavily damaged—the sails were split and the yards stripped—Columbus was forced to enter port. An armed ship full of soldiers approached. King João II requested a visit from Columbus; the cannons of the warship trained on the *Niña* lent additional weight to the request. Although the king certainly wanted to avoid war with Spain, he was nevertheless unwilling to hand over control of lands that the papal bull had guaranteed to Portugal. Columbus agreed to meet with the monarch. We might speculate that he found it amusing to tell him what he had found on the other side of the ocean, and what Portugal had forfeited when it had rejected his plan. Ultimately it was the Indians who persuaded King João II that Columbus had not trespassed on Portugal's African territories, for they bore no resemblance to the black slaves from Guinea.

The king allowed Columbus to travel on toward Palos, and on March 15, 1493, the *Niña* sailed up the Río Tinto. Two hundred twenty-four days had passed since she first set sail past La Rábida monastery. Only a few hours later, the *Pinta* also returned home. She had weathered the storm but had been driven to Vigo in northern Spain, from where Captain Pinzón, in yet another attempt to outmaneuver Columbus, had sent a hurriedly written letter to Ferdinand and Isabella in Barcelona, requesting an audience so that he might tell of the great discovery. Doubtless he would have informed Her Majesty how he, Pinzón, had assembled the crews, how he had found the islands, and how he had discovered gold. The queen replied that she would rather hear the news from Columbus. So dejected was Martín Alonso that he did not even report to Columbus when he arrived in Palos, although the *Niña* and the *Pinta* were berthed virtually side by side. Pinzón retired to his home and went to bed, whether from humiliation or exhaustion, or both, remains unknown. He died a month later.

After anchoring in Palos, Columbus rode to Seville, accompanied by his Indians and the gold. The people on the streets greeted him enthusiastically. More than merely a journey, his was a triumphal procession through Spain. He had reached the pinnacle of success and become a national hero. He was already drawing up new plans—involving bringing settlers to the islands, building a capital city, and carrying off as much gold as possible. He wondered what he should do with the Indians. He probably consulted Berardi the slave trader as to how he might organize a second voyage, though he suspected this would not be difficult. The king and queen had sent a letter, asking him to hasten to the court in Barcelona and tell them of his travels. The contents of the letter were less important than the form of address with which the monarchs had chosen to open it: "Don Cristóbal Colón, Admiral of the Ocean Sea, Viceroy and Governor of the Islands that he hath discovered in the Indies." Ferdinand and Isabella were granting him all the titles and rights he had longed for and a power unmatched by any grandee in Spain. At least for the moment, they were abiding by the Treaty of Santa Fe.

CHAPTER 6

The Fallen Hero

Columbus was supposed to have kept a log or diary on each of his voyages. Fernando spoke of "journals" that his father had written. However, none of the reports that may have been compiled during his second voyage to the New World survived the centuries. All that remains are a few letters and a detailed and very valuable contract Columbus sent back to the Spanish court from Hispaniola via his messenger Antonio de Torres. This contract now sits in the archives of Seville. What makes it so valuable is that the monarchs' replies also exist—one of those rare pieces of evidence showing how Isabella and Ferdinand treated their Admiral of the Ocean Sea and how he in turn dealt with his royal superiors.

However, the document itself reveals little about Columbus's second voyage. The story of this expedition has therefore been told from hearsay by Fernando and Bartolomé de Las Casas, as well by the witnesses Pietro Martire, Michele de Cuneo, and Nicolo Syllacio, whose reports are only marginally informative due to their subjective nature. Lastly, there is information supplied by the physician Diego Álvarez Chanca and Andrés Bernáldez. Chanca had long been the Spanish court physician, and his zeal earned him the right to participate in Columbus's second voyage.

His description of the first half of the voyage, recorded in a letter to the city of Seville, was skillful. Bernáldez, chaplain to the Archbishop of Seville, was a member of the Royal Council and a Grand Inquisitor. Bernáldez was a man of his time: he loved pomp and ceremonies, and he hated Jews and other nonbelievers. "They have been burned and shall burn in living flames until they be no more." Bernáldez had known and admired Columbus for years; he was, however, a rather idle chronicler at first, copying the first half of his report from Dr. Chanca; he was more meticulous during the second half of the voyage. There are also Fernando's accounts, of course. Fernando stood watching from the quay when the fleet left Spain, for he was not allowed to join his father. Although the original version of Columbus's log or journal has been lost, at the time when he compiled his own account, Fernando possessed all of his father's notes. Five hundred years later, his account remains the only available source.

During his sojourn in Spain, Columbus stayed in Castilian castles, spent three months in Barcelona, and visited his sons and his mistress. He bought himself clothing befitting a man in his position. His flowing cape, long gray hair, and complexion burnished from having spent eight months at sea all combined to give him "the appearance of a Roman Senator," wrote Samuel Eliot Morison. He could have continued to live well in Spain but thought he would fare even better at sea. In fulfillment of the vow he had made aboard the *Niña*, Columbus made a pilgrimage to Guadalupe in Extremadura, where he prayed to the Holy Virgin; the monks there asked him to name an island in her honor.

This time there was no shortage of volunteers willing to accompany Columbus. Juan Rodríguez de Fonseca, the Archbishop of Seville, was appointed the expedition's official organizer; he selected twelve hundred sailors, soldiers, and settlers. Fonseca purchased and chartered seventeen ships: the *Santa María la Galante*, also known by her nickname *Maríagalante,* would be the flagship. There were also two *naos* called *Colina* and the *Gallega,* as well as ten square-rigged caravels, two caravels with lateen sails, and a smaller rowing boat that could enter shallower waters. Each ship bore the royal standard, and every ship was decorated. This armada had been summoned to follow the call of gold—as well as all the other enticements. The naked women of the Indies that Columbus had mentioned in passing had created no less than a sensation in Spain's pious and straitlaced medieval society. Finally, and most importantly, in the fall of 1493 Columbus was regarded as a hero and a leader. It was only natural that any reasonably courageous sailor would wish to join his triumphal procession.

Columbus gave each of the captains in his fleet a letter, closed and sealed. It contained his orders in the event the fleet was separated during a storm. Naturally, Columbus wanted all of the ships to reach La Navidad, but he was unwilling to reveal the route to anyone. The captains were only permitted to open the letter in the event they got left behind.

The journey began in Cádiz on September 25, 1493, an hour before sundown. Favorable winds and mild breezes carried the fleet to Grand Canary Island, where they were forced to repair one of the ships before sailing on to La Gomera. Here they took on as much meat, timber, and water as they could. This time Columbus would certainly have had no time for Doña Beatriz, the island's governor; he had seventeen ships to load with fresh supplies of grain and wineskins, plants and ship's biscuits, salted pork and beef, as well as sheep, chicken, and twenty horses. The ships lay deep in the water when he sailed to Hierro on October 13, where he began his Atlantic crossing.

The light changed constantly, playing in the white sails, glimmering like gold in the sundown and silver in the moonlight, looking ominous when clouds loomed overhead. The sea was dark blue; flying fish jumped through the waves. During the day the ships sped across the ocean as fast as they could, racing each other, and at night the faster ships waited for the others to catch up. The Admiral had given precise orders for the night: every ship carried a lantern astern and the fleet had to sail in formation. Every thirty minutes the ship's boys would turn on the *ampolettas,* and at dawn the priest on the flagship celebrated a "dry

Mass," meaning no wine was served since it would only have spilled. The men on the other ships knelt and prayed, and then another day at sea began.

The fleet made an average speed of around five knots, managing twenty-five hundred nautical miles in twenty-one days. If only they hadn't had to keep waiting for the *Mariagalante*. Once again the flagship was one of the slowest vessels, and occasionally the other ships would have to shorten their sails because the Admiral was getting left too far behind.

On All Saints' Day, November 1, 1493, Columbus granted each man an extra ration of water. The next evening he ordered the ships to trim their sails. In the early morning light of November 3, one of the sailors on the *Mariagalante* climbed to the crow's nest and shouted, "Land in sight!"

There has probably never been a better sailor than Columbus. In a truly remarkable achievement, he had made landfall on the Antilles in exactly the same location where sailors using depth gauges and global positioning systems would land five hundred years later. There is only one favorable passage here, running straight and deep, otherwise the area is dotted with sandbanks and reefs. Columbus found this passage straight off. His friend Cuneo celebrated Columbus in his journal:

> *In my humble opinion, since Genoa was Genoa, no other man has been born so magnanimous and so keen in practical navigation as the above-mentioned Lord Admiral: for, when navigating, he only needed to see a cloud or star at night to know which direction to follow or if bad weather was on its way; he himself commanded and stood at the helm; and when the tempest had passed, he raised the sails while others slept.*

The Admiral named these first islands Dominica (having landed there on Sunday) and Mariagalante (because, despite her sluggish pace, he loved his flagship). Dr. Chanca described the islands as "very mountainous, very beautiful and very green down to the water's edge." The Spaniards anchored on the leeside, the downwind side of the island, and then went ashore dressed in festive attire. On the white sandy beaches of the Caribbean, and with the royal standard waving under the palm trees, Columbus planted wooden crosses and took possession of one island after another in the name of the Spanish crown. Fulfilling his vow to the monks, the Admiral named one of the next islands they reached Santa María de Guadeloupe. This was a spectacular island, with a volcano and a waterfall that seemed to come pouring straight down from the clouds. The sailors gazed in wonder at the jungle, the palm trees, and the spectacular colors. One captain was sent ashore with a scouting party to explore the island; all he found were deserted villages. He brought back, wrote Chanca, "four or five human arm and leg bones, and we suspected that these were the Carib islands, whose inhabitants eat human flesh."

Columbus sent more scouting parties onto the islands, and several returned with young men and women, whom they claimed had been captured by the cannibals. Some scout parties got lost, like Captain Diego Márquez and his six men; the others wondered whether they had been eaten by the cannibals.

The Spaniards spent eight days in the bay of Guadeloupe, eight days of complete chaos. "More than twenty women of the captives were fetched," recounted Chanca. And even Morison later wrote that the girls proved useful as interpreters and probably in other ways as well. "The customs of these Carib people are beastly," claimed Chanca. They could tell the Caribs by the two bands of cotton bound below the knee and above the ankle. They also wore their hair longer than other tribes and painted their faces in garish colors "to increase their ferocious appearance." They built their boats from one piece of wood and used them to hunt people, particularly young women, and they used fish bones, stones, and shells to turn their arrows into deadly weapons. Chanca wrote:

> These women say that they are treated with a cruelty that seems incredible. The Caribs eat the male children that they have by them, and only bring up the children of their own women; and as for the men they are able to capture, they bring those who are alive home to be slaughtered and eat those who are dead on the

*spot. They say that human flesh is so good that there is nothing
like it in the world; and this must be true, for the human bones
we found in their houses were so gnawed that no flesh was left
on them except what was too tough to be eaten. In one house
the neck of a man was found cooking in a pot. They castrate
the boys that they capture and use them as servants until they
are men. Then, when they want to make a feast, they kill and
eat them.*

Fernando recounted similar horror stories. "These men had had
their virile members cut off, for the Caribs capture them on the
other islands and castrate them, as we do to fatten capons, to improve their taste."

As to the truthfulness of these accounts, one cannot help won-
dering whether they really were cannibals—the Canibas or Caribs
they had been warned about during the first voyage—or whether
Columbus and his men used this to justify what would ensue.
Slaughtering cannibals would be fulfilling God's wrath. Morison,
for one, believed the stories and even wrote about "the man-
eating Caribs." Some archaeologists have written that no evidence
of cannibals in the Caribbean has ever been found. Linguists have
noted that the Spaniards wouldn't have understood the natives;
they would doubtless have misunderstood virtually everything.
Their imaginations might have made up for this. As Kirkpatrick
Sale pointed out, demonization of the victims was a way of justi-
fying genocide.

Captain Márquez and his scouts eventually resurfaced, looking disheveled and emaciated after spending four days lost in the
jungle. "The Admiral punished them for their rashness, ordering
the captain put in chains and placing the others on short rations,"
wrote Fernando.

On November 10, Columbus's fleet set sail again. Their expedition was turning into a spectacular tour. They saw mountains
reaching into the sky on nearly every island, with a single thick
cloud above them. The slopes were covered with vegetation;
palm trees sprawled along the beaches. Depending on the time of

day and the light, the colors of the Antilles would change dramatically. Columbus "discovered" Puerto Rico before returning to the side of Hispaniola that would later be called Haiti. "It contains many large rivers, great mountain ranges, wide open valleys and high mountains," reported Chanca. "I do not believe that there is winter either in this island or any of the others, for many bird's nests were found at Christmas, some containing fledglings and some eggs."

It was time for Columbus to return to where the *Santa María* had sank and where La Navidad had been built, the first town in the New World, the place where he had left many of his men. When he arrived, Columbus was attacked by six Indians, four men and two women in a canoe, who shot arrows at the fleet, killing a sailor before they were overpowered. Columbus took one look at his captured prize and presented one of the female Indians to his friend Michele de Cuneo as his slave. "When I had taken her to my cabin she was naked—as was their custom. I was filled with a desire to take my pleasure with her and attempted to satisfy my desire," wrote Cuneo. But the girl scratched him with her fingernails, and in the end he felt compelled to whip her with a piece of rope until she screamed. "Such incredible screams that you would not have believed your ears," described Cuneo. "Eventually we came to such terms, I assure you, that you would have thought she had been brought up in a school for whores."

The fleet anchored in a bay, named Monte Cristi by Columbus, some fifteen miles from La Navidad. He sent scouts ashore, and they returned with the news that they had found two dead bodies with beards. None of the natives, not even the supposed cannibals, wore beards. This was not a good sign. "Some of our men suspected the worst and with justification," wrote Chanca.

They set sail again. Everyone on board was subdued. It was the evening of November 27 when they finally arrived in the bay of La Navidad. In light of how amateurish they had been more than a year ago, when only a ship's boy had held watch and they had glided softly onto the sandbank and lost the *Santa María*, Columbus decided to wait until the next morning. This time the fleet stayed offshore and waited for daylight. A canoe bearing six Indians approached the fleet, but Columbus permitted nobody on board. He fired two bombards, in the hope that his men on land would recognize the cannonry and answer fire. But all remained still. The canoe approached again. In it was a cousin of Chief Guacanagarí. He sent greetings to the Admiral and presented him with masks of gold. Much as he might have welcomed the gifts, Columbus was incredulous when he heard the native's account. The man said there had been a war on the island. The tribe of Chief Caonabó and the tribe of Chief Mayreni had fought a bloody battle against Chief Guacanagarí, resulting in a massacre. The white men had been caught in the middle. Some of them had died of diseases, and some had killed each other. The truth, he said, was that there were no survivors.

Finding this hard to believe, Columbus painstakingly reconstructed the events that led to the death of his sailors. First the two lieutenants Pedro Gutierrez and Rodrigo de Escovedo had murdered their comrade Jacomo Rico. Columbus had liked all three men. Gutierrez had been the man ordered to tell Guacanagarí about the sinking of the *Santa María* the previous year, and he had also been at Columbus's side when the Admiral first set foot on land in the New World at Guanahani. Jacomo Rico had been the only Genoese sailor to accompany Columbus on that first voyage. The Admiral had trusted them, and now they had killed each other and nobody knew why.

But that was only the half of it. The houses of La Navidad had been "burned to the ground," wrote Fernando. They were blockhouses that were supposed to have been protected by an earth wall. Fernando recounted, "Next morning the Admiral went ashore and felt much grief at the sight of the ruins of the houses and the fort. Nothing remained of the houses except some smashed chests and such other wreckage as one sees in a land that has been devastated and put to the sack." Clothes were strewn around, some of it hanging in the Indians' huts, and in one hut they found the anchor belonging to the *Santa María*. Eleven corpses were found scattered throughout the area, which was overgrown by grass; their stench filled the air. A year before Columbus had left thirty-nine men here. Now all of them were dead, including his friend and confidant Diego de Arana.

Columbus's men demanded revenge. But Columbus hesitated. Chief Guacanagarí's men told him that most of the white men had been killed by the enemy tribes, those same tribes that had wounded Guacanagarí, who now lay in his hut with a serious leg injury and was being tended to by his seven concubines. Later Guacanagarí's men let slip that one of the Spaniards had taken three women for himself, another had taken four, and so on. "They said that soon after the Admiral's departure those men began to quarrel among themselves, each taking as many women and as much gold as he could," wrote Fernando. This was probably the true version of events. Under the Caribbean sun, the Spaniards had behaved like conquerors, and the Indians had dealt with them swiftly. According to Fernando, "Eight of them drowned; three others, whom these Indians could not identify, were killed ashore."

Chief Guacanagarí was sympathetic and friendly to Columbus and presented him with a fair amount of gold. But then his brother came on board to visit the Admiral, and when nobody was looking, he whispered something to the ten captive women whom the Spaniards had supposedly freed from the cannibals. The women jumped overboard. Accomplished swimmers, they easily made it to the shore three miles away, then disappeared into the jungle.

Columbus's men wanted vengeance. Columbus decided to set sail.

———————

Those who have searched for the Santa María and La Navidad in Cap Haitien—occasionally a few miles to the east, occasionally to the west—have been certain that the most famous ship in the world, apart from Noah's Ark and the Titanic, had to be there. And so, too, the fort—the first European settlement in America.

There are some certainties to go on: that the *Santa María* ran aground when Columbus and his crew were sleeping; that Columbus used the ship's wood to build La Navidad and that he left thirty-nine men behind to defend it; that only the bottom part of the hull and the ballast stones were left in the sea in 1492 and that it took only days for the *Santa María* to be wrecked; and that La Navidad was burned down and destroyed as early as 1493. What is not clear, however, is where all this occurred.

In the eighteenth century, French historian Moreau de Saint-Méry found an anchor in the riverbed of the Grand-Rivière, over a mile from the mouth of the river and some two miles from the fishing village Bord-de-Mer Limonade. Saint-Méry claimed that this must have been the anchor that Chanca had discovered in one of the native huts on Hispaniola. Any other theory would have been difficult to explain, for how could the *Santa María*'s anchor have ended up in a riverbed?

Samuel Eliot Morison turned up off the coast of Haiti a hundred and fifty years later, in the 1930s. Morison, as we've seen, had researched and analyzed Columbus's navigation avidly. Morison, then in his mid-forties, was teaching at Harvard and believed in a somewhat unusual code of professional ethics. He wasn't content with merely following Columbus's course with his finger on a sea chart; he wanted to do it with his hand on the tiller. It simply wasn't enough to study old documents to understand the past. Morison wanted to get out and see the places that Columbus had visited and described. Together with some friends, Morison purchased an old brigantine and equipped it for a global expedition. He set sail, first in the brigantine *Capitana* and later on the ketch *Mary Ann,* following the course laid down by Columbus, across the Atlantic, crisscrossing the Caribbean, and down to Central America. He noted everything he saw: the shoals, the distances, winds, currents, land formations, as well as the bad and the good anchoring grounds. Writing was like breathing to Morison: he wrote constantly. Later, as a lieutenant commander in the U.S. Navy, he authored fifteen volumes about marine missions during the Second World War. He also wrote three books on the four voyages of Christopher Columbus, winning the Pulitzer Prize for the first book.

Morison went to Haiti in 1939, equipped with sea charts and the accounts of the first and second voyages, and tried to reconstruct what had happened in 1492 and 1493. He knew that Columbus had told the Indian chief Guacanagarí of the shipwreck and, based on the assumption that it was by far the best location for a settlement, he sited Guacanagarí's village in the place where the fishing village Bord-de-Mer Limonade now lay. There was a mighty coral reef just off the coast as well as three shallow sandbanks. This, Morison believed, had to be the place. Unfortunately, the technology that would have helped him locate a 450-year-old wreck in the middle of the ocean hadn't yet been invented. Morison found nothing and sailed on.

Ten years later a pilot named Don Lungwitz flew over Cap Haitien and reported spotting a ship-shaped blur on the reef. In 1955 the oceanographers Edwin and Marion Link made their way to Haiti and began searching in those places that Morison had thought most likely. They found an anchor, without ring and side arms, but were able to ascertain that this anchor was made of iron—like the one found by Saint-Méry—and that both originated from the same era and had been built in the same way. Was it the anchor belonging to the *Santa María?* Twelve years after that, in 1967, the historian and treasure diver Fred Dickson arrived on the scene. He had received the exact coordinates of the oval blur from Lungwitz and—hidden under a thick layer of coral—found wood, ceramic shards, ballast stones, and pieces of iron. Eighty feet farther on, he found more of the same but also glass and thick iron rods. Unfortunately, radiocarbon dating showed that even the oldest artifact was only 320 years old. Rather than the *Santa María,* it was an eighteenth-century warship. Dickson wanted to extend the search but died in 1972, following a diving accident.

Kathleen Deagan came furthest in researching the whereabouts of the *Santa María.* Deagan earned her doctorate in anthropology and archaeology at the University of Florida in 1975 and stayed on to teach. Today an archaeologist with the Florida Museum of Natural History, she and her husband, Lawrence Harris—who shares her passion for research—have spent years living in tents and huts on beaches, looking for traces of Christopher Columbus. Following a tip by amateur archaeologist William Hodges, Kathleen Deagan spent three years living on Haiti's northern coast, near the village of Bord-de-Mer Limonade. There she discovered the ruins of an Indian village: En Bas Saline. She found twenty-one former gardens, and each of the gardens was surrounded by a kind of hedge that was "dense and prickly," Deagan wrote. In the middle was a kind of square, and underneath it she found a pit measuring ten feet deep and three feet in diameter. This pit must have been a former well shaft, but well shafts were unknown to the Indians of the Caribbean. In the well shaft, Deagan discovered shells, shards, and bones. A C14 analysis showed that these dated to 1440, give or take thirty-five years. This presented an unusual state of affairs. Usually the artifacts that archaeologists analyze are not as old as they would hope. This time, it was the other way around.

Then Deagan and her crew came upon the jawbone of a rat and the tooth of a pig. They were able to establish—with some certainty—that the pig came from the region around Seville, as did the rat. Here was evidence that trumped the C14 analysis. It was only a question of logic. The rat and the pig could have come with the first ship from Europe; they could hardly have swam the distance. "It could have been the first rat to leave a sinking ship in the New World," commented Deagan. She also found glass and clay shards. In the end, there was nothing that conclusively proved the site was La Navidad, though no one had ever come as close as Kathleen Deagan.

———————

After traveling for three months, it had become clear to one and all that this second voyage had been anything but successful. They had discovered twenty large islands and many more islets, but all the gold they had were nuggets given to them as gifts by the Indians. They had found no gold mines, and they had failed to establish any settlements; one of the prime objectives had been to begin building a metropolis near one of the inexhaustible gold veins. They achieved none of that. Now they were facing a head-wind and forced to tack, making little progress. It took them twenty-five days to sail thirty-two miles. The spray from the waves had made the sails slow and heavy, the close quarters seemed to be growing closer still, and all they had to eat were ship's biscuits. These conditions were bound to change their mood.

They were still in the north of Hispaniola when Columbus decided that the next halfway decent bay they chanced upon would be as good an anchoring ground as any. "It pleased Our Lord that through the foulness of weather which would not let us go farther, we had to land on the best site and lay-out that we were able to select," reported Chanca. There was an open bay with a few shoals and lots of fish; it was also protected from the winds. In short, it seemed perfect. Columbus called it La Isabela. It lay some ten miles east of Monte Cristi and fifty miles to the west of a beach that, in five hundred years' time, would be called Puerto Plata and be known as the star tourist attraction of the Dominican Republic. As Fernando wrote, "There he founded a town to which he gave the name Isabela, in honor of the Catholic Queen. They believed it to be an excellent site for a town, because it had a very large harbor, though open to the northwest, and a lovely river a crossbow shot in width, from which water channels could be led to the town; and beyond the river extended a very charming plain, not far from which, according to the Indians, were the mines of the Cibao." In truth, it was a terrible choice. There was only a slight opening toward the northwest and actually quite a number of reefs; there was also no protection from the storms. Nonetheless, it became the site of a second attempt to establish a settlement in the New World.

Here in La Isabela was where Diego Álvarez Chanca brought his account to a close. Describing the construction of the town, he noted that one side was protected by the ocean and the cliffs, the other side by a forest "so dense that hardly a rabbit can get through" and "so green that no fire could destroy it." There was a river, the Río Isabela, from which they could divert water to power the mills and waterwheels. Chanca also hinted at the men's feelings of discontent. Due to their long travels and the amount of time he knew it would take for the seeds they had sown to grow, Columbus rationed the food. The men were nonetheless being forced to build the kind of metropolis that Columbus had in mind, which was based on Cádiz. This meant that he needed a church, a governor's residence, and a plaza, as well as somewhere around two hundred stone houses. The men began to grow impatient. They had not traveled all this way simply to undertake construction work. There were cases of malaria and fish poisoning, and Chanca's supply of medicine was fast running out.

The physician also described the natives who watched the houses being built. They were naked, though the women wore a small band of cotton between their legs. Some had painted themselves black, others red and white, so that to the Spaniards they were such "sorry sights that we cannot help laughing at them." And their hair was long in places and shaved in others. What was considered a hairstyle befitting a lunatic in Spain here was an expression of honor and respect. These natives were rather stupid, thought Chanca, for they ate spiders and snakes and worms. They would prove to be easy to convert, he claimed, "for they imitate everything we do." But Chanca also described the beauty of his surroundings, noting that "the little that we have seen is marvelous," including trees that bore cotton, peach trees, ginger roots, bread trees, and Indian pepper.

Columbus sent off two scouting parties in either direction along the coast. Their task was to find gold. Alonso de Ojeda commanded one of the expeditions. He was a young man from Andalusia—athletic, good-looking, and cocky—who had caught the attention of Queen Isabella when he had walked out onto a beam projecting from the Giralda, one of the towers in Seville, and done a pirouette. The other expedition was led by Ginés de

Gorbolan. They returned on January 20 and 21, respectively. Chanca wrote that they had found "gold in more than fifty streams and rivers," which meant, he added, that "our sovereigns therefore can consider themselves henceforth the richest and most prosperous on earth, for nothing comparable has ever been seen or read of till now in the whole world."

Columbus decided to divide the fleet into three. He himself wanted to set sail again and discover new worlds. One-third of the men were to stay in La Isabela and establish the settlement. Twelve ships were allowed to return to Spain to deliver a report to the royal family, arrange for further supplies and provisions, deliver the sick to hospitals, and cut costs. Chanca joined the part of the fleet sailing home. One of the last things he wrote was "But as God is my witness I have not departed one iota from the truth."

Antonio de Torres, captain of the *Mariagalante,* was appointed commander of the fleet bound for home. It was decided that the twelve ships would set sail on February 2, 1494. Shortly before they left for Spain, Columbus fell ill and became so weak that between December 11 and March 12 he stopped writing in his journal. He did, however, manage to write a memorandum for Torres that he was to deliver to the king and queen. Columbus told Torres that it was important for him to "kiss for me their Royal feet and hands," and the hands and feet of "my natural Lords, in whose service I desire to end my days." Later the memorandum would include the king and queen's remarks, such as "Their Highnesses hold him in their favor," for they sent Torres back to Columbus with their reply. (The document reads like a question-and-answer game.) For his part, Columbus asked for provisions and equipment, praised his men, and recommended that they receive pay increases. He also advised on strategies and requested further instructions.

> *Because such signs and indications of spices have been found on the shores of the sea alone, without having gone inland, there is reason that very much better results may be hoped for. And this*

*also may be hoped for in the mines of gold, ... so many rivers
have been discovered so filled with gold, that all who saw it and
gathered specimens of it with the hands alone, came away so
pleased and say such things in regard to its abundance, ... for
this their Highnesses may give thanks to God, since He has been
so favorable to them in all their affairs.*

In their reply the sovereigns "give many thanks to God for this,
and consider as a very signal service all that the Admiral has done
in this matter and is doing." Columbus wrote that he had been
forced to abandon the gold mines as the Indians had threatened
him and his men had fallen sick: "It did not appear that it would
be a good idea to risk losing these people and the supplies." Their
Highnesses deigned to praise him for his actions and noted, "That
he did well." Columbus wrote that the Spanish must use caution
in these far-off lands and that they must build settlements. He
used the Arabic word *albarrada,* meaning mortarless dry-stone
walls. And he went on to note that the Indians were "not a people
to undertake anything unless they should find us sleeping, even
though they might have thought of it in the manner in which
they served the others who remained here. Only on account of
their [the Spaniards'] lack of caution—they being so few—and
the great opportunities they gave the Indians to have and do what
they did, they would never have dared to undertake to injure
them if they had seen that they were cautious." Albeit in a confused manner, Columbus was suggesting that the men he had left
behind in La Navidad had been to blame for their own demise;
they had not taken the proper precautions. He had thus not made
a mistake in leaving them there and was exonerating himself, in
the event that someone back in Spain might think to ask about
the fate of those poor men he was now leaving behind. Columbus went on to guarantee the safety of these men by writing that
it was his plan to protect the gold miners and, above all, the gold
by building a fort. (His tactic worked, for the sovereigns replied,
"That this is well and must be done in this manner.")

The memorandum went on for pages. Columbus requested wheat to sow and asked for wine, ship's biscuits, bacon, and salted meat, "better than that we brought on this journey." He also requested lambs, sheep—more females than males—as well as yearling calves and cows, linen, sack coats, and "cloths suitable for wearing apparel," as well as 200 cuirasses, 100 muskets, 100 crossbows, and a large quantity of ammunition. He would need 50 casks of molasses and laborers from the quicksilver mines at Almadén, for they were probably best suited for gold digging. He also asked for two caravels fully manned and wrote that everything he had requested be sent to sea by May. (Their Highnesses answered that they would assign these tasks to Don Juan Rodríguez de Fonseca, the Archbishop of Seville.)

Columbus also wrote Ferdinand and Isabella about the "cannibals" he was sending back to Spain, such that they "may cause them to abandon at once that inhuman custom," learn Spanish, and receive baptism and provide for the safety of their souls. Columbus also devised a scheme for a slave market, giving royal license to a number of caravels for use in transporting the slaves. He described the natives as "well-proportioned and of good intelligence." (The sovereigns replied that this project was to be held in abeyance for the present, and it is unclear whether this was because they were against slavery on principle or whether they thought Columbus was overstepping his authority. They were, however, offended that he was acting on his own authority by shipping Indians to Spain. Las Casas later speculated that this could have been one of the main reasons why Columbus did not remain governor of Hispaniola for long. One possibility was that this was Columbus's rather clumsy way of trying to settle debts with Gianotto Berardi, the slave trader and cofinancier of the first and second voyages, to whom he still owed a shipment of slaves. Ferdinand and Isabella were quite possibly annoyed that such business ventures were being set up without their involvement.)

Columbus then addressed other business matters, writing that he had purchased two ships, the *Gallega* and the *Santa María la Galante,* for purchasing ships cost less than chartering them. ("The Admiral has done well," answered the sovereigns.) Finally, Columbus raised the issue of money and individual requests. He praised his servant Pedro Margarite, writing, "I have been pleased to have him remain here," and the servants Gaspar and Beltrán, who had been entrusted to him by the royal family; he requested special care for the hardworking Margarite, who had a wife and children; and he praised Dr. Chanca, who had "acted with great diligence and charity." (Their Highnesses ordered that 30,000 *maravedís* be given to Margarite and that favorable examination be given to Dr. Chanca.) He signed off, "Written in the city of Isabela, January 30, 1494."

Their Highnesses acknowledged receipt of the letter and dated their reply April 13, 1494. Antonio de Torres had arrived in Cádiz on March 7. He departed for Hispaniola very soon after, accompanied by not two but four ships, bearing the supplies and provisions Columbus had requested.

Jealousy produces bad counselors, brotherly affection even worse. Over the course of his career, Columbus made a series of disastrous personnel decisions. He seldom seemed to learn from his mistakes.

While waiting for Torres to return, Columbus undertook various expeditions throughout Hispaniola. "He led his men out of Isabela and other places armed, in military formation, with trumpets sounding and banners displayed," reported Fernando. Eighteen miles from La Isabela, he built a fort named Saint Thomas and he left the aforementioned Pedro Margarite, "a very worthy man," in command of fifty-six men. He tried to bring the natives to heel. Five Indians who had been ordered to carry blankets across a river had suddenly turned around midway and fled back to their village, refusing to hand back the blankets. Columbus ordered that they be sentenced to death and had this announced among the natives. "At this the kind cacique shed so many tears that he at last obtained the lives of those men, promising they would never again offend," wrote Fernando.

In April Columbus decided that he wanted to discover more lands. That meant he had to entrust La Isabela, the town he had just founded, to someone else. Rather than appointing the most qualified man to ensure able leadership and stability, Columbus appointed a council, consisting of Fray Buil, Pedro Fernández Coronel, Alonso Sánchez de Carvajal, and Juan de Lujan. At the head of the council he placed Diego Colón, the least talented of the Colón brothers. Where Bartolomeo seems to have been a brilliant sailor and soldier, a veteran of storms and battles, Diego, according to Las Casas, a man who revered Columbus, was a peace-loving and rather simple man. He was probably the youngest of the brothers (the year assigned to his birth, 1466, has never been verified). Some have claimed that Diego was the older brother. What is more certain is that he had ambitions to join the church.

As head of La Isabela council, Diego Colón was surrounded by men who wanted gold and sex. These were men who had expected that Christopher Columbus would further their ambitions. Diego was another matter. In addition to appointing his brother, Columbus made the mistake of naming two highly ambitious men to lead the scouting missions and gold-digging operations, Pedro Margarite and Alonso de Ojeda. These were men who looked upon the natives as servants, the workers and the gold as their personal property, and Diego Colón as a weakling.

Columbus should have known that this setup was not going to work, but he was doubtless preoccupied with getting back out on the water and leaving his worries behind him on dry land. Columbus cleared "three caravels with square rigging," wrote Andrés Bernáldez. Las Casas noted that there was one *nao* and two caravels: the *Niña,* the *San Juan,* and the *Cardera.* Columbus was accompanied by a priest and the most obedient of his Indians, wittily baptized as Diego Colón, to act as interpreter. On April 24, he set sail toward the northeast, remembering there was land in that direction since he had been there before. It was Cuba, which Columbus was convinced was the Chinese province of Mangi, the South China described by Marco Polo. This part of his second voyage would later prove to be evidence of both Columbus's brilliance and his folly.

Sailing from what would later be known as Haiti, his fleet arrived at the southeastern tip of Cuba, at Cabo Alfaeto, and then cruised along the southern coast, where they took exact measurements. Skillfully navigating these treacherous waters, which are full of archipelagos and shoals, canals and reefs, they entered a harbor that Columbus named Puerto Grande and that later would be known as Guantánamo Bay. Columbus and his men spoke constantly of the Great Khan, of Mangi and Cathay, of Marco Polo and the treasures of Asia, of Russia and the Tartars, of the Ganges and the Arabian Gulf, of Ethiopia and Jerusalem. But the true magical words were "terra firma," the mainland. Cuba must be terra firma—South China.

They encountered Indians who "take no pleasure in anything save eating and women," wrote Bernáldez. They made a detour to the south and spent two days on the open seas, where, legend has it, Columbus sent his sailors below for some much-needed rest while he himself trimmed the sails. They then landed on what is today Jamaica, "the fairest island that eyes have beheld, mountainous and the land seems to touch the sky; very large, bigger than Sicily; it is very strong and extraordinarily populous," claimed Bernáldez. Fernando noted that Columbus had set sail "to learn if it was true, as they had been told on all the other islands, that Jamaica was very rich in gold." They presented the chiefs with gifts and received gifts in return, and they found one harbor "of extreme beauty" in the north of the island, where they anchored on May 5. Columbus christened it Santa Gloria. Columbus would return once more to the harbor. And on one occasion, he and his men were attacked. Bernáldez wrote that the Spaniards set dogs on their attackers, "for a dog is worth ten men against Indians." This was the first mention of the animals that would become one of the Spaniards' most effective weapons, very useful particularly against fleeing children.

The three ships turned north toward Cuba and then westward on May 15. The question that occupied Columbus most during this time was whether this was an island or the mainland. He asked Indian chiefs—who could hardly have understood what he was asking them—and when, eager to please, they assured him that the coast of their land was without end, he showered them with gifts. Yet the truth was there were islands everywhere. On one day during this expedition, they counted 164. There were so many that Columbus gave them the collective name El Jardín de la Reina, "garden of the queen," because the region was so beautiful. Fernando wrote:

> They saw many cranes of the size and shape of those of Castile, but bright red. On others they found turtles and many turtle eggs, resembling those of hens but having very hard shells. The turtles lay their eggs in a hole made in the sand, cover them up, and leave them until the heat of the day has hatched the baby turtles.... They also saw crows and cranes like those of Spain, cormorants, and a multitude of small birds that sang most sweetly. So fragrant was the air that our men seemed to be amid roses and the most delicate scents in the world. Yet the dangers to navigation were very great here, because there was such a maze of channels that it took a long time to find a way out.

On one occasion they saw natives using pilot fish to catch turtles. The trick was to tie a cord to the pilot fish's tail, and when it had attached itself to the turtle's shell with its sucker, to pull both the pilot fish and the turtle out together. The pilot fish received some of the turtle flesh as a reward and was placed back in its pail. Fernando, who seemed to forget that he had not even been on this journey, wrote, "I have seen them attach themselves to very large sharks in this manner."

On another occasion they saw a number of unclothed natives and took this as proof that they were in India. The Englishman John Mandeville had reported from his travels in India that its inhabitants seemed to be embarrassed to wear clothes. In one of those moments in his life that would become legend, Columbus decided he would prove he had found the mainland. He would use his men as witnesses, threatening to dock their wages if they didn't sign a statement affirming that Cuba was the mainland.

They reached areas in which the water was only a few feet deep; occasionally they were forced to kedge the ships over the sandbanks with cables. Las Casas reported that the color of the water changed from blue to green to white to jet black. While the crew was full of "gloom and anxiety," the Admiral "put on a cheerful countenance," wrote Fernando. "Some way beyond, the sea turned green and white, so that it seemed to be one great shoal, though it was two fathoms deep. They sailed over seven leagues of this sea, after which they came to another sea as white as milk; this caused them great surprise, as the water was very dirty." They saw mountains, overgrown with dense jungle, and passed by narrow channels between tiny islands. They saw lion tracks, though there have never been lions on Cuba.

In the end, Bernáldez estimated that they had "traveled 1288 miles from Cabo Alfaeto...on this course on which they discovered many islands and terra firma." On most days they had managed 200 miles. While Cuba is only 750 miles long, it is entirely possible to notch up many more miles than that when traveling in and out of every bay along the entire coastline. Columbus believed he had achieved great success. They had seen chieftains wearing feather headdresses and little else who had expressed the desire to accompany Columbus back to Spain, where they hoped to meet the most magnanimous sovereigns on the face of the earth. They had seen dolphins and palm trees and beautiful beaches. They had not found gold, but you might have to dig deep to find that. Most importantly, they had found the mainland, terra firma. Columbus believed all this and wrote it down in his journal, of which Bernáldez made ample use when compiling his own account.

Columbus estimated that he had sailed exactly halfway around the world. In truth, he was on the eighty-fourth degree of longitude west of Greenwich. As seen from Spain, that is less than a quarter of the earth's revolution. Nonetheless, provisions were growing scarce, the ships were in bad shape, and the crew was grumbling, and though he considered continuing the voyage and heading toward what is now Puerto Rico, Columbus decided to head home, choosing the simplest route for the return journey. He also decided against sailing back through the maze of narrow channels and against the continual trade wind, as well as "these mighty currents that flow in the same direction as the wind," but instead from Cabo de Santa Cruz south to Jamaica. He had by this point fallen ill, which would have factored into his decision to return. Fernando called the sickness "febbre pestilenziale"—plague fever—brought on by sleeplessness, for "he sometimes went eight days with less than three hours' sleep. This would seem impossible did he not himself tell it in his writings." Naturally, in Fernando's opinion, that counted as proof of authenticity. Morison claimed that Columbus might have suffered a nervous breakdown, perhaps brought upon by extreme exertion, lack of sleep, and poor nourishment. He also suffered from symptoms of arthritis.

Columbus's captains and crew conferred and quickly affirmed that they all wanted to sail home. First they sailed to the northeast, back to Hispaniola, where they carried Columbus ashore on September 29. They hoped that they could soon set sail for Spain. But when they reached La Isabela, Columbus was overjoyed to meet both of his brothers there. He had expected to see Diego, of course, but he had not expected to see Bartolomeo in La Isabela. The two had last seen each other six years before, when Bartolomeo left for France and Christopher headed west to China. Traveling, Bartolomeo had not heard of his brother's triumph for quite some time, returning to Castile too late to sign on any of the ships for the second voyage. The sovereigns held Bartolomeo in high regard, though they apparently were offended when Columbus appointed his brother "Adelantado de las Indias," feeling he had no authority to do so. Bartolomeo was from all accounts a courageous man; he could navigate and sail a ship, two qualities his older brother also possessed. He was a thoughtful man and a leader of men, qualities his brother now needed. And now he had arrived in La Isabela with fresh supplies and provisions.

At the end of 1494, Antonio de Torres had returned to La Isabela, accompanied by four caravels and everything Columbus had requested, as well as a reply from Isabella and Ferdinand, praising Columbus and respectfully requiring his return to Castile, so that he could be present during the continuing negotiations with Portugal over the division of the world.

Columbus disobeyed the order. There was trouble on Hispaniola. Spaniards had ill-treated some natives, and the natives were rising to their own defense; moreover, Spaniards were fighting Spaniards for control. Columbus wanted to address these problems before acceding to the royal family's request. In a letter to them, he wrote, "People who in Castile were not even able to hold one servant, here demanded six or seven men for their service and demanded from me that I should keep them and pay their wages. They were not satisfied with any common sense or any fairness." The reason for the island's "pitiful state," as Fernando described it, was that Pedro Margarite, whom Columbus had appointed commander of the fort at Saint Thomas, wanted more power. And, as Fernando went on to write, "most of the Christians [were] committing innumerable outrages for which they were mortally hated by the Indians, who refused to obey them. The kings and caciques of the island were united in refusing to serve the Christians."

Columbus had fifteen hundred natives—"peace-loving, harmless Indians," as he had previously called them—taken prisoner. Five hundred were loaded onto the ships, and he gave each of the Spaniards on La Isabela a choice: out of the one thousand remaining natives, each Spaniard could choose one slave, either male or female. The rest would magnanimously be spared. Two hundred Indians died en route due to the inhumane conditions on board; the rest died soon after arriving in Spain.

In Hispaniola Chief Guatiguana had united the inhabitants— about 250,000 lived on Hispaniola at the time—and attempted to storm La Isabela. The Spaniards were prepared and well armed. Along with Bartolomeo and Alonso de Ojeda, Columbus led two hundred soldiers, twenty horses, and twenty fighting dogs into battle. The Spaniards also had cannons. The natives, of course, had no chance, whatever their numbers. Fernando wrote that "Those cowardly Indians fled in all directions, hotly pursued by our men, who with God's aid soon gained a complete victory, killing many Indians and capturing others who were also killed." After a few weeks, the island was "secure," as Columbus called it. Fernando noted that "though they numbered only six hundred and thirty, most of them sick, with many children and women among them, the Admiral in the space of a year during which he marched through the country completely pacified the island without having to unsheathe his sword again."

After just a few months, small forts were built and exploitation was regimented into a colonial labor system called Repartimientos, with Spanish masters who wielded absolute control over the natives, who in turn owed them regular tributes. Columbus presumably considered the current state of affairs to be some kind of peace.

In the early 1990s, on the occasion of the five hundredth anniversary of the discovery of America, innumerable books were written on the subject of Columbus. One book in particular turned out to be a bestseller, Kirkpatrick Sale's *The Conquest of Paradise*, which damns and condemns Columbus. In it Columbus is depicted as a megalomaniac, a murderer, and a slave owner; moreover, Sale argued that Columbus's reputation as a navigator and sailor was overblown. Whatever the merits of its point of view, *The Conquest of Paradise* contains a number of mistakes. The translations from Spanish into English are inadequate, the assessment of routes and charts suspect, and the appraisal of Columbus as a navigator simply bizarre. But the book is brilliant, in its way, and it turned Sale into the Michael Moore of Columbus research.

"Columbus was a restless person," said Sale in an interview. "He wasn't nice, or good, and he had no respect. He was driven by greed and religious fervor. Columbus was a violent person. And while violence was part of that European era, Columbus was more violent than most. He wanted gold at all costs, and he had the ego to believe that he was the best in the world, the chosen one." On the subject of Columbus and his relations with the natives, Sale claimed that "the Taínos treated him in a friendly way, they welcomed him lovingly and he enslaved them. He demanded taxes and payments from anyone older than fourteen years. He arrived with an army and respected nobody." That was indeed the case. All natives living near the gold mines were forced to pay a tribute of three ounces of gold every three months. "Columbus was a liar," Sale continued. "He lied, when it came to his origins and his discoveries. He lied constantly. He respected nobody, only himself."

Columbus set sail for Castile on March 10, 1496. He appointed Bartolomeo as governor of Hispaniola and sailed off with the *Niña* and a caravel called the *India,* which his men had built on Hispaniola from the wrecks of two other vessels. Columbus was accompanied by 225 Spaniards and 30 slaves. They sailed past various islands, and on one occasion they saw an island inhabited only by women. Fernando described it:

> *Their women are excessively stout, ... in other respects their bodies are well proportioned. As soon as their sons can stand and walk, bows are placed in their hands so that they may learn to shoot. These Indians wear their hair long, flowing over their shoulders, and go about completely naked. The lady cacique who was made prisoner said the whole island belonged to*

women ... with the exception of four men who happened to be there because at a certain period of the year they come to lie with them.

There is of course no evidence to support Fernando's account.

When they reached what is today Guadeloupe, they were running low on provisions. Some of the men proposed eating the natives; these were, after all, cannibals and didn't deserve any better. Columbus forbade this, according to Fernando, who reported that the Admiral announced "that as Christians and human beings, they should not be treated worse than others."

The fleet arrived in Portugal on June 8; three days later they were in Cádiz. There Columbus heard the news that the king and queen were not amused. They had requested his return and had expected him to comply immediately. They had decided to defer on the issue of slaves, yet he had come back with hundreds of captive Indians.

Forty years after Columbus's arrival, no more than five hundred of the island's original inhabitants remained on Hispaniola.

———————————

Located on the northern coast of the Dominican Republic, Villa Isabela is a tiny village with a small market square, a cafeteria called Delicia, a drugstore, and a gas station. People play Bob Marley at full volume while standing on street corners, watching the cars drive by. Villa Isabela lies three miles from the ocean and the historic park, where there are walls, some a foot thick, others as high as six and a half feet. These walls used to consist of loosely stacked stones; over the years they have become encrusted and solidified. Kathleen Deagan undertook the task of excavating La Isabela. The remains of the first European settlement in the New World were discovered in 1987; Deagan arrived two years later to begin her work. Since then she has cataloged more than 1.5 million artifacts.

La Isabela survived from 1494 to 1498, a short span of time, though longer than La Navidad had. It was here that the Spaniards

lived and from which they set off in full armor into the mountains armed with trumpets, horses, and dogs. The colonization of
the continent began in La Isabela. It was the capital of Columbus's New World. For Deagan and her colleague José M. Cruxent,
a historian from the Universidad Nacional Experimental Francisco de Miranda in Venezuela, excavating La Isabela was one of
those projects that changed the lives of those who worked on it.
It meant working "in isolation, without fresh or running water,
no electricity, telephone, roads, postal service, medical care or
public transport," explained Deagan. But both she and her colleague admitted that it was wonderful work.

Wandering through La Isabela, one can make out the alleys
and the walls and get an idea of how things must have been. La
Isabela had the form of a rectangle, measuring somewhere
around a thousand by fifteen hundred feet. The bottom side of
the rectangle followed the coastline that curved outward. A wall
with watchtowers and gates encircled the settlement, and wind-
ing roads ran through it. Columbus lived on the northeastern
edge of La Isabela, in a house with a window facing the ocean.
His house was the largest—measuring thirteen by twenty feet—
as was fitting, and was built partly of thick limestone and partly
of packed dirt plastered on the inside with lime. The west side of
the house fell during Columbus's time, a victim to cliff erosion,
and only the foundations survived the centuries, but it still remains the best preserved frontier house in the New World.

When Columbus walked toward the central square, he would
have first passed the church, then the hospital, and then his officers' quarters, which also featured an ocean view. When he
walked toward the center of the settlement, he would have come
to the houses and huts belonging to the ships' crews. There exca-
vators found oil lamps, plates, belt buckles, mugs with two
handles, and cooking utensils. The largest building, a storehouse
120 feet in length, was located on the western wall. There they
found little silver balls and glass pearls, as well as quicksilver,
which had been stored in wooden casks and had seeped into the
ground over the centuries; quicksilver was used to melt gold.

Deagan and Cruxent found a kiln among the ruins. Until then historians believed that the Spaniards had brought all their bowls, pots, and plates with them; now they knew that the Spaniards were able to make those items themselves. The archaeologists also found casting molds and cast-iron cannonballs and chains. And they discovered a cemetery, in which most of the skeletons were found lying on their backs with their hands folded across their chests. However, one skeleton was found lying on his stomach, his hands on his back. "Possibly the victim of an execution," wrote Deagan. Only a month after founding La Isabela, Columbus had been forced to suppress an uprising. The men wanted to search for gold, not build a city. Bernal de Pisa, the leader of the rebels, landed in the prison of La Isabela; his followers ended up on the gallows.

The end for La Isabela came just five years later. The Spaniards were killed off by epidemics. A fire ruined two-thirds of the town and a hurricane destroyed the rest, even the ships lying at anchor in the harbor. Columbus was back in Spain at the time but wrote his brother Bartolomeo, instructing him to search for a better location, which is how the Spaniards went to Santo Domingo. The settlement deteriorated into a camp for mutineers and deserters, but even they soon moved on, and in 1498 the town finally fell to ruin. Deagan said she feels no doubt, based upon her work, that the Spaniards suffered from "hunger, disease, and weariness" in La Isabela.

For decades La Isabela's demise had been regarded as proof of Columbus's incompetence as a colonial governor; he had, some said, made a poor choice of location—lacking unprotected harbors and fresh water. Deagan believes these allegations of incompetence are unfair, for the conditions in La Isabela were actually very good, if one was in a position to make use of them. If one left the coconuts hanging in the palms instead of picking them, one starved; and if one walked along the beach at La Isabela dressed in full armor, one overheated. Deagan found that the "geographical and material conditions of life at La Isabela" had been excellent, but that the Spaniards were doomed to fail due to "their inability or unwillingness to accommodate the material and social actuality of life in America."

Michele de Cuneo, Columbus's friend, wrote in 1494 that the Taínos had papayas, guavas, pineapples, and more than forty other kinds of fruit to eat, as well as mussels, shrimp, and all kinds of fish. Moreover, de Cuneo reported, the turtles "were excellent to eat." He also noted that the soil had been very fertile and would have been easy to cultivate. "These rains are the cause of the wetness and consequently of the fertility of that island," Fernando commented. "So fertile was it that they ate fruit from the trees in November, at which time they flowered again, indicating that they bear fruit twice a year." The settlers were given "daily new confirmation of the wealth of the island." Yet the Spaniards made the choice of "starving in Paradise," as Deagan put it. Instead of cultivating the land, they ordered all provisions they needed from home: "Grain, ship's biscuits, wine, vinegar, oil, beans, ham, ... raisins ... salted fish, onions, garlic, sugar, mustard ... good honey, fifty pairs of chicken, and rose water ... for the Admiral and his household."

Columbus believed in living well and according to his social status. A delivery list for his household reveals a good deal about what he imagined should be found in the home of a viceroy, even one living beyond the pale of civilization:

> Clothing and footwear for himself;
> A bed made of six mattresses of fine Brittany linen;
> Pillows of cambric, 4;
> Bed sheets of half cambric, 3 pairs;
> A light quilt;
> Green and brownish serge silk cloth;
> A cushion (Alhambra);
> Cloth tapestries depicting trees;
> Door hangings of the same, 2;
> Coverings with his coat of arms, 4;

Decorated coffers, a couple;
Perfumes;
Paper, 10 quires;
Ordinary mattresses, 12;
Thick bed sheets, 12 pairs;
Ordinary blankets, 12;
Green and brownish cloth, 80 yards;
Shirts, 80;
Leggings and jackets, 4;
Vitre [coarse canvas], 100 yards;
Ordinary shoes, 120 pairs;
Black thread, 6 pounds;
Black twisted silk, 3 ounces.

Kathleen Deagan was surprised that she had found no traces of things that Hispaniola had to offer the Spaniards by way of surviving everyday life, such as fish bones or animal carcasses. Anyone who lived by the ocean and preferred to order salted fish from Spain rather than throw a fishing line into the Caribbean waters could not possibly have survived in La Isabela.

———————

Upon his return to Spain, Columbus was plagued by uncertainty. He had served his adopted country well and had led many heathen Indians to the true faith, from which his actions had not deviated. Nonetheless, the king and queen were allowing other men to travel to the New World, to bring gold back to Spain, and to set up the kind of slave market he had originally planned to set up. The sovereigns had granted him the title and the exclusive rights, and now he felt that God had turned against him.

Columbus took every ship that departed from Spain en route to the Caribbean as a personal affront and a sign of divine punishment. He concluded that they must be punishment for his pride and his vanity; he had let himself be carried away by the pomp and celebrations following upon his discovery of the New

World. Columbus was a pious man; some even described him as fanatically devout. He renounced his opulent lifestyle and began wearing a monk's robes. Forswearing pleasures of any sort, he avoided fancy balls and turned down invitations to the Castilian palace. Instead, he moved into a monastery, spending his days with Andrés Bernáldez, the chaplain to the Archbishop of Seville, praying, reading the Bible, and waiting. He had been promised a meeting with Isabella and Ferdinand, but time and time again, the audience was put off.

When he was finally given royal leave to travel to the palace in Valladolid, he used the occasion to display his diplomatic skills as well as his instinct for the dramatic gesture. He sent for two of the natives he had brought back from the second voyage—relatives of Chief Caonabó—and had them put on their most splendid and magnificent costumes. With painted faces and golden crowns on their heads, they rode to see Ferdinand and Isabella on mules. Columbus came bearing presents: gold nuggets the size of golf balls. In the presence of Their Majesties, he voiced his wish to sail to the New World for a third time. He could find no peace in Spain. The monarchs were hesitant. But when news came that Manuel I, the new king of Portugal, had equipped a fleet to be commanded by one Vasco da Gama to sail overseas, Isabella and Ferdinand grew nervous. By royal decree, the sovereigns of Castile decided to restore all of Columbus's titles and privileges. They ordered him to recruit three hundred soldiers and sailors for the settlement of Hispaniola and to take with him thirty women to create a new generation of colonists. The women would receive no wages for the voyage; it was enough that they were accorded the privilege to travel along and bear children.

Preparations proceeded slowly, the delays due to "neglect and mismanagement on the part of the royal officials," wrote Fernando. Another reason, undoubtedly, was that Columbus's reputation had suffered somewhat; his New World had not turned out to be all it had promised. Inhabited by wild natives, it was dangerous; gold was not simply lying around waiting to be picked up.

Columbus was forced to assemble his crew from inmates from Castile's prisons, making this third voyage the first known rehabilitation program on water. Only blackmailers and heretics were forbidden the privilege.

Columbus sent three caravels as an advance party to bring supplies to Hispaniola. The ships were captained by Alonso Sánchez de Carvajal; Giovanni Antonio Colombo, Columbus's cousin; and Pedro de Arana, the brother of his former mistress from Córdoba. As soon as they had left Spain, Columbus began equipping his ships. The *Santa María de Guía* would be his flagship. A *nao* with a capacity of 101 tons, it belonged to Cristóbal Quintero from Palos, who captained her. The caravel *La Gorda*, nicknamed *Correo*, also joined the fleet. She had a capacity of 60 tons and was captained by Hernán Pérez. The last of the three ships was the 70-ton caravel *La Castilla*, nicknamed *Vaqueños*, captained by Pedro de Terreros. Columbus planned to sail southward, toward what would later be Sierra Leone, and then westward, until he discovered something truly significant. He was aware that this might be his last chance. Morison wrote that at the time Columbus had taken to comparing himself to the biblical David, who had been commanded to perform nearly impossible tasks for Saul and succeeded at them; and yet, with each success, he had fallen deeper and deeper into disfavor.

> Columbus had discovered "the Indies," but that was not enough; he must colonize them and produce gold in quantities. He then successfully led a great fleet to Hispaniola, organized the colony there, discovered the Lesser Antilles, Puerto Rico and Jamaica, and explored the southern coast of Cuba; but these were not enough. He must now discover something more spectacular, and produce more gold; yet even when the continent and the Pearl Coast were discovered, these did not prevent his being sent home in disgrace. A fourth voyage in search of a passage to India was still necessary. Never could he do enough to satisfy his Sovereigns....Columbus would have been well advised at this juncture to settle for a good round pension and a

*castle in the conquered kingdom of Granada. . . . But he was not
that sort of man. If he had been, he would not have discovered
America.*

The expedition finally set sail during the last week in May 1498,
pausing in Porto Santo, "where he heard Mass and stayed long
enough to take on water, wood, and other necessities," as Fernando noted. The fleet also stopped at the neighboring island of
Madeira, where Columbus was still considered a hero. For seven
days they were received "with much kindness and courtesy by
the captain of the island," according to Fernando. La Gomera
was the next stopover, though certainly not for amorous reasons.
"We loaded cheese," wrote Columbus tersely. The affair with
Doña Beatriz, if it had ever actually taken place, was over. And
that was just as well, claimed Morison, for "Doña Beatriz was as
cruel as she was beautiful." A man who had once spread rumors
questioning her chastity was invited to call on Doña Beatriz and
then was hanged from a rafter in the hall of the castle. His life-
less body was later dumped outside his residence.

Columbus's fleet sailed south and managed to make 750 nautical miles in six days en route to the Cape Verde Islands, where
they planned to take meat on board. But the natives had little to
sell. The Cape Verde Islands, Fernando commented, "were a miserable and melancholy place," and over the centuries little would
change. Las Casas cited Columbus as writing about "how the lepers came there to be cured because of the great abundance of
turtles on that island, which commonly are as large as shields. By
eating the flesh and constantly bathing in the blood of these
turtles, the lepers become cured."

On July 7, Columbus set out on the transatlantic crossing, following a southwesterly course, "intending to sail until he was
below the Equator and then sail due west until he struck land,"
wrote Fernando. Shortly afterward they hit the doldrums. The
men waited and sweated—there was little shade on deck and they
were still wearing their woolen uniforms. "None could endure
staying below deck, and but for an occasional rain that obscured

the sun I believe they would have been burned alive together with their ships," commented Fernando. This went on for two endless weeks. On July 22, the trade winds from the northeast finally returned, and from then on they were able to make an average of six knots. On July 31, Columbus announced that they were now level with the Lesser Antilles, which was as remarkable an announcement as it was true. Columbus erred constantly whenever he used a quadrant. His ideas about the configuration of the earth—five-sixths mainland and one-sixth water—were grotesquely wrong. Yet somehow he was able to orient himself, even without the presence of a mainland. Indeed, the ocean was the one place where Columbus found his way around with relative ease.

Almost out of water, Columbus changed the course to northeast, so that they could take water on board at Dominica. Then suddenly they heard the shout "Land ho!" Up in the crow's nest sat Alonso Pérez Nizardo, a sailor from Huelva. He kept shouting until the others also saw three hills in the distance. They all sank to their knees and thanked God and the Virgin Mary. All that remained of their provisions before sighting land was one barrel of drinking water for three ships. The land had been sighted at nearly the last minute. Things had been about to turn desperate.

Columbus named this island Trinidad. They found a bay, and the men went ashore to wash themselves and their clothes. They drank, sailed on, and went ashore again, where they fished and collected oysters. Columbus believed he had finally reached Asia and was bitterly disappointed when all he saw were naked natives. Then strange things began to occur. Natives approached the fleet in a canoe but remained a lombard shot away—even when Columbus ordered his crew to play a welcome concert with drums and trumpets, and even when his men held up their usual array of worthless junk. Instead, the natives shot arrows at the entertainers. They must have interpreted the music as a prelude to an attack by the white men. No sooner had the Spanish cannonballs driven away the assailants than the ships were struck by two gigantic waves, perhaps triggered by a volcanic disturbance. It lifted the ships thirty to fifty feet, then threw them down. Fortunately, there was only a little damage: one anchor lost and one anchor line snapped. Columbus christened the bay La Boca de la Sierpe, "the serpent's mouth," and then left quickly.

Elsewhere they came across natives who served them "a liquor white as milk" and another that tasted like unripe grapes, wrote Fernando. The males wore gold mirrors on chains around their necks. This made the Spaniards greedy. The females wore nothing; they "cover nothing, not even their genitals," Fernando noted. And that made the Spaniards uncontrollable. Perhaps because of all the excitement, Columbus failed to comprehend what happened next; in any event, he ignored it.

Trinidad is J-shaped, the vertical portion being much wider than the horizontal. Located off the coast of South America, it is not far from what would later become Venezuela. Here, on August 5, 1498, Columbus first set foot on the American mainland, an event with enormous repercussions during all the centuries to come. There is a very long headland on the coast of modern Venezuela, a mixture of cliffs, jungle, and sandy beaches. Here the Spaniards landed. In 1498 the natives called this peninsula Paria, which it is still named five hundred years later. The Spaniards saw huts and fire pits, but the natives had apparently spotted the strange ships and fled. The only things left sitting on the beach were monkeys. Columbus may have thought this place identical to the hundreds of islands he had discovered and claimed. Perhaps he was too embarrassed to go ashore with flags and banners waving, carrying all his trinkets, to declare this land the possession of the Castilian crown before an audience of monkeys. Perhaps he was weary of all these formalities. Whatever the reason, he canceled the banner-waving ceremony, which would have been the first on the American continent, and sailed on.

There were natives on other islands who made their jewelry from a mixture of gold and copper. The alloy could be melted over a campfire. They were also happy to exchange their gold for copper, for they had plenty of gold and only a little copper. One of the natural harbors they found Columbus named Los Jardines, "the gardens." The female natives wore very little aside from beautiful jewelry made of pearls, which they revealed they had found in the water's plentiful oysters. Columbus might have amassed incredible wealth had he harvested the pearls—they were apparently so abundant that all you had to do was dive down and pick them up—but he seemed uninterested in doing so. He permitted his crew to exchange a few goods, then on they sailed through the straits between Trinidad and the mainland. He had sent the caravel *Correo* on to scout; it had the lowest draft, an advantage when reconnoitering in coastal waters. When the *Correo* returned to the fleet, her captain, Hernán Pérez, reported having seen something amazing: four river mouths side by side and one broad estuary a few miles farther on that would later be called the Orinoco River. This must have been the mainland, though Columbus never mentioned this. It was now August 11. He had the fleet change course once again and sail in an easterly direction. Four days later the Spaniards sailed north and then left the Gulf of Paria.

Columbus's mind worked in peculiar ways. He had sailed along the coast of South America for two weeks, noting this island or that island. Only when he had left it behind did it dawn on him that this had been the mainland. Here was the New World. Naturally he defended his new theory as obstinately and as vehemently as he had defended his old theory:

> *I believe that this is a very great continent, which until today has been unknown. And reason aids me greatly because of that so great river and fresh-water sea, and next the saying of Esdras in his fourth book chapter six, which says that the six parts of the world are of dry land, and one of water. . . . And if this be a continent it is a marvelous thing, and will be so among all the wise, since so great a river flows that it makes a fresh-water sea of forty-eight leagues.*

Rather than calling it El Nuevo Mundo, "the New World," Columbus called this continent an Other World—"Otro Mundo." (Amerigo Vespucci later brought news of the New World, and of course it would come to be named for him. But Columbus termed it "Otro Mundo" and mentioned it only in passing.) "And Your Highnesses will win these lands, which are an Other World, and where Christianity will have so much enjoyment," he wrote the king and queen. A few days after that, Columbus started to obsess about the discovery he had initially all but ignored. It was as if something had broken in him. As Morison observed, Columbus "was not one to put two and two together to make four; rather, in the Admiral's way of reasoning, two and two made ten." Columbus sailed to and fro off the coast of South America, confiding to his journal that he had not only found a new continent; he had found the "Terrestrial Paradise." There, where monkeys sat under palm trees, was the Garden of Eden itself.

Columbus's theory was groundless. *Imago mundi* had based its entire view of the world on Genesis. "And God created a garden east of Eden," it says, at the first point of the Far East, where the sun rose on the day of creation; and where magnificent trees grew and a river parted with four heads, which was, of course, what the scouts on the *Correo* had reported. Like others of his day, Columbus believed that here the earth rose up and took the form of a nipple, bringing Paradise closer to heaven than any other spot on earth. In his report to Isabella and Ferdinand, Columbus wrote:

> *Ptolemy and the other geographers believed that the world was spherical and that the other hemisphere was as round as the one in which they lived. . . . I do not in the least question the roundness of that hemisphere, but I affirm that the other hemisphere resembles the half of a round pear with a raised stalk, as I have said, like a woman's nipple on a round ball. Neither Ptolemy nor any of the other geographers had knowledge of this other hemisphere. . . . I do not hold that the earthly Paradise has the*

form of a rugged mountain, as it is shown in pictures, but that
it lies at the summit of what I have described as the stalk of a
pear, that by gradually approaching it one begins, while still at
a great distance, to climb towards it.

In his account of his father's life, Fernando made every effort
to ignore his father's train of thought. "The Admiral writes that he
could not give as full an account of it as he wished because continual watching had made his eyes bloodshot, and therefore he had to
write down what he was told by his sailors and pilots." Columbus
suffered from arthritis, and his eyes were swollen. Some would
later suggest that he suffered from Reiter's syndrome, a combination of several chronic inflammations. Ever the dutiful son, Fernando devoted only one sentence to this episode, writing only that
his father "concluded that all that land that he had taken for islands
was really but a single continent." Las Casas, for his part, emphasized Columbus's heroic efforts and the sacrifices he was making.
"There the eyes of the Admiral became very bad from not sleeping. Because always, as he was in so many dangers sailing among
islands, it was his custom himself to watch on deck." Las Casas
made no mention of the pear, the nipple, or Paradise.

On August 15, Columbus returned to what he did best—sailing. He set a northwesterly course toward Hispaniola and Santo
Domingo, the capital that Bartolomeo had founded and named
after their father, Domenico. To get there Columbus had to battle
the equatorial currents that had pushed him westward. They
seemed to have grown stronger; he ordered his fleet to haul in
the sails every night, for fear of being pushed onto the many reefs
and sandbanks. He finally landed in Alta Vela, 120 miles southwest of Santo Domingo. Never before had he been so navigation-
ally wide of the mark. Las Casas wrote, "It weighed much on him
to have fallen off so much."

On August 21, Columbus anchored in a bay he named
Madama Beata. From there he spotted a caravel approaching, a
rare and joyous occasion for a discoverer in these times. On board

was Bartolomeo. They embraced with great happiness and relief, then set sail for Santo Domingo, fighting currents and wind the whole way. The journey took eight days; it wasn't until August 31 that they anchored in the mouth of the Ozama, the bay of Santo Domingo.

Thirty months had passed since Columbus left Hispaniola, and a lot had happened. "All the families of the island were infected with a disorderly and rebellious spirit," reported Fernando. Moreover, life in the Caribbean had proven hard for the Spaniards. They were low on provisions and felt vulnerable, despite the fact that there were plenty of coconuts and bananas around. They became ill. Feeling trapped, they had become disaffected. "They became discontented with their present lot and despaired of the future," wrote Fernando. It was the hour of the rebels, and the chief among the rebels was Francisco Roldán, from Torredonjimeno. Roldán was ambitious and had long been a loyal follower of Columbus, which is why before he returned to Spain, the Admiral had appointed him mayor and chief justice. As soon as Columbus left, Roldán acquired "so much prestige and authority among both Indians and Christians that he was obeyed as if he were the Admiral himself," reported Fernando.

While Bartolomeo was in the province of Xaragua and Diego was supervising the town, Roldán drew up his troops. He founded Concepción, both a fortress and a settlement, and won the natives over by telling them that the Colón brothers wanted to increase the natives' tributes, but that he, Roldán, would protect them. Civil war erupted. There were bloody fights and atrocities. Bartolomeo made every effort to retain his troops' loyalty, and in the end he promised each of them two slaves if they were victorious. The three ships that Columbus had sent ahead, loaded with provisions, arrived at this time from Spain, and the mood in Santo Domingo changed. Roldán and his rebels were cut off. Such was the state of affairs when Columbus arrived.

During the following weeks, he governed in a manner utterly unlike the way he commanded a ship at sea. He became indecisive.

Fernando, naturally, saw this in a positive light. "At the same time he resolved to be as moderate as he could in this affair, that the rebels might more easily be reduced to obedience." Disaster struck when Columbus sent a messenger, Miguel Ballester, to meet with Roldán and initiate negotiations. Roldán refused any negotiations until all prisoners had been released, adding that he could easily destroy Columbus if he so chose. He would speak with Captain Sánchez de Carvajal or nobody at all. Naturally, Roldán also demanded safe conduct. On October 26, Columbus acceded to all of Roldán's demands, including safe conduct. Eventually, Columbus signed an agreement whose terms were humiliating. "First, that the Lord Admiral will give him two good ships, vouched by seamen to be properly equipped," it read. Columbus had to guarantee Roldán that he would continue to receive his wages, grant him and his rebels safe conduct, and give him slaves as compensation for the hard years he had spent on La Isabela. Columbus also had to write a letter to Queen Isabella attesting to the rebel leader's good conduct. In return, Columbus received no more than a promise that Roldán would sail to Castile with two ships and that he would refrain from enticing men away from the Admiral's troops for ten days. The agreement ended, "Done in Concepción this day, Saturday, November 16, 1498."

Roldán waited in Xaragua for the ships. Because they were delayed, he terminated the contract and for nearly a year things reverted to where they had started. Finally, Roldán decided that he no longer wanted to return home and presented Columbus with a new list of requests. "First, he should allow fifteen of them to return to Castile in the first ships that should come from Spain; second, those who chose to stay should be given houses and grants of land in lieu of their pay; third, he should publicly proclaim that all that had happened had been caused by false testimony of a few evil men; fourth, he should restore Roldán to his office of perpetual *alcalde* [mayor]." Eager to bring an end to this whole wretched business, Columbus submitted to the demands and appointed Roldán mayor for life. "On Tuesday, November 5,

Roldán began to exercise the duties of his office," wrote Fernando. The humiliating debacle brought Columbus, viceroy and governor and Admiral of the Ocean Sea, to the lowest point of his career. There were now only two people left on Hispaniola who took him seriously, Diego and Bartolomeo.

Essentially, Columbus's moment had passed. Ferdinand and Isabella had grown tired of all the bad news from overseas. The sailors and settlers complained constantly that the Colón brothers were incapable of governing; that they were lining their own pockets; that they had formed alliances with foreign princes and were working against the interests of the Spanish crown. There was intrigue everywhere. Columbus's sons were pages at the Castilian court and later remembered how people had pointed at them in ridicule. "There go the sons of the Admiral of the Mosquitoes, of him who discovered lands of vanity and illusion, the grave and ruin of Castilian gentlemen!"

As a result, Ferdinand and Isabella sent a royal commissioner, Francisco de Bobadilla, to Hispaniola. He arrived in Santo Domingo on August 24, 1500. At the time Columbus was in La Vega and Bartolomeo in Xaragua, leaving only Diego in charge of the settlement. Bobadilla was greeted by the sight of seven dead Spaniards hanging from a gallows. Diego informed him that another five would be hanged the following day. That was enough for Bobadilla. He took over the fort and the government, he had Diego arrested and taken aboard a ship, and then he won the hearts of the people by allowing everyone to search for gold whenever they wished. He could hardly have made a more popular decision. A messenger was sent to bring Columbus, bearing a letter: "Don Cristóbal Colón, our Admiral of the Ocean Sea. We have sent the Knight Commander Francisco de Bobadilla, the bearer of this letter, to say certain things to you in our behalf. We desire you to give him full faith and credit and to act accordingly. From Madrid, May 26, 1499. I, the King. I, the Queen."

Upon his return, Columbus probably paid Bobadilla little respect, and as a result the new commissioner had Columbus locked up. Bartolomeo returned soon afterward and for a while considered organizing a rebellion and freeing his brother, which of course would have been tantamount to treason against the crown. Bartolomeo also landed in prison. Fernando later complained that Bobadilla "neither held a hearing nor took any evidence," and that "he forbade anyone publicly to mention them, on pain of very severe penalties." Bobadilla wanted to take Columbus to court in Spain and had the Admiral of the Ocean Sea put aboard the caravel *La Gorda* in chains. Diego was put with his brother. Bartolomeo, also in chains, was put on the other caravel. "I had no more conversation with him and he has allowed no one to speak to me this day. I swear on oath that I cannot imagine why I have been made prisoner," wrote Columbus.

Fernando noted that the captain of *La Gorda* offered to unchain Columbus, but that the Admiral declined the offer, saying that "he had been placed in chains in the Sovereigns' name, . . . and would wear them until the Sovereigns ordered them removed." He lay in the hold while the ship pitched and tossed. In a letter to his friend Doña Juana de Torres, Columbus later complained how it came to be that he, God's messenger of "the new heaven and the new earth," had been so misunderstood. He had, after all, "placed under the sovereignty of the King and Queen our lords, an Other World, whereby Spain, which was reckoned poor, is become the richest of countries."

Our Lord is in heaven, who saved Daniel and the three children, with all His wisdom and power. May it please Him to save me also by a similar manifestation of His will. I should have been able to repair all this and everything else that has been said and done since I came to the Indies if I had allowed myself to act for my own advantage and if it had been honorable for me to do so. But the continuous maintenance of justice and the increase of their Highnesses' estates has brought me to ruin.

Just at the moment when so much gold is being found, men argue whether it is better to go about plundering or go to the mines. The cost of a woman is 100 castellanos, the same as that of a farm. The trade is very common and there are now many merchants who go about looking for girls; some of nine or ten are now on sale, but whatever their age they command a good price.

I declare that the slanders of disaffected persons have done me more harm than my services have done me good. This is a bad example both for now and the future. I swear on oath that there are plenty who have come to the Indies who were not deserving of baptism in the eyes of God and the world and now they are returning home.

At least the fleet had a following wind and made good progress. Columbus arrived in Cádiz in October 1500, still in chains, and was taken to the monastery at Las Cuevas. While he naturally considered himself a martyr, nobody seems to have been terribly interested in or sympathetic about his plight. Six weeks passed before Ferdinand and Isabella deigned to issue the order to have Columbus's chains removed. Fernando wrote that the Admiral "was resolved to keep those chains as a memorial of how well he had been rewarded for his many services. And this he did, for I always saw them in his bedroom, and he wanted them buried with his bones."

The three Colón brothers were finally brought before the king and queen shortly before Christmas. His wrists and ankles scarred from the chains, Columbus wore a gray Franciscan monk's habit. Ferdinand and Isabella promised a solution to his problems, but then more time passed and nothing happened. Columbus grew more and more nervous. After all, he had discovered the New World and felt he had earned his privileges and titles pertaining thereto. He was unable to comprehend that time had not stood still during his absence; that he was now regarded as living in the past; that there were others, younger men than he, ready to capitalize on his discoveries; and that he had made too many mistakes. Hispaniola was in a terrible state, and Ferdinand and Isabella had no intention of reinstating Columbus as governor of the island. They were glad that calm and order now reigned there.

Had he possessed any diplomatic skills, Columbus would have realized it was time to step aside. The king and queen would have given him a castle, some kind of title, and a pension. After all, the sovereigns wanted calm and order to reign in Castile too. But that was apparently not what Columbus wanted. He waited until the New Year, 1501, ignoring all recommendations to be flexible in his demands. Ferdinand and Isabella decided that Columbus would retain his titles of viceroy and admiral, both worthless, but that his position as governor of Hispaniola would be given to Nicolás de Ovando. Ovando promptly set sail with a fleet of thirty ships and twenty-five hundred men. Columbus was permitted to send only one representative, to make sure that all the wealth and goods owed to him found their way back to Spain. The man who had opened up an entire world, and to whom an entire world had been opened up, was left stranded.

———————

"He was a marvelous sailor and a terrible governor," said Stuart Schwartz, who teaches history at Yale and is one of the leading experts in the study of colonial Latin America, Brazil, and slavery in the Americas. The yellow walls of his office in the Hall of Graduate Studies are barely visible; books stretch up to the ceiling. "His model for the colonization of America was exactly the same as the Portuguese model, the same model of a 'factoría,' trading settlement, that he had seen on Madeira and on the western coast of Africa, in what is now Ghana." He continued, "Columbus saw himself as a factory owner and he regarded the Spaniards who accompanied him as his workers. The natives, of course, he considered to be his slaves. Their job was to mine the gold, and the Spaniards would earn wages. But this model was doomed to fail because the Spaniards who traveled to the New World wanted nothing more than to become wealthy noblemen. The last thing they wanted and could accept was to be subordinated to an Italian."

Schwartz is an authority on colonization. He grew up in Springfield, Massachusetts, the son of poor Jewish immigrants whose relatives died in Romania during the Holocaust. His father was the first in the family to graduate from college and became a doctor. He provided his son with the kinds of books that young Stuart loved—history books. Schwartz's dream was to become like Heinrich Schliemann, the famous German archaeologist and discoverer of Troy. Schwartz studied at Middlebury College, later went to Columbia, and was then offered a professorship at Yale. Columbus is one of his specialties, and indeed he is one of the reasons for the changes that have taken place in Columbus research over the past few years.

The truth is, no one is much concerned with the so-called landfall theory of 1492, but, rather, with what happened after Columbus went ashore, how the interconnection between Europe and the Americas unfolded, and how the Europeans and the natives communicated or miscommunicated with each other. Modern science of history deals with the clash of two worlds. "I'm interested in contact and conflict" was the way Schwartz put it. In 1892 historians considered Columbus "the greatest man ever to have lived," said Schwartz. "Just name any ethnic group and I'll find the book in our library that claims Columbus originated from that ethnic group. At the time immigrants were forced to prove their connection to the United States, and that was best done by establishing a connection to Christopher Columbus." Researchers in 1992 went in another direction. "Suddenly it was all about political correctness, and Columbus was portrayed as the worst person who ever lived," explained Schwartz. Columbus was the first mass murderer, the first anti-ecologist. Anti-Americans regarded Columbus in his early years as a kind of symbol of all that they hated, although he hadn't even discovered America at that time. Asked about the truth behind Columbus, Schwartz contended that there were many truths. He offered his suggestions as to what some of them might be.

Columbus was originally from Genoa. "He was born in 1451, not necessarily in Genoa, but somewhere in Liguria, and then the family moved to Genoa," said Schwartz. Columbus could have had Jewish ancestors, he continued. There are enough findings to substantiate this. "Converted Jews took care of the financing and Columbus set sail on the very day that Jews were forced to leave the country. But the evidence is missing," added Schwartz, "and that will keep researchers occupied for a while."

Columbus wasn't shipwrecked and didn't wash ashore in Portugal. "To my mind there are too many coincidences. It makes no sense that he should happen to be the only one to survive this battle at sea and that he should happen to come to Lisbon, where his brother had already established a business. I have yet to see the evidence. I think—quite simply—that both of them emigrated."

Columbus knew his destination. "If he or the crown really thought that he would make it to China, why didn't he take any opulent gifts? Why were there no ambassadors aboard? He knew from Marco Polo how the Great Khan lived, so why did he take glass baubles and cheap beads? Why were there no diplomats? After his return the queen and Columbus both spoke of 'the Indies.' I think they weren't certain of where they were, but they knew that it wasn't China."

Columbus was ahead of his time. "In Columbus's time it was an established fact that the earth was round. Everyone knew that, yet Columbus still dwelled on the concepts of the Bible; he really believed he had found Paradise on earth, and to him that looked like a woman's nipple. He carried all these Christian mysticisms and apocalyptic ideas around with him; his thinking was bizarre."

Columbus's true achievement was his ability to market his discovery. "The Vikings traveled to Iceland and found fish and ice; they went to Greenland and found fish and ice; they went to Canada and found fish and ice. It was of little interest to the rest of Europe, and it was of little interest to the Vikings where they had been. Columbus spoke of the gold, and after only one year, the entire continent knew his story."

Columbus wanted to found a new society. "He took over one thousand men on his second voyage, and not one single woman. It is unquestionable that there was only one thought behind that: the white men would get involved with the native women; and it was in the nature of the voyage that they would no doubt simply take and rape them."

Columbus's view of the natives was enlightened. "In the beginning he was impressed. He described them as friendly and intelligent. It goes without saying that he considered himself to be civilized and the Indians not, but he nevertheless appreciated them and the beauty of the region. But when he was unable to find gold, when he was forced to fight the rebels, he sacrificed the Indians—he gave them away to the Spaniards; he kidnapped them and brought them to Spain. And it is certainly true that he had no scruples. After all, slavery was commonplace in the fifteenth century."

Columbus turned into a liar after becoming famous. "Suddenly he embellished his past; suddenly he began making up stories. His world became one of exaggeration and invention."

Columbus was a man without a home. "He wasn't interested in Genoa, not in Santo Domingo, not in Porto Santo or Seville. He traveled around and never spoke of his home."

Columbus died in poverty. "It is merely a legend that he was destitute when he died. He was the Admiral of the Ocean Sea and had managed to salvage his wealth."

But, with that last point, we're jumping too far ahead in the story.

CHAPTER 7

——————

The Last Voyage

Nilda Vázquez enjoys surprising people. When you visit her house in Portobelo, she will sometimes wait for you out front, dressed in her pajamas—occasionally in a short pink nightgown. Sometimes she calls her guard dogs. The last time we met her, she cupped her hands together and made a machine-gun noise, like a kid pretending to be in combat. It was as if she were gunning down anything or anyone that got in her way.

In the tiny Copa Airlines aircraft, flying from Miami to Panama City in October 2003, Vázquez was sitting with her lawyer Saturio Segarra and her son Ernesto Cordovez. Across the aisle was Gassan Salama, then the governor of Colón; he quickly left to take his seat in business class. This time Vázquez was quite polite. She explained that she and her team had been to Florida, speaking to scientists and filmmakers and hiring divers, since they planned to raise the *Vizcaína*. "We can begin the salvage operation in November," announced Vázquez. "The ship will go to a museum in Portobelo, where it will lie in an aquarium, just like it does in the ocean now."

A race was on by this point; the shipwreck was the prize. Marine archaeologists from Texas A&M had teamed up with Carlos Fitzgerald from the Instituto Nacional de Cultura in Panama City,

and they were pitted against Nilda Vázquez and her team of treasure hunters. We wondered whether Warren White, the man who
claimed to have discovered the *Vizcaína,* was still in the picture.

"Warren White is a damned liar; he's an ignoramus," said
Vázquez. "He claims to have discovered the ship, but I was the
one who told him it was the *Vizcaína.*

"By the way, what are you doing back in our pleasant land?"
she asked us.

We told her we were going to visit Warren White.

"Give him my best regards."

———————

Christopher Columbus is not a particularly popular figure in
South and Latin America. They have other heroes there. Only
one town in Panama bears his name—Colón, where the Panama
Canal connects to the Caribbean. Colón lives for the seafaring
industry and from it. At any given moment, a hundred ships sit
offshore, waiting to enter the canal. Nonetheless, Colón is a poor
town; the houses are derelict and unemployment is high. Some
200,000 people live there, either in the half of the town they call
Cristóbal or on the other side, Colón. In the center, a few hundred feet from the boardwalk, is a bronze statue of Columbus on
a marble plinth. He looks messianic with his flowing long hair.
His left hand is opened in a gesture of generosity or benevolence,
while his right hand rests on the shoulder of a naked, large-
breasted, and very frightened-looking Indian woman. The inscription reads: "For the immortal discoverer of the New World."
The statue stands beside a local garbage dump.

It is a distance of some fifteen miles from the statue to the
Panama Canal Yacht Club, the home of Warren White. Over the
years White has developed his own theories about Columbus:
"I've learned to understand him, and it even feels as if I have his
phone number." White's first theory about the discoverer is that
the archival approach toward finding his shipwrecks may not be
the best. Analyzing each text and going through every letter and

document, word for word, to isolate the exact location of the wreck can lead to misleading results. Columbus wasn't interested in revealing the location of his ships; he wanted to cover his tracks. He left his own crew in the dark as to the route and the destination, and he lived in constant fear of envious competitors. Such a man, in White's view, doesn't want anyone else finding sunken ships, for when he returned he would do the salvaging himself. In White's opinion, Columbus was always thinking about his next journey.

White's second theory is that one has to understand Columbus as a sailor and take the sources as evidence. The best underwater detectives in the world have searched for the *Gallega* in Belén, for the *Capitana* and the *Santiago de Palos* in Saint Ann's Bay, and for the *Vizcaína* in Portobelo. They found nothing not because nothing is left of the wrecks but because, in White's view, they are lying somewhere else. He has himself claimed that he could find them all. Then he qualified this. "Well, three of them. I've already found one while out lobster fishing."

White is nothing if not supremely self-confident. He has also gotten on the wrong side of Columbus scholars and researchers, for he is a treasure hunter; he works for himself, not for posterity. Yet when you talk to him, it is impossible not to see how well he understands Columbus. In Jamaica, for example, divers had been searching for years in Saint Ann's Bay to find either the *Capitana* or the *Santiago de Palos*. Ultimately, researchers came to the sad conclusion that a hurricane must have destroyed the vessels. How else could one explain that there was nothing left? "Columbus had put Saint Ann's Bay at a longitude of 23, but in reality it is 22.6. Did he slip up because he lacked the proper instruments? I don't think so. He had twelve months to check the longitude. After all, he was marooned in Jamaica. But maybe Columbus's longitude was right after all. Maybe it just wasn't Saint Ann's Bay but another bay. Give me $100,000, or even less, and I'll find the ships." As regards to Belén, Columbus wrote that he had left the *Gallega* in the river because his men were unable to kedge it over the sandbank. All subsequent diving expeditions have searched the entire river, up to its source, foot by foot. "It was the dry season, and every dry season ends. I am certain the river washed the *Gallega* out to sea at the start of the rainy season." He explained that natives found a wreck out in the bay of Belén, a really ancient wreck, and that "there were no cannons on board." White said this makes sense, "for if they were pulling a ship over a sandbank, they would have removed anything heavy." The *Gallega's* cannons have been lying on the *Vizcaína* for five hundred years: were the wreck off Nombre de Dios the *Vizcaína*, that theory would fit. "It is the *Vizcaína*. I'm one hundred percent certain. Well, ninety-nine point nine percent."

White rocked back and forth on a leather chair in his office. His yacht, the *Makado*, lay at anchor by the pier. Five companies share the building, and the rooms are little more than tiny cells. White has two rooms. The back room contains his desk, a computer, a telephone, and his art supplies. Paints and varnishes are strewn about. The front room, with yellow crumbling walls and pink carpet, contains his pictures. White began painting more than ten years ago. His style might best be described as "romantic" or "naive": depictions of women standing on cliffs; of Eve and the serpent; famous naval battles—and of Columbus. White painted Columbus in the bay off Nombre de Dios, his men standing on the *Vizcaína* pointing toward the other ships. The *Vizcaína*, as White has painted her, is bare. There are no sails, simply two enormous anchors lying in the bow. Three masts protrude from the tiny vessel, and you can see water seeping in through the cracks on the sinking ship. Was this how it happened?

"Of course that's how it happened. I painted it in the same way the wreck is lying on the ocean bed." According to White, he found the wreck in 1995. Since then a few cannons have disappeared after being salvaged, as well as a few pieces of wood. Not much else has transpired, except for a whole lot of trouble. "It's so sad. Columbus discovered a whole new world, and we could discover his world. But all we do is argue."

From White's point of view, it began when he approached
Carlos Fitzgerald of Panama's Instituto Nacional de Cultura,
INAC. Initially, Fitzgerald failed to realize the significance of the
find. "The state of Panama lacks the financial means to salvage a
wreck of that kind" was all he said, according to White. Time
passed. White spoke to Nilda Vázquez, who immediately recognized the importance of the discovery. Things began to get complicated. Vázquez worked as a volunteer in the local office of
INAC, but her son Ernesto was head of a treasure-hunting company called Investigaciones Marinas del Istmo, which is backed by
several wealthy U.S. investors. White joined the company but
later left because he was disappointed with all the delays and the
infighting.

Nilda Vázquez's backers have proven impossible to locate.
Isaac Nunn, spokesmen for the investors, issued only one statement to the *Los Angeles Times* in June 2002, portraying the exploration as good for the Panamanian government. The investors
put up the money while the government reaped the rewards. "It's
a good deal," he said. They could then launch a spectacular salvage operation, produce a documentary, give interviews, and
organize a world exhibition.

Nonetheless, the wreck still lay on the ocean floor off Nombre de Dios. The courts would have to decide who possessed the
legal rights to the ship. Cannons, shards, and pieces of wood already salvaged would remain where they were, in the freshwater
basins on Nilda's property in Portobelo, rather than in the labo-
ratories of an archaeological institute. Nilda Vázquez remained
in possession of her contracts. One of them states that in the case
of a salvage operation, the investors would receive 65 percent and
the government 35 percent of all proceeds. Another stipulates that
Nilda's team has the right to report on the wreck in words and in
pictures. The contract doesn't state that these rights are exclusive,
which is why the government and Nilda Vázquez are now locked
in a court battle. For when the significance of the wreck finally
dawned on Carlos Fitzgerald, a law was quickly passed declaring

this wreck and all wrecks found off the Panamanian coast as National Heritage sites.

White commissioned one of the first scientific analyses of the wreck. He took a piece of wood from one of the freshwater tanks, placed it in a plastic bag, and asked Brendan Buckley, a friend of his and a specialist at Columbia University, where he might send the sample. The name White got was Dr. Bernd Kromer, of the radiometry laboratory at the University of Heidelberg in Germany. After conducting a radiocarbon C14 analysis, Kromer and his assistant Sahra Talamo estimated that the tree from which this sample had been taken was felled between the years 1480 and 1520. "It seems that the wood could have grown close to the date of the proposed abandonment of the Columbus fleet," Kromer wrote in a letter. "Of course that would not be proof, but it certainly supports an early sixteenth-century date for the ship." That removed any trace of doubt from the mind of Warren White.

To sailors like White, Columbus remains a legend. "Of course I don't admire the way he practiced local politics, but one has to admire these men for all their discoveries. They sailed off into unknown regions filled with courage and conviction. This man had terrible ships, and the ships grew more awful with each voyage. And yet he managed to do it four times.

"Man, those were real adventurers," he added, gazing out over the ocean. "You can feel it even five hundred years on. Just read the diaries and documents on the fourth voyage, then you'll know what I mean."

As mentioned, while conducting research in the Archivo General in Simancas, Consuelo Varela managed to find the names of twenty-five crew members on the *Vizcaína*. These were men whom Columbus trusted. Some had accompanied him on the first three voyages. Among them were gold diggers and adventurers; for the most part, however, they were men who had nothing better to do and who needed the money. They signed on knowing that the risks were especially great: the ships Columbus had been given for this voyage were third rate; this signified that he had no support from the royal family. The crew was the youngest ever to have accompanied Columbus. There were fifty-eight ship's boys and fourteen soldiers; seventy-two were twenty or younger. Some—for example, Esteban Mateos and Antón Quintero—later testified that they were thirteen years old. Quintero, however, would have found it easier to deal with the inevitable bouts of homesickness; his father had also signed on for the voyage.

The crew was organized hierarchically; roles were clearly defined. Some brought along their personal assistants, though nobody had as many as Columbus, who took eleven servants, among them two valets. Wages were also strictly hierarchical: Bartolomeo Colón earned 100,000 *maravedís* a year; Fernando received 60,000 (the general rule was that captains received 48,000 *maravedís*). The scribe Diego de Porras was paid 34,000; steersmen received 24,000; boatswains, 18,000; soldiers, 12,000; and ship's boys, 8,000. Also among the crew were two caulkers, three cannoneers, two trumpeters, two coopers, two carpenters, and one physician, Maese Bernal.

Varela has been able to demonstrate that no women and no pardoned murderers accompanied Columbus on this voyage. There were, however, twenty Italians and eighteen men from the harbor town of Palos. Thirty-five members of the crew later testified at the Pleitos—11 for the crown and 24 for the Columbus family. Around half of the crew, or 70 men, returned to Spain; 38 remained on Hispaniola and 35 died during the wild and chaotic journey that was the High Voyage.

———

Things were set in motion when Columbus received a letter from the king and queen, a letter Fernando cited in his account. "We are even more resolved to honor and treat you very well...you and your heirs shall enjoy them [all privileges], as is just, without any contravention....And be assured we shall look after your sons and brothers as is just, and your office shall be vested in your son." Sailing off with such assurances must have alleviated some of Columbus's anxieties. Of course, it also helped enormously that he knew the route, how long the journey would take, and what awaited him at his destination. This time he was accompanied by Fernando, then thirteen years of age. The small and somewhat disheveled-looking fleet was made ready: the spacious *Capitana,* the four-masted *Gallega,* the *Santiago de Palos*—whom everyone called by her nickname *Bermuda*—and the *Vizcaína,* the baby of the fleet, measuring approximately sixty-five feet and with a capacity of fifty tons.

Father and son boarded the *Capitana* in Cádiz, but the fleet's departure was delayed for three weeks; the winds were either too weak or blowing in from the south. A north wind arrived on May 11, and they set sail, for a second time, toward Las Palmas. They reached Grand Canary Island on May 25, and then set a record for crossing the Atlantic that would remain unbroken for years: twenty-one days. They dropped anchor off Martinique on June 15; there they rested for three days, loading fresh water and provisions under the watchful eyes of the natives.

In June the four ships finally reached Santo Domingo. This, of course, was the settlement Columbus had put his brother Diego in charge of. It was also where Columbus had been held prisoner. Santo Domingo was the nearest thing to a home he had in the New World. There was a new governor of the town—Nicolás de Ovando. He refused to allow Columbus or his ships to dock there.

————

Today, the Palacio Nicolás de Ovando in Santo Domingo is a first-class hotel. Made of bright white stone, it has large arches and spacious walkways, a pool overlooking the ocean, and lots of deck chairs for lounging. The Palacio gives the impression that it was the Spaniards who had brought style and elegance to the Caribbean. From here the stark realities of life in the Dominican Republic seem distant. The Palacio stands where the real governor's palace once stood five centuries before, but it is a replica, of course. That's the problem with most of the houses up on the cliff overlooking the mouth of the Río Ozama. They all seem unreal compared with the rest of Santo Domingo, whose high-rise buildings are dirty and wooden shacks seem crooked. The city, whose population is approaching three million, is noisy and stifling. But in the old part of the city, La Zona Colonial, everything seems picturesque and charming. Locals seldom venture there.

La Zona Colonial also features El Alcázar de Colón, the house that Diego supposedly built in 1510. It is, in fact, a very large brick building with five arches on the first and second floors. "If we were being honest, we'd have to admit that we have no idea what Diego's house once looked like," said the historian Tristán Colente. The Pantheon, a tomb for colonial heroes, also stands in La Zona Colonial, as does Las Casas Reales, a museum featuring maps and letters that date back five hundred years. Quadrants, hourglasses, sugar presses, and other artifacts have been assembled here. Visitors can see what the Spaniards—depicted sweating under their flowing capes in the hundred-degree heat—brought along to subjugate the natives: shackles and forceps, wooden blocks for head and hands, whips and neck irons with holes through which nails could be driven until the torturers got what they wanted or the nonbelievers got what they deserved.

La Zona Colonial has statues of both adversaries from ages past: the one of Nicolás de Ovando stands on a square named La Atarazana. He is depicted as an old, balding man; his head is thrown back, his expression skeptical and somewhat grim. Columbus's statue stands in the Parque Colón, the marketplace and center of La Zona Colonial. He is depicted gazing into the distance, his left hand pointing west; next to him is a bollard with a rope and an anchor. One part of this bronze statue depicts a female native, shown leaning toward Columbus, as if offering herself to him; apart from a headdress and tiny loincloth, she is naked, although she is holding a pen and writing "Cristóbal Colón" in the plinth. Ernesto Gilbert completed this statue in February 1887. His depiction of Columbus speaks volumes about how the colonial masters perceived themselves—as well as about race, class, and sex.

About 150 feet from the statue is the Catedral Basílica Menor de Santa María, the first church to have been built by the Spaniards in the New World. Constructed in 1540 as a tomb for Don Juan Mosquera, mayor of Santo Domingo, it was restored in 1992, on the anniversary of Columbus's first landfall. Here is where Columbus was once buried, or is said to have once been buried.

Sitting in the Columbus Plaza café, Tristán Colente, a history teacher, told us he believed that "Columbus could have had it all." He continued, "The Taínos baked bread called casabe. They hunted, fished, and grew yucca. They even welcomed the Spaniards. Columbus should have accepted and entered into relations with the Taínos. But because he wasn't familiar with their bread and their fruits, he went hungry. And because he didn't understand the language and their gestures, he viewed the Taínos as enemies and slaughtered them. No, Columbus didn't discover this world. It already existed and was already settled. And, no, he didn't bring Europe and America together. He came here and murdered. Could you explain one thing to me? Why do you Europeans idolize this man?"

Colente gazed across at the church. "It could have been so simple if Columbus had just opened his eyes."

———————

Hurricanes are fairly easy to spot: darker-than-normal rain clouds; increasing wind velocity; large, dark, and fast-moving spots on the water. What is more difficult is sensing when they lie beyond the horizon. The only signs are a drop in barometric pressure and a minimal increase in temperature. You have to register the existence of thin clouds high in the atmosphere and monitor changes in the wind. If you can sense a hurricane coming, there is usually enough time to make it to land. If you can already see one approaching, you might be able to make a narrow escape. But fail to read the signs and you're in trouble. Many ships have sunk because their captains only noticed when the hurricane was upon them. Few have sunk because their captains willfully ignored the warning signs. This, however, was one of those occasions.

Governor Ovando forbade Columbus entry into the mouth of the Río Ozama, Santo Domingo's new harbor. Columbus knew there was a hurricane approaching; he could sense it. He also knew that Ovando was planning to send a fleet of thirty ships back to Spain, one of which was carrying the entire fortune the Admiral had amassed in the New World. Columbus also needed a new ship. "I begged as a favor that a ship should be supplied me at my own cost in lieu of one of those that I had brought with me, which had become unseaworthy, and could no longer carry sail," he wrote. He was referring to the *Gallega,* whose sail area was too small; she was also carrying too little ballast, which prevents the wind from pushing the ship to the side. "She was a crank and a dull sailer; not only was she slow but she could not load sails without bringing the side of the ship almost under water, which caused a good deal of trouble on that voyage" was how Fernando described the *Gallega.*

Columbus sent Pedro de Terreros, the captain of the crippled vessel, ashore with the letter for the governor. The letter requested permission to land and urged Ovando to detain the homeward-bound fleet in port for eight days or until the hurricane had passed. Ovando laughed out loud when he read Columbus's letter, dismissing Columbus as a "soothsayer." Ovando's fleet immediately set sail for Spain, while a saddened Columbus wrote, "What mortal man...would not have died of despair? Even for the safety of myself, my son, my brother and friends, I was forbidden in such weather to put into land or enter harbors that I had gained for Spain by my own blood and sweat." We might conjecture that feelings of gloating and schadenfreude might not be entirely alien to a man like Columbus, but his letters at least contain no such sentiments. Instead, he ordered his four ships to sail to the mouth of the Río Jaina, to wait out the storm in a bay that provided plenty of room for the ships to maneuver without the danger of running onto the reefs.

The hurricane approached from the northwest. "The tempest was terrible throughout the night," Columbus reported. "All the ships were separated, and each one driven to the last extremity, without hope of anything but death; each of them also looked upon the loss of the rest as a matter of certainty." Fernando recounted, "It appeared that the Adelantado [Bartolomeo], experienced seaman that he was, had weathered that great storm by going out to sea, while the Admiral had saved his ship by lying close to shore."

Twenty of Ovando's ships sank, killing all on board, among them Antonio de Torres and Francisco de Bobadilla, Columbus's chief rivals. Other ships were driven ashore and smashed on the rocks, killing some five hundred souls. Only four ships made it back to Santo Domingo. "God was pleased to close the eyes and minds of all those men so that they did not heed the Admiral's good advice. I am certain that this was Divine Providence, for had they arrived in Castile, they would never have been punished as their crimes deserved," commented Fernando. Only one ship from Ovando's fleet made it through to Spain undamaged. This was the *Aguja,* the boat that happened to be carrying Columbus's fortune.

Columbus and all of his men survived. All they had lost were three anchors and a small boat. He granted his crews a week's rest, during which the men from the *Vizcaína* caught a giant stingray, lying asleep on the surface. They struck it with a harpoon and tied it to a lifeboat until it died. A feast followed. A week's rest must have been a welcome respite for the men, but to Columbus—impatient and spurred on by self-doubt—it would have seemed like an eternity.

At some point during his three previous voyages westward, Columbus must have realized that he had not reached India; that there was a reason that wherever he landed he was greeted by dark-skinned naked men rather than by minions of the emperor of China. One indication that Columbus might now have sensed he had discovered a new and unknown continent was that he hardly mentioned Asia in his accounts of the fourth voyage. Gone were the references to the Great Khan and gold-roofed palaces. Nonetheless, he could not admit as much, as his negotiations with the king and queen had always been based on his discoveries of Asia and "the Indies." Columbus wanted a share in the profits and knew that the sovereigns would take advantage of any loophole offered them. There was no percentage for him if it turned out he had not reached India.

Moreover, acknowledging as much would have required a magnanimity Columbus simply didn't possess. He was unable to laugh at his own weakness, to admit to his own mistakes. But he must have known. He may have been an obstinate man and a fanatic, but he was no idiot.

His four ships sailed through the Windward Passage and down to the southern coast of Jamaica, against "the wind and a fearful contrary current," as Columbus wrote. Then they took a northwesterly route to the southern coast of Cuba, where the winds were finally to Columbus's liking. They managed 360 nautical miles in just three days, and they were able to begin searching for the opening through the mainland—a river that would take them through to the other side. They sailed up and down the coast, exploring estuaries and sending out reconnaissance patrols. It was late July 1503, on the coast of a region that would later be called Honduras.

Here they spotted a canoe larger than any they had ever seen before. It was carved from a single tree trunk. Resembling a galley, it featured a protective awning and was rowed by twenty-five natives. The sight excited Columbus, for he interpreted it as a sign of civilization—an indication of a more developed race of people. Fernando described the contents of the impressive canoe, which included cotton mantles and embroidered sleeveless shirts, long wooden swords, copper hatchets, wine made of maize that tasted like English beer—as well as "many of the almonds which the Indians of New Spain use as currency." Fernando attested that they "displayed admirable modesty, for if one had his breechclout taken from him, he would immediately cover his genitals with his hands; and the women covered their faces like the Moorish women of Granada."

Spaniards and natives exchanged goods. Through hand signals, Columbus asked about gold, and the natives pointed east. He asked about their home, and they pointed to the west. The natives invited the Spaniards to follow them but Columbus declined, though he did shanghai the canoe's pilot, an old man named Jumbe, whom Columbus renamed Juan Pérez. He needed his services as a translator.

The question looming before him was where the passage he sought might be located. Going west offered the easier route, for the wind blew constantly from the east; the problem would have been with the return journey, and good sailors always think about the homeward trip, when they might be low on provisions, their crew tired, and their ships no longer seaworthy. From his spot on the deck, Columbus would have seen bay after bay, densely covered slopes, thick rain forests, sheer cliffs, and sandy beaches. He ordered the fleet to sail east.

A storm at sea robs sailors of their orientation; their world becomes unhinged. In 1502 a man overboard was a dead man. The storm that Columbus and his ships confronted swept in from the east, the direction Columbus wanted to take. The ships were forced to tack—moving toward shore and then back out to sea—which meant they made no headway; indeed, they were pushed steadily backward. "The course was navigable though difficult," wrote Fernando. Columbus noted:

> *Nor was there any cessation of the tempest, which was one continuation of rain, thunder and lightning; indeed it seemed as if*

it were the end of the world. . . . Eighty-eight days did this fear-
ful tempest continue, during which I was at sea, and saw nei-
ther sun nor stars; my ships lay exposed, with sails torn, and
anchors, rigging, cables, boats and a great quantity of provi-
sions lost; my people were very weak and humbled in spirit,
many of them promising to lead a religious life, and all making
vows and promising to perform pilgrimages, while some of
them would frequently go to their messmates to make confes-
sion. . . . The distress of my son who was with me grieved me to
the soul, and the more when I considered his tender age, for he
was but thirteen years old, and he enduring so much toil for so
long a time. Our Lord, however, gave him strength even to en-
able him to encourage the rest, and he worked as if he had been
eighty years at sea, and all this was a consolation to me. I my-
self had fallen sick, and was many times at the point of death,
but from a little cabin that I had caused to be constructed on
deck, I directed our course.

The ships were small and with a low draft, so they rolled and
pitched unmercifully from one side to the other. There was no
dry place on any of them. The crew had no cabins and hence
slept anywhere they could—among provisions, on coiled ropes,
in puddles. It took the fleet twenty-eight days to sail 170 miles. Finally, on September 14, the fleet rounded a cape leading south
that Columbus named Gracias Dios, consisting of a long gradual
curve full of cliffs in an area that would later be called Nicaragua.
From here, being able to sail southward and with a crosswind
from the east, the four ships made good progress.

They anchored 120 miles south of Gracias Dios. Boats were
sent ashore to take on water, provisions, and wood. When the
wind built surf up over a sandbar in the mouth of a river—"the
wind having freshened from seaward and the sea became heavy,"
as Fernando wrote—one of the boats was swamped and her two-
man crew drowned. With a sense for the symbolic, Columbus
named the river Río de los Desastres. They came to another es-

tuary, but it was night and they dared not enter. Coincidences like that turned this fourth voyage into a disaster. Had they entered the estuary and persevered, they would have reached what is today called Lake Nicaragua. And had they found a native with whom they could communicate, he might have told them that they only needed to walk for fifteen miles to reach open water. Columbus would have realized his dream. He would have reached the Pacific Ocean. Instead, as it was night, they sailed past the estuary until they reached an area the Indians called Cariai, later known as Costa Rica.

The Spaniards, for once, seemed to accord the natives some respect. Although the natives seemed eager to trade their goods, approaching the ships with cotton shirts, spears with fish-bone tips, and worthless guanin pendants made of gold alloy, "the Admiral did not allow his people to accept any of their articles, since he wanted to show them that we did not covet their possessions," wrote Fernando. It would turn out to be just one of many misunderstandings that dogged this voyage. And for once it would turn out to be a mistake. The natives then sent two young girls to the ships, one about eight, the other about fourteen. Both carried gold chains. Fernando noted, "The girls displayed much courage, for though the Christians were completely strange to them in aspect, manners, and race, they showed no fear or grief but always looked pleasant and modest. On this account they were well treated by the Admiral, who caused them to be clothed and fed and then sent them ashore." His father, curiously, described the same encounter in an entirely different manner. "Both exhibited so much immodesty," claimed Columbus, "that more could not be expected from public women; they carried concealed about them a magic powder; when they came I gave them some articles to dress themselves out with, and directly sent them back to the shore."

The natives deposited the articles Columbus had given them on the shore and left them there. They suspected the Spaniards were sorcerers and fled into the jungle. Later, in return for the release of two captured Indians, the natives presented the Spaniards with two peccaries, wild boars. On board the *Capitana,* the crew pitted the two boars against a spider monkey they had captured by cutting off its leg, providing a "fine sport," as Fernando described it, although he called the monkey "the cat." Columbus then had a boar and the "cat" thrown together. The ensuing fight was won by the "cat," which choked and bit the pig, using its tail as a coil; "from this we concluded that these cats hunt other animals, like the wolves and greyhounds of Spain."

On October 5, 1502, Columbus resumed his search for a strait. Yet again he was thwarted by an inability to communicate in any meaningful way with the natives. "They go completely naked, only covering their genitals with cotton clouts," wrote Fernando. The Spaniards were only interested in the golden mirrors the natives wore on chains around their necks. But the natives were reluctant to part with their jewelry, even when the Spaniards offered them glass beads in exchange. Shots fell, and natives were injured before they finally grasped the laws of free trade and exchanged their goods.

Some natives led Columbus to a lagoon, the Chiriquí Lagoon, and told him that they were standing on an isthmus between two oceans, but that the other ocean was inaccessible due to a high mountain range. Then they said something that Columbus obviously misunderstood. He thought they told him that he was in the biblical land of Ophir, the region where the servants of Hiram presented King Solomon with a cargo of gold. Columbus asked his interpreter, Jumbe/Juan Pérez, who told Columbus about the wealthiest country in the world. It was located deep within the continent; its people wore robes, crowns, anklets, and chains of gold. This land had harbors and city walls and the name of the country was Quiriquiamba. "Others assert that their ships carry cannon," wrote Columbus about this distant land, "and that the men go clothed and use bows and arrows, swords and cuirasses, and that on shore they have horses which they use in battle, and that they wear rich clothes and have good things. They also say that the sea surrounds Ciguare, and that at ten days' journey from hence is the river Ganges."

Here, in what would later be called Costa Rica, Columbus changed his plan again. He decided to abandon the idea of finding a passage to the Pacific and instead renewed his efforts to find gold and establish a trading settlement. He set sail again for the region that would later be called Panama.

The *Capitana,* the *Santiago de Palos,* the *Gallega,* and the *Vizcaína* left the Chiriquí Lagoon on October 17, 1502, accompanied by a westward wind. They sailed on, passing various islands where natives lined the shores, beating drums and brandishing spears. On November 2, the four ships sailed into a wide and deep bay, protected on three sides by mountains and rain forests. Fernando described it as "very large, beautiful, thickly populated, and surrounded by cultivated country,...as pretty as a picture." Columbus named it Puerto Bello.

Puerto Bello, later Portobelo, would of course become one of the most important bases in the New World. The Spaniard Vasco Núñez de Balboa would anchor here, as would the Englishman Francis Drake; a ring of protective barriers would be built until Portobelo was virtually impregnable (that is, until Henry Morgan came up with the simple idea of attacking Portobelo from land and conquered the town). Portobelo later became a reloading point for all the gold that would be found in this region and then transported back to Spain or England. But all that was in the future. Columbus's reality was the natives. At first they were friendly. They brought fruit, bread, and small pieces of gold, and they were delighted by the Spaniards' glass beads. The Spaniards stayed for a week, taking cotton on board. Then the first skirmishes with the natives flared up, and Columbus decided to sail on rather than establish a settlement there. This would later prove to be one of his many missed opportunities, for they would not find a more suitable and more beautiful bay than Puerto Bello.

On November 9, the fleet left Portobelo, but contrary winds pushed them back, forcing them to seek refuge in a bay that Columbus called Porto de Bastimentos, the "harbor of provisions." Three small islands lay beyond the bay, whose sandy beach was shaped like a giant sweeping sickle; behind it was a narrow cultivated strip of coast. This is the bay that Diego de Nicuesa would later christen Nombre de Dios. But Columbus put in; "much against my will," he noted, "the storm and a rapid current kept me in for fourteen days." Natives approached the ships, but when they saw the Spaniards rowing toward them, they jumped into the water and swam away. The ensuing chase by the Spaniards "was comical to behold," commented Fernando.

The crews undertook some much-needed repairs to the ships. The waters of the Caribbean had badly damaged the caravels; their timbers were rotting, no match for the dreaded shipworm. The Spaniards built huts for themselves or slept on the beach. There were dangerous animals in the area, and once, in the middle of the night, they awoke to the screams of a man being dragged away by a crocodile. Fernando watched these animals and described them as "so ravenous and cruel that if they find a man asleep they will drag him into the water to eat him." Neither Columbus nor Diego Méndez de Segura mentioned these killer crocodiles in their accounts.

The fleet anchored a few miles farther on, and Columbus named the bay Puerto del Retrete. The entrance was narrow, "with rocks as sharp as the points of a diamond sticking up on either side," but the channel was "so deep in the middle," wrote Fernando, that the four ships managed to squeeze in. A few of the Spaniards sneaked ashore with their weapons and stole from one of the villages. "A greedy and dissolute set of men," claimed Fernando. Soon many of the villagers stood by the shore, threatening the fleet with their spears. Columbus "tried to placate them by patience and civility," as his son noted. But when Columbus perceived "their arrogance," he lost patience and civility and ordered a cannon fired at them.

The situation aboard was bad. It rained ceaselessly. The sailors formed groups and whispered among themselves, flashing vitriolic glances at Columbus. Rumors started and spread: they had been bewitched; they were in a region where the sun never shone; the Great Khan had sent his armies to enslave them all. It was a mutinous atmosphere. But Columbus, still intent on finding gold, was unwilling to sail home. He gave the order to sail east. Perhaps his men were simply too tired to rebel.

Back and forth they sailed. When the wind came from the west, they sailed east; when the wind came from the east, they sailed to the west. The changing winds also meant a change in the direction of the currents. This voyage was turning into an odyssey. "There, my wound reopened," wrote Columbus, "and for nine days my life was despaired of; never was the sea seen so high, so terrific, and so covered with foam." This "wound" continues to baffle scholars. None of the scribes or chroniclers mentioned it, though Las Casas noted that Columbus did suffer from gout. Today most feel that Columbus must have meant "wound" in a symbolic sense; it represented all his suffering during the fourth voyage. Fernando reported, "The Admiral, perceiving that the violence of the east and northeast winds did not abate and that no trade could be carried on with these people, decided to turn back and verify what the Indians had said about the mines of Veragua."

They returned to Portobelo on December 5, but this offered them no respite. Two days later they were caught in the middle of a hurricane. Frightened sailors gave each other confession; most simply wanted their suffering to end quickly. "The ships were no longer in a sailing condition, and my people were either dying or very sick," wrote Columbus. So terrible were the thunder and lightning, recounted Fernando, that "the men dared not open their eyes and it seemed the ships were sinking and the heavens coming down.... They could not get even half an hour's rest, being wet through for days on end."

On December 10, a cyclone was seen approaching the fleet. Columbus prayed, reciting the passage about the tempest in

Capernaum from the Book of John, saying, "Fear not, it is I!" With the Bible in his left hand and a sword in his right, he stood on the deck of the *Capitana* and drew a circle around his fleet with his sword. He must have looked like a cross between Moses and Captain Ahab. The waterspout bypassed the fleet. Fernando described this weather as "an enemy that lies in wait for a man."

That same night the fleet lost sight of the *Vizcaína*. For three long days, Captain Bartolomeo Fieschi and his twenty-five-man crew fought the churning seas. They lost a boat and were forced to anchor but had to cut the cable before being able to return to the other ships. Two days later, on December 13, the fleet was becalmed. Sharks circled the ship, which was "frightening, especially to those who believe in omens," wrote Fernando. Using a red cloth as bait, the men caught several sharks. In the stomach of one they found a live turtle. Here was a feast after the long months of nothing but ship's biscuits, which as Fernando noted, were "so full of worms that, God help me, I saw many wait until nightfall to eat the porridge made of it so as not to see the worms."

On December 22, they anchored in the estuary of the Río Chagres, and here they found fresh fruit and water. The natives called this harbor Huiva; later it would be called Colón. Centuries later ships would lie at anchor at the mouth of the Río Chagres, waiting to cross from the Atlantic to the Pacific, for this is where the Panama Canal begins.

Here again was one of those moments when matters might have turned for the better. Columbus would have needed no more than a few canoes and the ability to communicate with the natives, who might have shown him the route upstream. From there Columbus and his men would only have needed to walk twelve miles to find the Pacific Ocean. Again, however, Columbus was his own worst enemy. In a letter he wrote from Jamaica, he said, "The world is but small; out of seven divisions of it the dry part occupies six, and the seventh is entirely covered by water." An acquaintance with the Pacific would have changed this, of course. He was so close to achieving his goal, here in the river estuary, and he even seemed to sense this, writing that his destination, the other side, "appears to hold the same relation to Veragua as Pisa to Venice." This was a surprisingly accurate description of Panama. But Columbus let the opportunity pass. He and the ships remained in the bay.

———

There have been decades when Columbus's name has fallen into oblivion, such as those immediately following his death. And there have also been entire centuries when he was celebrated as a man of undaunted courage who had accomplished one of the greatest feats of all time. He was many things to many people, and these were often in direct contradiction: great man and pathetic loser, Renaissance visionary and slave trader, navigating genius and feckless fool.

"One cannot see one without seeing the other," said Diógenes Cedeño Cenci. "One cannot view the discoveries and the contact between nations without also seeing the arrogance and the genocide. Columbus was everything and both at the same time." Historian and former president of the University of Panama, Cenci has written books about Columbus and the effects of his discovery. He sat at the bar of the Hotel Ejecutivo in Panama City, drinking coffee and water, and expounding his favorite subject. "One must see his courage and his determination. Columbus was definitely the best sailor of his time. He was pedantic and he was well informed. And yet he was greedy. Gold was the meaning behind his life. He killed for gold. He was blind and ignorant. He was a very bad leader and politician." The fourth voyage was the most significant of them all, according to Cenci. For the first time, the Europeans actually made it to the mainland of Central America. For the first time, moreover, the natives revolted against the discoverers. The main focus of the fourth voyage was finding the link between the Atlantic and the Pacific, making it the expedition with the most "historical repercussions," as Cenci put it modestly.

Columbus sailed up and down the coast of Panama, but he failed to find the opening, which would not be discovered until Núñez de Balboa took Columbus's idea to its furthest point. Balboa wasn't thinking about an isthmus but, rather, about an overland link, which he discovered and claimed for Spain in 1513. It was here that the idea for a passage was born. "That is why," explained Cenci, "the eighth wonder of the world, the Panama Canal, is the realization of Columbus's dream."

The project really only got under way in 1848 after the first golden nuggets were discovered in California and people by the thousands wanted to make it to the other side of the world. First the United States built a railway across Panama; it was completed in 1855. Some twenty-three years later, in 1878, French engineers Napoleon Bonaparte Wyse, Armand Reclus, and Pedro J. Sosa, working for Ferdinand de Lesseps, founded the Panama Canal Project, which was designed as a canal at sea level. The problem was that Panama's interior is very mountainous; excavation work would have had to have gone very deep and would have been very expensive. As a result, the French sold their assets to the United States, which completed the canal and celebrated its official opening on August 15, 1914. Three sets of canal locks lift ships up into the mountains and back down to sea level on the other side. The canal measures approximately fifty-one miles. The first ship to cross it took nine hours and forty minutes. Instrument of power and a source of revenue, particularly in times of war, the Panama Canal was relinquished by the United States to the Republic of Panama in January 2000.

"What a success story, what an achievement," said Cenci. He paused before adding, "What a contrast to the experiences Columbus made on his fourth voyage." During this fourth journey, explained Cenci, "Columbus was weak and sick. He suffered from arthritis and malaria. He lay in bed, virtually blind and lame. He hardly went ashore at all. And he must have known that he wasn't in India. After all, he wasn't stupid. But he couldn't admit it, because then he would have lost his fame and his fortune. Both were based on his finding India." He was, according to Cenci, "a beaten, embittered, and broken man."

———————

Columbus inspected his ships in the estuary of the Río Chagres; what he found did not lift his spirits. The boats were rotting. The dreaded shipworm had eaten its way through the hulls and was inching forward. He knew that they had no time to lose, for the homebound journey would be long. "I do not know if any one else ever suffered greater trials," wrote Columbus. Repairing what they could, he and his crews sailed westward along the coast, past bay after bay, along the hilly jungles of Panama.

On January 6, 1503, the four ships reached a region Columbus christened Veragua, which features a wide estuary. They had approached from the east and turned port side into the mouth of the river. On January 9, the flood tide carried the *Capitana* and the *Vizcaína* across the sandbank, and a day later the two other ships followed. To the right of the ships lay hills and to the left lay jungle, which stretched down to the riverbank, where there were fields of maize and some thirty huts. The natives called this river Yebra; Columbus named it Río Belén—"Belén" being the Spanish word for Bethlehem—because they had just celebrated Epiphany and the Feast of the Three Kings. They sailed across a sandbank and into the estuary, for the water was high enough. The four ships anchored side by side behind the sandbank. The current was gentle and the weather cleared; the heavens opened to reveal the sun. The omens seemed promising. In actuality it was in Belén that the fourth journey went disastrously wrong.

It all began with a hail of arrows when the Spaniards first went ashore. The crews returned fire but tried to avoid a massacre. The next morning things seemed to have calmed down, and the Spaniards began erecting huts. By the third and fourth days, the natives had begun to approach the camp; by the fifth day, the usual bartering of goods began. Business boomed: glass beads, hawk's bells, and colorful cloths in exchange for gold. The natives told Columbus about the great wealth to be found in the gold mines. The custodian of these mines was Quibián, a chieftain, a warrior, a trickster, and the leader of some eighty thousand men. Five hundred years later, scholars continue to debate whether Quibián was a name or a title, for some reports refer to him as "the Quibián." Fernando simply noted that "Quibián" was "the name those Indians give to their king." Today in Belén he is revered as a man who resisted Columbus in 1503.

Diego Méndez de Segura was one of the sailors on this fourth voyage, having signed on to serve on the *Santiago de Palos*. He was apparently one of Columbus's favorites. He later wrote an account of the voyage, published in 1536 in Valladolid. In his version of events, Méndez, who calls himself "a citizen of Santo Domingo on the island of Hispaniola," wrote extensively about the role he played in saving the lives of Columbus and his crew. These exploits, in his view, went unrecognized. Méndez's reason for writing his account was to show that he had been cheated of his rightful proceeds. In any event, Méndez noted that he had misgivings about what the natives were up to. "But no one in the fleet noticed this except myself. I went to the Admiral and said: 'My Lord, these men who have been going about here in battle array say that they are going to join the men of Veragua to attack the people of Cobrava and Aurira, but I do not believe them. On the contrary, they are gathering to burn the ships and kill us all.' And this was the truth."

Yet another storm passed through. The attendant floodwaters struck the *Capitana* with such force that the *Capitana*'s foremast and cables broke and she collided with the *Gallega*. When the seas had calmed, on February 6, Bartolomeo and Méndez took command of two boats and sixty-eight men, who rowed upriver to the interior. In his version of the events, Méndez reported that he was alone "with a single companion" and that "strange Indians informed me very clearly that these people were going to burn our ships and kill us all." According to Méndez, he arrived at the chieftain's village, which had "a large space around it and was surrounded by the heads of 300 warriors whom they had killed in battle. When I crossed the whole open space and reached the cacique's house, there was a great commotion among the women and children gathered around the door and they went screaming into the palace."

The truth was slightly different. After Bartolomeo and Méndez had rowed up the Río Veragua for three hours, together with their sixty-eight men, they came to a village where the chieftain greeted them, naked and visibly unarmed. Quibián entertained the men and offered to send three guides to accompany them to the mines. They marched through the jungle for five hours, and although they had mistrusted Quibián, they reached the mines and collected all the gold they could carry from among the roots of the trees. Columbus himself wrote that he had sent seventy men ashore to head into the interior and find the mines and that his brother had been placed in command of these men. Columbus made no mention of Méndez.

The men collected as much gold as they could carry and loaded it onto the ships. The share belonging to the Spanish crown was loaded aboard the *Vizcaína*. After that the *Gallega* was fully loaded. Columbus believed he had finally reached his goal and was already planning his fifth voyage. Then things began to go dreadfully wrong.

Quibián was in fact at war with the neighboring tribe of Urirá and had led the Spaniards not to his own mines but to those belonging to his enemies, as Columbus learned sometime later. Moreover, Columbus decided that the mouth of the Río Belén would be the perfect location to build a splendid harbor. He assigned his brother Bartolomeo with the responsibility of taking control of the region and organizing the settlement while he himself, as Fernando put it, "returned to Spain for reinforcements and supplies."

The Spaniards began work and had soon erected twelve thatched huts. The name of the settlement was to be Santa María de Belén. Having returned from his scouting trip, Bartolomeo decided that the best place for the new town was right beside the mouth of the river. Half of the crew, some eighty men, would stay behind. They built a large structure—half storehouse, half armory—and several smaller huts. They were so busy that they failed to notice that the Indians had stopped coming to the camp but were watching them from a distance, constantly chewing on something that they "decided must be the cause of their rotten teeth" and having painted their bodies red and their faces black. Alarmed, the settlers retreated to their ships, from which they heard the sound of beating drums.

Columbus told the story in a slightly different way, noting that he had predicted the ensuing events. "I established a settlement, and made many presents to Quibián.... I plainly saw that harmony would not last long, for the natives are of a very rough disposition, and the Spaniards very encroaching; and, moreover, I had taken possession of land belonging to the Quibián." For all his foresight, Columbus had failed to keep an escape route open. The rains had stopped, leading to a drop in the level of water. The sandbank between the river estuary and the ocean was too high to sail across. In fact, the heavy rainfall of the previous months had washed so much sand into the estuary, that "we thus found ourselves trapped and without hope of relief," Fernando reported. They were stuck in ships that were no longer stable, that looked like "honeycombs, riddled through and through by the shipworm," as Fernando described them; and "forced to remain here by the violent seas and winds which swept in and piled up sand in such quantities as to block the entrance to the harbor," as Méndez noted.

The natives approached on foot and in canoes, circling the boats and beating their drums but not attacking. This went on for three days. Méndez and Bartolomeo discussed the situation while Columbus was seemingly indisposed. Méndez wrote that he went ashore to negotiate with Quibián, accompanied by Rodrigo de Escobar, a ship's boy on the Vizcaína. On their way into the jungle, they took along a pair of scissors, a comb, and a mirror.

"I pretended that I had come to him [Quibián] as a surgeon to treat a wound that he had in his leg, and in return for the presents I gave them they let me go to his house." When they arrived at Quibián's village, the villagers threatened them. To show they had come in peace, Escobar began to cut Méndez's hair. Although Quibián later agreed to have his locks shorn, this apparently did not appease anyone, though the chieftain allowed the two men to return to their ships.

Méndez wrote that Columbus ordered Quibián be taken prisoner. "Next morning the Admiral sent for me to discuss what should now be done about the Indians. My opinion was that we must seize the cacique and all his captains, because once we had them in our power the common people would be subdued. His Lordship was of the same opinion." Predictably, Fernando told a completely different story, one in which Diego Méndez played no role. According to Fernando's account, on March 30, the interpreters said that they had learned Quibián planned to burn down the houses built by the Spaniards. Columbus decided to "teach him a lesson and strike fear into his neighbors by taking him and all his leading men prisoners and sending them to Castile, and to make his people serve the Christians."

Bartolomeo marched toward the native village with seventy-four men, taking only five of his closest companions as they grew close. He arrived at Quibián's hut and pretended to be interested in tending to Quibián's wounded leg. The men then overpowered and captured Quibián and several of the villagers, and, as Fernando noted, "the Adelantado felt no fear." Méndez naturally said that he alone had overpowered and captured the Indian chieftain.

Later the two versions of the story converged, for the chroniclers needed a scapegoat for the failure of this mission. They found one in Juan Sánchez, the helmsman. Quibián was captured and brought to the river estuary in shackles, where Sánchez was already waiting for the group. He took charge of Quibián in the early hours of the morning, bringing him aboard the *Capitana*. The other men hid in the forests until they could board the ship under the cover of darkness. Quibián began to wail and complained bitterly about the pain in his leg. No sooner had Sánchez taken pity on the chieftain and loosened the chains, than Quibián jumped overboard. And with his hands still chained, he swam to the shore. Over the centuries it was this feat that turned him into a national hero in Panama. "We took him prisoner, together with his wives, his children, and his servants. His captivity, it is true, lasted but a short time, for he eluded the custody of a trustworthy man, into whose charge he had been given, with a guard of men," wrote Columbus.

By the time the sun had set and Méndez and his men were able to leave the forest, the battle of Belén was already under way. Quibián had sworn revenge upon his captors. Columbus and his captains had managed to maneuver three ships across the sandbanks. The sailors stood in the water and pulled the ships across, leaving much of their provisions behind to lighten the loads, taking instead the gold they had found. But the *Gallega* still lay in the river estuary. She was supposed to serve as a fortress for the men who were to build the colony. The natives attacked the *Gallega* with spears, torches, and arrows. Méndez had already surrendered the huts and retreated to the *Gallega* with his fifty-six remaining men. They tried to pull the ship across the sandbank but failed. "Suddenly I was attacked by a host of about 400 natives armed with spears, darts and slings," Méndez reported in his testament. He lost seven men, and the battle lasted for three hours. Then, "by a miracle the Lord gave us victory, for we were very few and they were very many."

Outside the harbor Columbus stood aboard the *Capitana* and experienced what must have been one of the strangest and most surreal scenes on this voyage. Whether from strategic self-defense or as further evidence that he was suffering from malaria, he wrote:

> *I toiled up to the highest part of the ship, and, with a voice of fear crying, and very urgently, I called upon your Highnesses' war-captains....At length, groaning with exhaustion, I fell*

asleep, and heard a compassionate voice address me thus: "O fool, and slow to believe and to serve thy God, the God of all! What more did He do for Moses, or for David his servant, than He has done for thee? From thine infancy He has kept thee under His constant and watchful care.... He gave thee for thine own the Indies, which form so rich a portion of the world.... What more did he do for the people of Israel, when he brought them out of Egypt?"

This "compassionate voice" ended with the words "Fear not, but trust; all these tribulations are recorded on marble, and not without cause."

Columbus and the three remaining ships lay outside the bay of Belén for a week, while his brother and Méndez and the other men fought for their lives. "We remained on the shore among the huts we had built and they on the wooded mountain an arrow's flight away," recounted Méndez. "They began to shoot their arrows and hurl their darts as if attacking a bull. The arrows and darts fell thick as hail, and some warriors left the woods to come and attack us with clubs, but none of them returned, for all lost an arm or a leg or were killed outright by our swords. At this the rest took such fright that they ran away, having killed seven of the twenty men with whom we had started the battle." (Fernando reported that one Christian was killed and seven were wounded.)

Méndez saw that help was on the way, for a boat carrying Diego Tristán, captain of the *Capitana,* and ten of his men approached the river estuary. The natives attacked the boat, mortally wounding Tristán and killing the others. "They finally killed Tristán with a spear stroke through the eye," wrote Fernando. Méndez took two canoes, bound them together with branches, and then his men tied the provisions—the wine, oil, and ship's biscuits—to the boats and rowed to and fro, bringing all the provisions and the men across the sandbank. "The men who had been left with me were also taken out a few at a time and I remained with five men to the last and entered the last boat at nightfall. The Admiral was highly delighted with this action and repeatedly embraced me, kissing me on both cheeks, in gratitude for the service I had done him. He gave me command of the *Capitana* and of its whole crew, to take responsibility for the voyage, and I accepted this in order to oblige him as it was a service of great responsibility." The *Gallega* remained behind—the first of Columbus's ships to be lost on the High Voyage.

The stories vary, depending upon who was narrating. Columbus, for example, wrote that after the fighting was over, he collected all his men and set sail. "I sailed in the name of the Holy Trinity on the night of Easter Monday in ships that were rotten, leaky, and worm-eaten...." His version makes no mention of Diego Méndez. He did, however, appoint Méndez to succeed Tristán as captain of the *Capitana*—but evidently not to take "responsibility for the voyage," as Méndez had written in his testament. Fernando noted that the remaining captives belonging to Quibián's tribe hanged themselves below deck. "Their death was no great loss to us of the fleet." He added, "In two days nothing remained ashore except the worm-eaten hulk of the *Gallega*."

The village of Belén is located in a river estuary, looking much as it might have five hundred years before. It seems, even today, very isolated—an outpost on the margins of the world, on the edge of a huge rain forest. No road leads to Belén, not even a dirt road. It takes two days on horseback to get there from Colón. It essentially consists of forty-five wooden huts built on stilts to protect its three hundred or so inhabitants during the rainy season. There is one church and one newsstand. The inhabitants subsist on what they can fish out of the river's muddy waters and the coconuts they collect.

The village is about a third of a mile long, the footpath leading through about six feet wide. "That is our town hall." Arthur Saunders, the village chief, was pointing to a corrugated sheet roof atop four wooden supports. Saunders originally came from Colón, where there were jobs and bars and soccer. But the love of his life was from Belén, so he followed her and has lived here, at the end of the world, for the past thirty-five years. "Belén is democratic, which means that if we have any problems, we meet here to discuss them, things like who should drive the next boat to Colón." Saunders was wearing a baseball cap, a blue polo shirt, and gray pants rolled up to the knees. He wore flip-flops; everyone else walked around barefoot.

He showed us the village park, little more than a concrete square with twelve benches surrounding a plinth for a memorial. We asked him whether it was a memorial to Columbus. "Columbus was a killer, a murderer. He would have done anything for gold, he wiped out the native Indians, he felt he was superior to them, and he felt he could do anything he wanted. I wish he'd never turned up here. The memorial," Saunders went on to explain, "is for Quibián, of course. For the man who offered resistance. They captured him and shackled him, and he jumped overboard with his hands still tied. They shot at him but he escaped. He is our hero. We don't celebrate Columbus Day here. We celebrate February 28, Quibián Day." What happened to Quibián, we ask him. "Unfortunately, we don't know, and the archaeologists are only ever interested in Columbus."

In 1987 some archaeologists did come to Belén. Among them was Donald H. Keith, who was associated with Texas A&M. (Following that, he became president of the company Ships of Discovery, an underwater archaeological institute founded in Corpus Christi, Texas, in 1989.) Keith was among those who have long dreamed of finding one of Columbus's wrecks. And he is extremely fastidious about his work. Before committing themselves to a full-scale search, Keith and his team had to decide upon a wreck and a location. The *Santa María*, Columbus's flagship and the ultimate ship of discovery, was ruled out because Columbus's men had stripped the ship in 1492, in order to build the fortress La Navidad. Moreover, the Haitian coast had undergone considerable geomorphological changes over the past centuries. The two or three ships that Columbus lost on his second voyage during the hurricane off Bahía de Isabela on the north coast of Hispaniola in late 1494 and early 1495 didn't seem suitable either; the wreck's remains had been used to build a new ship, the *Santa Cruz*. In addition to that, there were insufficient sources and no reliable data on the precise locations. Nonetheless, Keith set off and found several water sites at which his search instruments registered an anomaly. However, the stone and coral layers in these areas measured several feet. The chances of finding anything were minimal.

Then, of course, there were the wrecks from the fourth voyage. The *Capitana* and the *Santiago de Palos* were said to lie off Jamaica, and a number of teams had searched for them, but, as Keith put it, "that is an incredibly difficult task due to the extensive geomorphological changes on Jamaica's shoreline." Keith knows what he's talking about. He himself went to Saint Ann's Bay in Jamaica to join his colleagues, but they failed to find anything relating to the two wrecks.

What about the *Vizcaína*? Keith maintains that the *Vizcaína* should be lying off Portobelo. However, because Portobelo had not been used as a seaport for centuries, the murky waters were choked with silt. He believes it highly likely that the wreck was "deeply buried under centuries of debris," either destroyed and rotted or untraceable.

That left the *Gallega*. "It was clear that the Río Belén offered the best opportunity to discover a well-preserved, identifiable, unsalvaged, discovery-period caravel." The team from Texas A&M began their search in the spring of 1987. They started by reconnoitering Panama's northern coast by air, searching for the region that matched accounts written by Columbus, Fernando, Diego Méndez, and Diego de Porras. They were searching for a river with a high hill located on the western bank and a clearing to the east, as well as sufficient depth at the mouth to enter and enough space within it for four vessels to lie at anchor. The Río Miguel de la Borda was too small; the Río Veragua too narrow; and there were no hills on either side of the Coclé del Norte. It soon became clear to the team that the Belén of today was also the historical Belén.

But then Keith found that his efforts were thwarted. He had signed a lucrative contract with Panama's Instituto Nacional de Cultura, granting him exclusive rights to excavate, dig, conserve, and research for seven years. For that purpose he had brought some of the best people in for the job, including a surveyor named Ric Hajovsky and sonar expert Bob Adams, who rigged a high-resolution sonar in a dugout canoe to sound out changes in the riverbed. For months Adams rowed up and down the bay. Keith brought in his students, and they camped by the river and spent six hours underwater every day. Keith then brought in Antonio Tourino, a geomorphologist with the University of Panama, to determine whether the riverbed had migrated over the centuries. Tourino found that the mouth of the river had not changed appreciably during the last several millennia.

There are those who believe that while the *Gallega* was certainly abandoned in the riverbed, the next rainy season would have washed the wreck out to sea. Treasure hunter Warren White is among them. "You have to search out in the ocean and not in the river." He claimed some divers recently told him they had discovered a really ancient wreck outside the bay of Belén. Keith didn't believe this. Seven years after the *Gallega* was abandoned, a Spaniard reported that he could still see what remained of the ship in the river. "That indicates that the ship sank while riding at anchor. In addition, the ship had tons of stone ballast that would have been sufficient to press the *Gallega* into the muddy riverbed. After seven years the ship would have decomposed. It would not have been washed out to sea."

For seven years Keith searched for the *Gallega*, unsuccessfully. He found some shards, probably dating from the days of Santa María de Belén, the fledgling settlement that was to become the new colony and that only survived a few days before Quibián burned it down. These were of no consolation to Keith. "There are wonderful theories, but sometimes in practice, things work out differently."

"Unfortunately," said Arthur Saunders. "Of course, we hate Columbus, of course we despise him. But if they had found the *Gallega,* then Columbus would at least have brought us something, a little fame and a little fortune."

CHAPTER 8

———

Shipwrecks and Mutiny

*Solitary in my trouble, sick, and in daily expectation of death,
surrounded by a million hostile savages full of cruelty, and
thus separated from the blessed sacraments of our holy
Church, how will my soul be forgotten if it be separated
from the body in this foreign land? Weep for me,
whoever has charity, truth and justice!*

—Columbus, in a letter from Jamaica

On Easter Sunday Columbus's depleted fleet got under way again, traveling along the coast of what is now Panama. The ships made a sorry spectacle as they sailed from one bay to the next. Heavily loaded—the crew of the *Gallega* had been divided up among the three remaining ships—the *Capitana*, the *Santiago de Palos*, and the *Vizcaína* were rotting from shipworm. Rain fell and storms thundered down upon the men, who spent all day and night pumping water while their commander kept slipping in and out of a feverish delirium, occasionally losing himself in religious prophecies.

Incredibly, through it all, Columbus retained his sailing skills. Everyone wanted to return home as quickly as possible by heading north; Columbus planned to sail eastward along the coast until they were directly south of Santo Domingo. He had calculated the current and the winds. The men were close to mutiny; they didn't believe Columbus was telling them the truth and suspected that he had ulterior motives. They thought they had long ago reached the point directly south of Santo Domingo. For a while Columbus managed to keep the upper hand. Shortly after Easter, however, catastrophe struck.

The *Vizcaína* was full of holes and literally falling apart; the water in the bilge was climbing higher and higher despite their attempts to pump it out. It was becoming clear to everyone that she would never be able to sail across the open seas to Hispaniola. The fleet anchored side by side in a bay; the crews removed the gold and provisions, as well as the sails from the *Vizcaína*, leaving only the heavy cannons, which, in 1503, were of inestimable worth to anyone thinking of constructing a settlement. However, the men knew that if they packed the *Vizcaína's* cannons aboard the *Capitana* and the *Santiago de Palos*, the chances of reaching Santo Domingo were slight. There was no alternative. The *Vizcaína* was stripped bare until only the shell was left. The men abandoned her. She drifted off and sank.

Columbus made reference to the events of these days in a letter he later wrote from Jamaica. "I departed, in the name of the Holy Trinity, on Easter night, with the ships rotten, worm-eaten and full of holes. One of them I left at Belén, with a supply of necessities; I did the same at Belpuerto [Portobelo]." His terseness suggests that ships were nothing more to him than a means of transportation. Once they were lost, they were forgotten about. Columbus had purchased the *Vizcaína* from Juan de Orquiva, a full burgher of Guetaria, for 40,000 *maravedís* on February 15. He had owned her for a mere two months before she sank.

Diego Méndez elaborated on things in his testament:

On the last day of April 1503 we left Veragua with three ships, intending to return to Castile, but as the ships were all riddled and worm-eaten we could not keep them afloat, and after mak-

ing thirty leagues we abandoned one of them, remaining with two, which were in an even worse condition. With all hands at the pumps, pots and cauldrons, we were still unable to draw off all the water that entered through the wormholes.

One surprising thing about his account was that Méndez didn't bother to note the location of the wreck. Fernando described it as follows: "We held on our course till we reached Portobelo; there we had to abandon the *Vizcaína* because she was drawing much water and because her planking was completely riddled by the shipworm. Following the coast, we sailed on beyond Retrete."

As we've seen, these passages buttress the argument of those people who don't believe the shipwreck off Nombre de Dios to be the *Vizcaína*. Nombre de Dios lies twenty miles to the east of Portobelo, and in April 1503 that meant a day's journey. And, finally, there is also Diego de Nicuesa, who noted in his account that he had discovered the *Vizcaína* in the bay of Portobelo.

There are five counterarguments to the Portobelo theory. First, the only convincing source is Columbus himself. Reduced to a semiconscious state by the fever, he might well have failed to register the *Vizcaína*'s exact location. He might also have had no intention of revealing the site because he was already planning his fifth voyage and never divulged this kind of information. There were many cannons aboard the *Vizcaína*. Why would he provide his enemies with a blueprint for recovering these valuable weapons? It is entirely possible that the words "in Puerto Bello" were meant to throw people off the scent. Second, Portobelo or Puerto Bello was a name that meant something to the people of Spain. Nombre de Dios was still called Bastimentos in 1503. It seems plausible that Columbus wanted to refer to a place that would have seemed familiar to the queen and also have provided a rough indication of the site. Third, at the time these events occurred, Fernando was fourteen years old, and it seems unlikely that he would have recalled the exact location of the bay decades later, when he was writing his book. Very likely he had his father's letter to hand; it is possible he simply copied it from his father, and that some later copied it from him and so on. A carelessly dropped or deliberately false remark can turn into a fact. Fourth, research based upon five hundred–year-old documents—written in a long-forgotten Spanish, copied by hand, then transcribed and translated over and over—is a precarious matter. "In Puerto Bello" might well have started as "near Puerto Bello." Fifth, in truth, Diego de Nicuesa didn't really see the *Vizcaína* in the bay of Portobelo. His sighting was simply a rumor that he had seen masts jutting out of the water. All he did see was an anchor, which he attributed to the *Vizcaína* because he thought Columbus had abandoned her here. At least that is what Nicuesa reported.

No single source claims that the *Vizcaína* was left behind off Bastimentos alias Nombre de Dios. No one ever claimed the *Vizcaína* could only be found off Nombre de Dios. But it seems equally true that the evidence favoring Portobelo remains extremely tenuous, tenuous enough to lead us to conclude that the *Vizcaína* could be lying off Nombre de Dios.

The citizens of Nombre de Dios learned of the miracle in October 2001. An uncle of a brother of one of the villagers in Nombre de Dios had gotten hold of an old newspaper in Panama City. In it was an article reporting that Christopher Columbus's *Vizcaína* had been discovered off Nombre de Dios. When the villagers heard about this, they called a meeting. Most led subsistence-level lives, scraping by on what they could fish and what they could grow. The cafés and bars were empty; young people loitered in the marketplace. After the United States left Panama, Nombre de Dios lost its tourists; lacking any kind of industry, it seemed to have lost its future. The beaches could be enchantingly beautiful—if they weren't covered with garbage and excrement.

The house of Juana Rojas, a local administrator, consists of two rooms; it has a corrugated-iron roof. Nine people live with her.

"We thought this ship would be our big chance. We thought, 'It's our bay; it's our history.' If this ship was salvaged, then people will come, tourists and researchers. We thought they would build a museum. We thought this ship would help us shape our future."

The inhabitants soon saw boats floating over the site. They saw divers going into the water and heard cars driving through the town late at night. Deciding to take matters into their own hands, they called a law firm. The response they got was to remain patient; they had no claim to the wreck.

Nilda Vázquez wants to sell the artifacts to the highest bidder. Carlos Fitzgerald wants to build a museum, either in Portobelo or in Panama City. The people of Nombre de Dios are waiting to see what happens.

———

On May 1, 1503, Columbus's two remaining ships reached a cluster of white cliffs he called El Mármol. Centuries later this region would become the border between Colombia and Panama. Once again the captains and crew on the *Capitana* and the *Santiago de Palos* gathered to demand that Columbus change his route and head north. They continued to believe they were already south of Santo Domingo and had been for quite some time; they even suspected they might already have passed Guadeloupe. Columbus felt they were mistaken, but he was so weakened by illness that he was unable to resist them.

Columbus turned out to have been right. They were south of Jamaica, and some nine hundred miles west of Guadeloupe. They should have sailed east along the coast for a few more weeks and then turned north. But the fleet changed course. Although they were sailing as close to the wind as they could, the winds blew from the east, pushing them farther west. On this course, they had no hope of ever reaching Santo Domingo.

On May 10, they were level with Little Cayman Island, northwest of Jamaica. Two days later they reached the Cuban archipelago that Columbus had named El Jardín de la Reina. Life was anything but idyllic. The men were starving; the only provisions they had left were ship's biscuits and oil. They argued among themselves. They pumped water from both of the ships, but the wormholes kept growing and growing. They were "exhausted by working three pumps day and night to keep the vessels afloat," wrote Fernando.

And then the storms hit. One of the anchor cables securing the *Santiago de Palos* broke, sending it crashing into the *Capitana,* splintering its bow and rupturing the stern of the *Santiago de Palos,* locking them together. Then the *Santiago de Palos* smashed the *Capitana*'s rudder. The crew of the *Capitana* threw ropes across to attach the ship's anchor, which now had to hold both vessels.

By June 10, Columbus realized that the two ships would not be able to stay the course. In an act of desperation, he decided to try his luck one more time and took them out onto open water. He pinned all his hopes on catching a breeze that would carry them to Hispaniola. He lost. The waters rose. Everyone could see that the *Santiago de Palos* would not make it. All they could do was to make for the nearest bay.

Five hundred years later, this long, curved bay would be called Saint Ann's Bay. Columbus had named it Santa Gloria when he'd anchored there on his second voyage. On June 25, Columbus took both ships into the bay side by side, separated only by a few feet. "Having got in, since we were no longer able to keep the ships afloat, we ran them ashore as far as we could, grounding them close together board and board, and shoring them up on both sides so they could not budge; and the ships being in this position the tide rose almost to the decks," Fernando recounted. The crew used ropes to tie the beached vessels together. Then they built huts with roofs of palm fronds. One hundred and six-teen men were stranded on Jamaica, a world that was as foreign to them as it was full of danger.

Columbus ordered the ships turned into fortresses and placed men on sentry duty. The natives had waved in a friendly way from the shore, but he warned his men that their mood could turn. At the same time, he thought his own men "naturally disobedient," as Fernando noted, quite capable of escalating the violence. As a result, he confined everyone to the ships.

There they sat, stranded in two beached vessels. The question was what should they do now? According to his own account—which as we now know was highly fictional—this was when Diego Méndez turned into a hero. Undermining his account's veracity is the fact that it is the only available source. He was at best a vain man who regarded the rest of humanity as cowards. He decided to set off into the wilderness, "since no one had yet dared to search for food for the Admiral and his men." Picking a sword and three of the best men to accompany him, he left. They reached a village called Aguacadiba, where friendly seeming natives greeted them and immediately began trading goods. Ten dried fish for a piece of string, one loaf of cassava bread for two glass beads, and a whole boatload of fish for one knife. It had been ages since the Spaniards had had such a feast.

Méndez managed to arrange for the natives to bring bread and fruit to the ships in Saint Ann's Bay each day. He then traveled on, eventually reaching the eastern tip of Jamaica, a region ruled by a chieftain named Ameyro. Méndez and Ameyro became friends, "giving him my name and taking his, which is considered a great sign of brotherhood among them," as the Spaniard observed in his account. The two began exchanging goods. In return for a canoe and six rowers, Méndez gave the chieftain a shirt, a brass helmet, and a coat. The Spaniard then put out to sea and returned to Columbus. For ten days the men sat in Saint Ann's Bay. They had enough to eat, but they still had no idea as to how they would leave the island. In his testament Méndez reported that Columbus took him aside and said, "Diego Méndez, my lad, none of my people realize the danger of our situation except you and myself. We are very few, these savage Indians are very many....One day," Columbus continued, "when the fancy seizes them, they may come and burn us here in these two ships that we have turned into houses.... It is true that you have made this arrangement with them to bring us food every day, and at present they are doing so willingly. But tomorrow fancy may seize them to act otherwise, and supplies will cease.... I have thought of a remedy," Columbus went on, "about which I should like your opinion. Suppose that in this canoe you have brought someone were to risk making the crossing to the island of Hispaniola. He could buy there a ship in which we could escape from our very great danger. Let me hear your opinion about this."

And Méndez replied, "Sir, I can clearly see our danger, which may be even greater than it appears. To cross from this island to Hispaniola in a vessel as small as this canoe would in my opinion be not merely dangerous, but impossible. I know no one who would dare to make the passage across those forty leagues of sea. For since among these islands the waters are subject to violent currents, and seldom calm, the dangers are only too obvious."

Columbus insisted that there was only one man who could accomplish this feat. Méndez said that he could. "My Lord, I have often put my life in danger to save yours and those of your companions, and Our Lord has marvelously preserved me." However, he also asked that the Admiral assemble all the men to ask whether there was anyone among them who possessed enough courage for such an undertaking, "which I doubt, and if they all hold back, as they will, I shall risk my life once more in your service as I have done many times already." Columbus called for volunteers, but no one came forward. Only Méndez rose to the challenge. "My Lord, I have only one life but I will risk it in your Lordship's service and for the good of all those here present. For I trust the Lord God, that being witness to the motives from which I act, He will preserve me as He has done many times before."

He began preparing for the journey by caulking the canoe, strengthening the prow and stern with planks, adding a drop keel, putting up a mast, and sewing a sail. Although it was July by this time and the hurricane season had passed, the seas were still rough. Santo Domingo was 108 miles away, and Méndez planned to row across in a canoe.

Méndez would have us believe there was one canoe on this heroic if foolhardy expedition. Fernando wrote that there were two volunteers and two canoes, and that his father's plan had been to allow Méndez to proceed to Santo Domingo, where he was ordered to charter a ship. Accompanying him was Bartolomeo Fieschi, the Genoan who had been captain of the *Vizcaína;* he was to return immediately to Jamaica with news of Méndez's safe arrival. Two men, two canoes, each with six Spanish sailors and ten natives at the paddles: that is how Fernando described the band of men who rowed off. It would still have been a heroic act, regardless of how many went. In his version Méndez never mentioned Bartolomeo Fieschi.

Knowing he faced a dangerous journey, Méndez sat down in Jamaica and wrote his obituary, leaving unspecified the date of his demise. "Here lies the Honorable Gentleman DIEGO MÉNDEZ. He greatly served the royal crown of Spain in the discovery and conquest of the Indies with the Admiral Don Christopher Columbus of glorious memory who discovered them, and afterwards by himself, with his own ships, at his own expense. He died...and begs from charity a Paternoster and an Ave María."

Columbus also sat down and composed a letter. Although he entrusted it to Méndez, Columbus makes no mention of his messenger, simply saying, "I send this letter by means of and by the hands of Indians; it will be a miracle if it reaches its destination." It would become one of the most famous documents he ever composed—his "Lettera Rarissima." Addressed to Isabella and Ferdinand, it offered an account of his life as well as a complaint: he had been wronged by his rivals, by the royal family, and by life in general. "Such is my fate, that the twenty years of service through which I have passed with so much toil and danger, have profited me nothing, and at this very day I do not possess a roof in Spain that I can call my own; if I wish to eat or sleep, I have nowhere to go but to the inn or tavern, and most times lack wherewith to pay the bill." This part of the letter is scarcely accurate. He possessed an enormous amount of gold and a steady income; the reason he didn't own a house was that it would have stood empty while he went off in search of India.

He made much of his most recent discoveries, and in particular of the coast of Veragua, where "I saw more signs of gold in the first two days than I saw in Hispaniola during four years." There was, he attested, no "more fertile or better cultivated country in all the world." He was in fact referring to the stretch of coast upon which he had lost two ships and many of his sailors, and where he had never felt more wretched in all his life. The gold received special attention, for, as he claimed, "he who possesses it does all he wishes to in this world, and succeeds in helping souls into paradise." He praised his sailors and wrote, "I beseech your Highnesses, since they are poor, to pay them promptly." He made one final complaint:

> I was twenty-eight years old when I came into your Highnesses' service, and now I have not a hair upon me that is not gray; my body is infirm, and all that was left to me, as well as to my brothers, has been taken away and sold, even to the frock I wore, to my great dishonor. I cannot believe that this was done without your royal permission. The restitution of my honor, the reparation of my losses ... will redound to the honor of your royal character.

He ended with a poignant plea:

> I am indeed in as ruined a condition as I have related; hitherto I have wept over others;—may Heaven now have mercy upon me, and may the earth weep for me....
>
> I did not come out on this voyage to gain to myself honor or wealth; this is a certain fact, for at that time all hope of such a thing was dead. I do not lie when I say, that I went to your Highnesses with honest purpose of heart, and sincere zeal in your cause. I humbly beseech your Highnesses, that if it please

God to rescue me from this place, you will graciously sanction my pilgrimage to Rome and other holy places. May the Holy Trinity protect your Highnesses' lives, and add to the prosperity of your exalted position.

    Done in the Indies, in the island of Jamaica, on the seventh of July, in the year one thousand five hundred and three.

Six Spaniards and ten natives sat in each canoe, wrote Fernando. Méndez reported that the canoe held "myself, one other Christian, and six Indians." From the distance of more than five centuries, it is hard to know who was right. Fernando's version is more plausible; he had no reason to concoct a heroic tale. The only person who cared whether there were two canoes or just one was Diego Méndez, and he was unwilling to share the limelight.

Méndez's first attempt soon failed. The Spaniards had planned to row to Jamaica's outermost tip and wait there for favorable winds and calm seas, but they were attacked by natives. Méndez told of "great hardships and dangers," for he was "taken prisoner by Indian sea-raiders, from whom God miraculously delivered me." Again, as was so often the case, his account was uncorroborated. The Spaniards returned to Saint Ann's Bay. Undaunted, Méndez decided to try again. Columbus ordered an armed guard of seventy men to escort him to the eastern tip of Jamaica. This time, they took the overland route, and when they arrived at the outermost tip of the island, the seas had grown calm and Méndez was able to set off again.

The journey took five days and four nights. There was no protection from the glaring sun and few provisions. The natives had used up their own supply of fresh water after paddling without rest after only one night. Fernando later wrote, "By good fortune the captains had each brought along a small water cask from which they kept doling out a few drops of water to their Indians." Sometimes the natives took turns swimming to refresh themselves. On the second night, one died of thirst. The others were too weak and despondent to do much else than lie at the bottom of the canoe. They were convinced that they had gone off course; by their reckoning, they had paddled sixty-four miles and should have sighted the island by now. After the third day in the sweltering heat, Méndez observed that at the rising of the moon, "a small island covered its lower part like an eclipse." They landed on a bare rock, with no trees and no springs, but from the high cliffs the men caught sight of Cape Tiburón to the east, some miles away. The men collected water in gourds, drank their fill, and rested until the afternoon before launching the canoes for the final leg of the journey to Hispaniola.

Whether Méndez was heroic or heroically self-aggrandizing, his journey was an incredible feat. He—they—had traveled 108 miles at a pace of one mile per hour.

Mutinies don't only occur at sea. They can also occur on a beached ship. Stranded in Saint Ann's Bay, Columbus and his men had no idea whether they would ever see the coast of Spain again. Their mood was grim. The men had little to eat, no meat, and no wine. They were haggard and exhausted, and some of them were sick. Columbus lay on his blankets, unable to move from the pain brought on by an attack of gout. Méndez and Fieschi had been gone for months, and there was still no news of their safe arrival.

A rumor spread that two empty canoes had been seen drifting on the ocean. One man said this was the end. Another claimed that Columbus wasn't planning to return to Spain at all. One thing led to another. The mutiny was instigated by the Porras brothers. Diego de Porras had been the fleet's scribe; his brother Francisco was captain of the Santiago de Palos. Both men made a simple calculation. Given that Governor Nicolás de Ovando was a sworn enemy of Columbus, it seemed unlikely he would punish anyone for starting a mutiny against the Admiral. Moreover, they were connected. Bishop Juan de Fonseca in Castile had been a friend of the Porras family for years. One of their sisters was a mistress of Señor Alonso de Morales, high treasurer to Castile. They believed they had nothing to fear.

On the morning of January 2, according to Fernando, Francisco stormed into Columbus's quarters and cried, "Señor, what do you mean by making no effort to get to Castile? Do you wish to keep us here to perish?" Weakened by illness, the Admiral replied that "he knew no way of going home until a ship was sent; that he was second to no man in his desire to leave, both for his own good and that of the men for whom he was responsible." Columbus then proposed a council of officers to decide on a plan, but the mutineer lifted his sword and shouted, "It's no time to talk; embark quickly, or stay here with God." Then Porras turned to the men and said, "I'm for Castile, who's with me?" Outside on the deck of the ramshackle *Capitana,* the men shouted, "We're with you." Columbus struggled up from his blankets and attempted to intervene, but those attending him held him back. His brother Bartolomeo came running, armed with a lance; the men wrested it from him and locked him in the cabin with Columbus. According to Fernando, Columbus's attendants "begged Captain Porras to go with God and not be the cause of a murder which was bound to harm them all."

The battle cry of the mutineers became "To Castile!" Shouting encouragement to each other, they took ten dugout canoes, shanghaied several natives, and began rowing away. They planned to head east, unaware that the winds were blowing from that direction. When water began to wash over the sides of the canoe, they threw their provisions overboard to lighten the load. When the seas grew rougher, they decided to kill the natives and throw them overboard. Some of the natives tried to cling to the canoes; the Spaniards hacked off their hands. The mutineers returned to the northeastern tip of Jamaica before attempting another crossing. And then they gave up. Their battle cry "To Castile!" was reduced to absurdity, as they now set up camp in a village in the northeast of Jamaica, called Aomaquique. From there the rebels waged war on the natives and on Columbus.

Columbus, meanwhile, was still stranded in Saint Ann's Bay, along with fifty loyal followers. All they had to eat was what the natives brought them. There were coconuts, bananas, pineapples, and fish, but the Spaniards would surely have starved had the natives not brought them bread and water every morning. But the natives soon lost interest in supplying the outsiders with food, for, as Fernando noted, "we consumed more in a day than they in twenty." Moreover, they had run out of glass beads and no longer had anything to exchange. When the natives realized this, they stopped bringing provisions. "This posed a serious problem," wrote Fernando.

Columbus concocted his most famous and ingenious ruse, the "eclipse trick." Various witnesses described it in later years, but Fernando provided the best account. Knowing that there would be a total eclipse of the moon on the night of February 29, 1504, Columbus summoned the native chief aboard what was once the *Capitana* and told him that he was a messenger of God and that God was angry with them because they had refused to bring more food. He told them to watch the moon that night, for God would send them a sign. The moon would remain dark with a flaming circle around it, a sign of God's wrath. Columbus then withdrew to his bed, for his joints were inflamed.

That night, when the dark moon rose, howling and wailing reverberated around Saint Ann's Bay. The natives returned and begged Columbus to speak to his god and ask for forgiveness. Columbus repaired to his quarters. When the eclipse was on the wane, he reappeared and spoke to the natives, telling them that if they treated the Spaniards well and brought them what was rightfully theirs, then God would remove the shadow from the moon. The natives pledged to do this. Then the sun rose. On March 1, 1504, Columbus and his remaining crew held a banquet.

Méndez and Fieschi finally arrived in Hispaniola. Fernando wrote that Fieschi immediately wanted to return to Jamaica; those were, after all, his orders. He was to accompany Méndez and then bring news of the journey's success back to the men stranded in Saint Ann's Bay. No one volunteered to accompany him, however. Those who had survived were exhausted and unable to endure more hardship. Fieschi never returned to Jamaica.

Méndez was suffering from fever and ague. He gave himself two days' rest and then took his rowers along the coast of Hispaniola to find the governor. On the way Méndez heard that Nicolás de Ovando was traveling in the western province of Xaragua, where he was waging war against insurgents.

It was a bloody war. The Spaniards were behaving like the master race. In the province of Xaragua was a woman named Anacaona, the widow of Chief Caonabó and the sister of the deceased chieftain Behechio. According to reports, Anacaona was a compelling figure. Las Casas called her "cultivated" and "talented"; others described her as being courageous, clever, and powerful. Méndez even called her "the greatest chieftain in all the island." Yet Ovando had had her murdered. He had invited the native chieftains and their attendants to a feast in a large hut, which he then barricaded and set on fire. According to Méndez's account, Ovando burned or hanged eighty-four ruling caciques. Las Casas mentioned only eighty, but the difference seems of no importance.

Nicolás de Ovando never kept a diary or a journal. When judging him, one must bear in mind that accounts of what happened were written by his enemies. And yet the evidence, the stakes and gallows upon which many natives died, was there for all to see.

When Méndez finally reached Ovando at his field headquarters in Xaragua, the governor took him prisoner. He refused to send a ship to Jamaica to rescue his old enemy. Humanity counted for little in the New World; all that mattered was power.

There could hardly have been a more cruel sight than the one that the marooned sailors, sitting on the beach in Jamaica, were forced to witness. A ship sailed into the bay, dropped off some scant supplies, turned around, and left. It was a small Spanish caravel, and at first the men on the beach cheered and waved, falling into each other's arms in relief. Nicolás de Ovando had sent the boat, captained by Diego de Escobar. Escobar's orders were to verify that Columbus was still alive and to check on the overall situation. He brought along two casks of wine and a slab of salt pork, as well as a letter from Méndez, who confirmed that he was doing everything in his power to procure a ship to rescue the stranded men. Escobar was under strict orders to take nobody on board. After unloading his scant provisions, he quickly weighed anchor and sailed off again.

Although Columbus's men were dejected and despondent, they knew at least that Méndez had made it to Hispaniola. Then, day after day, week after week, and month after month, they sat on the beach and waited. Finally, they were forced to fight.

Columbus had offered to negotiate with the mutineers. It was dangerous to have his enemies roaming the island, and he knew that he would not be forgiven if he returned to Spain without the Porras brothers. He sent two messengers to the mutineers with an offer of safe conduct and a pardon as well as a portion of the salt pork. The Porras brothers, who considered Columbus to be delusional, wanted power more than anything else. They mistrusted Columbus and demanded that if Méndez sent two ships, they should get one. If Méndez sent only one ship, then half of it belonged to them. Knowing this was humiliation, Columbus broke off negotiations. Fueled by the fear of being left stranded in Jamaica, the mutineers attacked on May 20, 1504. Loyalists fought against insurgents. Bartolomeo commanded fifty men loyal to Columbus armed with swords and knives. Watching from a distance, the natives could presumably only wonder at this carnage. Columbus's personal valet was killed and the mutineers Juan Sánchez and Juan Barva also died. Sánchez had been a pilot, steersman, and officer, and Barva a cannoneer on the Capitana. The vanquished mutineers were put in chains. Bartolomeo wanted to mete out harsh punishment. The others urged him to show restraint. If too many Spaniards were executed, they argued, the natives could attack and easily overwhelm the survivors.

Seven months passed before Governor Ovando eventually released Diego Méndez, permitting him to make his way to Santo Domingo, where three ships lay at anchor. Méndez purchased one of the ships; had it loaded with bread, wine, pork, lamb, and fruit; and dispatched it to Jamaica. Captain Diego de Salcedo received precise instructions as to where he would find the marooned Columbus. Méndez himself embarked on one of the two remaining ships bound for Castile, where he planned to give a full accounting of the High Voyage to the king and queen.

The victors in this scaled-down version of the Spanish civil war fought out in Jamaica were reluctant to celebrate until they saw a caravel enter Saint Ann's Bay in late June. Even then they remained wary. The caravel was deep in the water, groaning and pitching and so obviously beset by shipworms that it would be a miracle if it saw the year through. It was a relief that Captain Salcedo was a loyal follower of Columbus and that Méndez had issued orders to take everyone who wanted to leave on board.

On June 28, 1504, Columbus was finally rescued. He had been on Jamaica for a year and four days. The hulks of the two ships that had carried Columbus and his men from Spain to the New World, or at least as far as Jamaica, were left behind.

One side of Saint Ann's Bay is bordered by sharp stones and heavy gray boulders that reach down to the water's edge. Car parts and tires have been dumped on the boulders. The other side of the bay is lined with fine Caribbean sand. Saint Ann's Bay lies in the north of Jamaica, the side with the bays, the jungle, the palm trees, and the sand. Despite the beauty of the surroundings, people here are just as poor as anywhere else on the island. The sandy beaches are lined with garbage. A few Rastafarians sit outside beachside bars, drinking, smoking, and panhandling. "For a dollar we'll clean the beach for you," they offered. Five centuries after Columbus was marooned here, Saint Ann's Bay is still a sad place.

Two hundred yards inland, there is a polo field on which cows roam freely, a Paul's Millennium Supermart, the Columbus Beach Cottages, and the inevitable memorial. The statue of Columbus was erected in 1957. Perched atop nine steps, the bronze figure stands with legs wide apart. This Jamaican version of Columbus has short hair, wears long stockings, carries a naval staff, and gazes into the distance. He holds his chin slightly aloft, presumably to convey pride and determination, though the result is arrogance. This figure of Columbus is rather small. A plant has sprouted from his head. Shards of glass lie at his feet. The fence surrounding the small park is rusting.

Next to the park stands the Columbus Preparatory School. Behind it is Marcus Garvey High School, named for the famous revolutionary leader and preacher; in Jamaica he is still regarded with almost religious reverence. The founders of the school, however, must have been confused, for although the school's motto reads: "Strive for excellence," its coat of arms shows three ships riding the high waves.

Saint Ann's Bay conceals what to underwater archaeologists would certainly rank as among the greatest treasures, the *Capitana* and the *Santiago de Palos*. They lay beached in the surf, driven ashore by Columbus himself, and that is exactly how he left them in June 1504. Centuries later one man was convinced he would succeed in finding them.

Roger Smith can spend hours talking about old ships and the configuration of ribs and planks in their hulls. His office at the Florida Office of Cultural and Historical Programs in Tallahassee is crammed full with books about old ships and the hulls of old ships. Baseball hats with the names of various expeditions, such as "Sunken Treasures" or "U.S.S. Florida," line his shelf, along with various certificates and commendations. Underwater archaeology has been Smith's life. He loves everything about it: the legends and myths behind sunken boats, the romance and the tragedy, the treasures. Ships transport "objects, clothing, animals, technologies, diseases, and people. They transport an idea and a philosophy of life, and when they sink, all of this is frozen," he explained.

Underwater archaeology also holds deep frustrations. There are far more defeats than victories, "much more detective work than John Wayne work," as Smith put it. "Underwater archaeology means comparing discoveries with things that are already known, endless reading, delicate work, for one can never put something back into its original state. When I salvage something, it's out, and you can cause a lot of damage down there."

Smith was born in Salt Lake City. The son of a diplomat, Smith and his family moved around a great deal, and Roger grew up in Japan and Germany. He never knew what to make of his life. "I was a cowboy and a hippie, but nothing seemed real." Until one day he came across a book called *The Lost Ships* by Peter Throckmorton; it changed his life. He started off at the University of Pennsylvania and then jumped at the chance when he was accepted into the new program at Texas A&M, which was already considered the elite place for underwater archaeology. Smith did his doctorate there and then went to Florida as a state underwater archaeologist. He now teaches at the University of West Florida and at Florida State University. Today Smith is one of four or five great figures in the small circle of the world's premier underwater archaeologists. He puts in sixteen-hour days; he writes books that, when published, sell a few hundred copies; and he likes nothing better than to dive in the murky waters of river estuaries.

Finding one of Columbus's ships would be a "milestone in archaeology" and "one of the greatest gifts to history," Smith said. We know next to nothing about the ships from the great Age of Discovery, a very short period in maritime history—only thirty to fifty years by some calculations. These ships had to be nimble yet stable. A large hold was not required, as the purpose of these voyages was discovery and not exploitation. And they needed to be able to deal with adverse winds on the homeward journey. The caravels—"ships that changed the world"—were built according to these requirements. When the New World had been discovered, when gold and slaves had become the focus, these ships gradually disappeared from the waters. Europeans built transport ships with massive holds.

The key features of these caravels were the rigging, hull, and rudder. The Spaniards copied the triangular sails known as lateens from the Arabs. They were rigged to two, three, sometimes even four masts and used in combination with the classic foursquare sails. This enabled the discoverers to respond better to variable winds, rather than being forced to drift along passively. Were a captain clever, he would have had the sails trimmed, so that the foresails guided the wind into the main sails. Because the demands placed upon the ships and its load increased, the hulls were strengthened. Planks were nailed to a preconstructed skeleton frame, elevated at the prow and stern. "That was the start of a strong European hull tradition," according to Smith. The depth of the caravels measured 2.3 times the width of the ship; their keel was around 2.4 times longer than the maximum width. The deck was 3.3 times longer than the width. In order to keep these ships on course in tropical storms, the Spaniards incorporated a stern rudder. "The rigging, the hull, and the rudder were all very skillful accomplishments," observed Smith.

Scholars are also fairly certain that weapons were stowed below deck. Normally, these consisted of two heavy cannons called *bombardettas* and twenty smaller cannons. Shortly before they reached land, the crews would have hauled the weapons above deck.

It is telling that when replicas of these caravels have been built, based upon research and speculation, they have often turned out either too far removed from reality or to have overlooked certain important features. Enrico d'Albertis, a member of the Italian Columbus commission, produced the first constructional drawings in 1892. He had little to base them on. He was followed by a Spanish commission, and then by Cesáreo Fernández Duro, who sketched the next models. Duro's drawings were the basis for replicas of the *Santa María*, the *Pinta*, and the *Niña*, built for the World Columbian Exposition held in Chicago in 1893 and sailed across the ocean for the occasion. The *Santa María* pitched and rolled and tended to miss her course by ninety degrees, although she did always finally make it to her destination. The other two ships had to be towed, presenting a sorry sight when they arrived in America. In 1962 the Spaniard Carlos Etayo Elizondo built a better version of the *Niña*. Though outfitted with both lateen and square riggings, the replica needed ninety-seven days to go from Palos de la Frontera to San Salvador. Columbus sailed the distance in thirty-six.

"Genuine and good reconstructions have to be based on the authentic fragments of the time capsules that still lie on the ocean floor off Haiti, the Dominican Republic, Panama, and Jamaica." Smith looks upon the ships of the fifteenth and sixteenth centuries as a family—albeit a small family, given that so many have yet to be found. What ones have turned up, of whatever age, he has seen; when a newborn arrives, he invariably compares it to the older models. "And, naturally, we're always hoping it turns out to be one of Columbus's ships. His name is omnipresent, but every time it has turned out to be someone else's baby."

Nonetheless, despite his "omnipresence," Columbus is not a figure of particular interest to Smith. "Columbus was merely an Italian businessman who followed in the footsteps of others. He was not a great sailor. After all, Oriental visitors and European fisherman had reached America before him. But, of course, he has the fame. He has the history. I'm less interested in him as a man, but rather more in his ships." To Smith, Columbus "wasn't extraordinary, but his ships were."

Smith began to recount his first visit to Saint Ann's Bay in 1981. "We should go back a little further in history." The role of Santa Gloria, now called Saint Ann's Bay, where Columbus abandoned the *Capitana* and the *Santiago de Palos*, diminished over the centuries. Diego Colón, appointed governor in 1509, wanted to establish a town there and even had a few houses built. The settlement was named Sevilla la Nueva. But after a few years, the Spaniards moved farther to the south of Jamaica. The teeming rain forest quickly overgrew the settlement, and soon all the houses had disappeared. In 1692 a huge earthquake struck the region, rocking the island and completely destroying Port Royal, where, during the golden age of piracy, Henry Morgan and his hordes spent their pirated booty in the bordellos and taverns. Buried under silt and mud, Port Royal is located in the southeast of Jamaica; Saint Ann's Bay lies two hours to the north by car. Smith described the 1692 earthquake as just another one of those incidents that makes underwater archaeology such a lottery. It was very possible it had destroyed all that was left of the ships or altered the coastline to such an extent that it no longer resembled the shore Columbus had known. Where now there was a road, five hundred years ago there might have been a beach. There might have been other earthquakes, smaller perhaps and unrecorded, whose epicenter happened to be in Saint Ann's Bay.

Archaeologists depend upon luck. In 1932 an overseer on a British plantation was riding a horse that stumbled over a stone. The stone belonged to a cistern, and the cistern once belonged to Sevilla la Nueva. The archaeologist C. S. Cotter began excavating the site; he soon uncovered the foundations of houses built by Diego Colón.

The first to search for the two ships was the amateur archaeologist William Goodwin. Goodwin was convinced that the ships were lying not in Saint Ann's Bay but in nearby Don Christopher's Cove, a narrow and shallow bay. Why else, he argued, would the place have been given its name? Goodwin began excavating the site in 1935. He bored 150 test holes. After three years of effort, he gave up.

Samuel Eliot Morison was the next to arrive. In 1940, during preparations for his expedition that would later become the basis of his Columbus books, Morison came to Saint Ann's Bay. An experienced sailor, as we've seen, Morison immediately disproved Goodwin's theory of Don Christopher's Cove being the final anchorage for Columbus's ships. He argued that the cove was too shallow and narrow for Columbus ever to have risked landing there. He pointed out that the cove might have been named after Don Cristóbal Ysassi, the last Spanish governor of Jamaica, a rebel and a buccaneer who had used the bay as his hideout. Morison concluded that Columbus had driven his ships to the west side of Saint Ann's Bay, where the waters were deep and wide and therefore there was enough room to maneuver. The question remained as to whether his worm-ridden ships actually left Columbus much choice as to where he could land.

The first team from Texas arrived in 1968, led by Robert Marx, a pioneer of underwater archaeology. Marx found wood, stones, ceramics, and obsidian (naturally formed glass) in the area favored by Morison. He then conducted a sonar survey and turned up several targets in the bay. These artifacts included glass, pieces of iron, charcoal, and flint. Newspapers around the world announced that the first ship belonging to the discoverer of America had at last been found. The Jamaican government called for support, and the French diver Frédéric Dumas arrived. He located ballast stones, glass, and other artifacts, including wine bottles. Analysis of the bottles showed that they dated to the eighteenth century. Dumas confirmed that in the past this had probably been a popular anchorage site; he also admitted to finding no traces of the *Capitana* or the *Santiago de Palos*.

Roger Smith came to Jamaica in 1981 accompanied by his colleague, geologist John Gifford. They began by comparing maps, aerial photographs, and historical documentation in order to ascertain to what degree the coastline had changed over the centuries. The results showed that the coast had changed considerably. "There was the possibility that Columbus's ships lay buried under the present-day beach or even under the freeway."

The team began dividing the area into grid squares. They sketched maps and began searching the waters and the beach, foot by foot, with magnetometers and subbottom sonar. They were able to prove that the area to the west of the bay had indeed been a well-used anchorage site. They found a number of artifacts from various periods, though nothing that excited anyone. Buried under a six-foot layer of clay and mud, Smith and his team found an extremely well-preserved English merchant ship from the eighteenth century. The interest this generated among the community of underwater archaeologists was fleeting, however.

The team cheered when they saw the changes in the bedrock; when they had three-dimensional images drawn up, the changes seemed to indicate two ships lying side by side. Joy turned to despondency when they explored the site and found only debris, stones, and iron; no trace of a wreck.

Smith and Gifford persevered, even boring test holes underneath historic Sevilla la Nueva and the freeway. Eventually they were forced to admit defeat. "We didn't discover anything that was older than 1692, and we utilized all the means at our disposal." The *Capitana* and the *Santiago de Palos* remain unfound.

———————

It took six and a half weeks for Columbus and his men to reach Santo Domingo on the caravel. Governor Ovando welcomed Columbus with a smile and offered to lodge him at his own house. As Fernando put it, "It was a scorpion's kiss." The moment they landed, he released Francisco de Porras, the ringleader of the mutineers. Columbus remained calm, however. He may have been unwilling to delay his departure or may have realized who had the upper hand. He chartered a caravel and, on September 12, he set sail for his final journey home. Accompanying him were his brother, his son, and twenty-two men. The others all remained on Hispaniola. They had had enough. Their homeward journey began inauspiciously when the mainmast split and had to be repaired. After fifty-six days fraught with the usual storms and dangers, they finally arrived in Sanlúcar de Barrameda, Spain.

In a letter to his son Diego, Columbus wrote that he had wanted "to gain Paradise and more," but that it had been "impossible or that my knowledge and strength were not sufficient." The High Voyage had lasted two and a half years. He was a sick man in the final stages of his life.

The royal family also concluded that the High Voyage had been a complete disaster. They had lost four ships and gained virtually nothing. A statement of accounts was included in Queen Isabella's files, housed in the Archivo General in Simancas. Juan Gil found the statement in October 2003. He had not been searching for it, of course, but that is how things often go in relation to Columbus. "There are tons of paper stored in these archives, and much of it has yet to be filed and compiled." Gil had been rummaging through other documents when he came across those belonging to Alonso de Morales, high treasurer to Queen Isabella during Columbus's fourth voyage. Here was the money trail.

The good thing about accountants like Morales is that they tend to keep excellent records; these files had wandered into the archives in an orderly state. The problem is that accountants and treasurers produce a staggering amount of paper, most of which is the most boring reading material imaginable. Gil was lucky. The archive shelves in Simancas possessed all of the files left by Morales. Soon his desk was surrounded by piles of documents that Morales had left to posterity. "A royal treasurer probably paid some twenty people a day," explained Gil. "There are expenses, invoices, wage statements. He accounted for every single payment." Gil's job was deciphering and classifying every single entry. Among the piles of paper, he found three and a half pages of figures—the cost estimation for Columbus's fourth voyage.

Prior to his departure, Columbus had estimated how many sailors and officers he would need and how much it would cost. The amount came to 3,163,600 *maravedís*. But the accountants were tenacious. Over the next few weeks, Morales's cronies nickel-and-dimed Columbus, eventually beating down the cost by nearly a third, granting the Admiral of the Ocean Sea 2,259,239 *maravedís*. This would explain why Columbus had fewer ship's carpenters on board than would have been necessary, as well as fewer caulkers, who might have sealed the leaking hulls. That is doubtless also why he had to make do with only one chief pilot for all four ships—Juan Sánchez—and had no subalterns. Moreover, it could be the reason why he had more ship's boys on board than adult sailors. Ship's boys received only 666 *maravedís* a month whereas a sailor was paid 1,000 *maravedís*. "Columbus's last crew was nothing more than a bunch of adolescents."

The tragedy of this fourth voyage fascinates Anunciada Colón de Carvajal most about her famous ancestor. An aristocratic woman, Carvajal is always careful not to jump to conclusions about Columbus. She has spent her life trying to understand the man and is unwilling to condemn him as a ruthless egomaniac. But she remains equally wary of revering him as a hero. Her brother, Cristóbal Colón, not only inherited the discoverer's name, as family tradition dictates, he also holds the title Duke of Veragua. Until recently he served as an officer in the Spanish navy. He loves the sea, helicopters, ships, in fact anything fast moving—a down-to-earth man who would never say anything inappropriate in a speech. This is why he has become a welcome guest at festivities, such as the 1992 anniversary of Columbus's first voyage. He is well known in Spain's high society; his name appears often in the media. The prominence of his family name also has its drawbacks. Anunciada and Cristóbal's father was murdered in 1986 by Basque separatists belonging to ETA. "Just like that, just because he was famous," according to Anunciada. "And it had nothing to do with Columbus."

Anunciada is the intellectual force in the family. A historian, she is the assistant director of the Mapfre Tavera Foundation, which is funded by an insurance company and publishes historical documents on CD-ROM, so that the children of the Internet generation can learn something about their country's history. She began by looking for information on everything her famous predecessor had destroyed. She read anything she could find on the culture of the Taínos, the Maya, the Aztecs, and the Incas—anything at all about those people who perished when the conquistadors followed in Columbus's wake. She is also a close friend of Consuelo Varela and therefore familiar with the historian's extensive files on Columbus. It was in these documents that she first learned about the gold-grubbing side of Columbus—the Admiral of the Ocean Sea as ruthless conqueror with a keen eye for the slave trade—the man whom Varela maintains she has sometimes come to hate. While not specifically condemning her ancestor, Anunciada Colón claimed that these were all various aspects of a complex personality. "We historians have a kind of magnifying glass which we hold over a certain section of a person's life to enlarge the details and then we can say, aha, that's what the man was like. But if we held the glass over another portion, then this person might take on a completely different aspect."

When she holds her magnifying glass over the fourth voyage, she finds that Columbus looks like anything but a ruthless conquistador. "The fourth voyage was his biggest battle. It is the most impressive chapter, because his men suffered so much." Columbus himself had placed his highest hopes in his High Voyage. It had been his chance to prove that something he believed was there truly existed, meaning a passage to India. He approached this voyage with greater resolution and focus. He had even wanted to design the ships himself—to build them with a lower draft than the other caravels, making them faster, more maneuverable, and better suited to enter the shallower coastal waters and the rivers where he hoped to find a westward passage.

A tiny worm had brought the Admiral of the Ocean Sea to his knees—the worm the Spaniards called *broma* at the time. She explained that the Spanish word *abrumado* meant "crushed," "afflicted," "tormented," and "tortured." Columbus had been crushed, afflicted, tormented, and tortured on his final voyage. And yet, according to Anunciada, he behaved in a noble and generous way. "His behavior in Jamaica was not that of an autocrat. He was beaten and he was docile. He even begged the Spanish crown not to punish the mutineers. Would a despot act that way?"

CHAPTER 9

A Ship Without a Name

The question remained as to whether the wreck lying off the Panama coast really is the *Vizcaína*. Might someone else have anchored in the bay of Playa Damas, off Nombre de Dios, during the same period and abandoned it there?

The Treaty of Tordesillas, signed in 1494, divided the world along a north-south meridian, according Spain the western and Portugal the eastern half of the world. In 1498 King Ferdinand and Queen Isabella realized that the Spanish half was far too vast for Columbus to explore alone. A year later the crown authorized four more expeditions. Although these voyages were expensive and financing was tricky, anyone who could afford to do so simply left. Those unable to finance an expedition also set sail, turning to piracy instead. Alonso de Ojeda, for example, seized the ship that eventually took him to the New World.

This did not remain an exclusively Spanish boom. The British, and in particular John Cabot, were not far behind. In 1509 Cabot's son Sebastian announced that he had discovered Canada. Feeling cheated, the Portuguese ceased to show respect for the Tordesillas dividing line and sent the Côrte-Real brothers racing across the Atlantic. Nonetheless, Spain remained the leader in the chase for new lands. Between 1499 and 1505, according to Donald

Keith, Spain organized at least eleven voyages of discovery into the New World.

Alonso de Ojeda, Juan de la Cosa, and Amerigo Vespucci all set off from Spain in 1499, parting ways off the coast of South America. Vespucci sailed farther south, past the Amazon delta, while the other two sailed north. A few days later, Pedro Alonso Niño and Cristóbal Guerra arrived at the same spot but missed the others. (Chance meetings in the New World were extremely rare occurrences, given the amount of territory being explored.) Commanded by Vicente Yáñez Pinzón, a third fleet also set sail but lost two ships near the Bahamas. Diego de Lepe later followed Pinzón's route. Nonetheless, he failed to discover any islands of note.

In 1500 Alonso Vélez de Mendoza and Juan Luis Guerra sailed along the Brazilian coast and claimed the country for the Spanish crown, oblivious to the fact that Pedro Álvars Cabral had already claimed the territory for Portugal. At the same time, Amerigo Vespucci was en route across the Atlantic, this time sailing in a Portuguese ship. The man after whom America was later named was somewhat of a mercenary among discoverers.

Around 1502 Rodrigo de Bastidas and Juan de la Cosa sailed north in the service of the Spanish crown, passing the Isthmus of Panama until they reached Hispaniola, where they lost all four ships in a storm. They eventually made it to Santo Domingo, where they signed on with the homeward-bound fleet belonging to Francisco de Bobadilla. But they were struck by a hurricane that engulfed nineteen ships, the same hurricane that Columbus had warned Governor Ovando about. Bastidas and Cosa were lucky. They were on the only ship that made it back to Spain.

There was thus a fair amount of maritime traffic in the Caribbean, and the waterways into the New World were soon chock-full, becoming busy travel lanes. Cuba was encircled and conquered; Puerto Rico became a Spanish colony; and Ovando and his successor Diego Colón pressed for expansion. In 1512 King Ferdinand ordered his discoverers to search for the Western Passage to Asia.

According to Donald Keith, it is possible that Ponce de León discovered Florida during one of these forays. What eluded him, however, was Asia. Vasco Núñez de Balboa was more successful in this respect. He discovered the Pacific Ocean, a glorious achievement, certainly. King Ferdinand then ordered his sailors to sail around South America. Balboa's captain, Juan Díaz de Solís, filled his three ships with provisions for two and a half years but only made it as far as the Río de la Plata, where he died. One of the ships sank, and even ten years later, passing vessels were still picking up survivors who had been shipwrecked in 1516.

In 1517 the Spaniards discovered the treasures of the Aztecs. Francisco Fernández de Córdoba saw enormous wealth but paid for this discovery with his life. The natives put up fierce resistance and killed fifty-seven soldiers. In January 1518 another expedition set sail for the Yucatán, led by Juan de Grijalva, a nephew of the Cuban governor. There was no news from Grijalva for eight months, so Hernán Cortés was sent to follow his trail. Cortés took eleven ships and six hundred men on the voyage that was to mark the end of the Aztecs' legendary empire in the Yucatán. Alonso Álvarez de Pineda sailed along the Gulf Coast of North America, where he discovered the Mississippi River and Texas. He was followed by Ferdinand Magellan, also looking for a sea passage to India.

These were all formidable efforts. They were expansive and dangerous adventures. Not all of the conquistadors survived, and not all ships returned home. The question is, where are they?

Donald Keith spent years rummaging in archives, reading everything he could find: letters, court files, tax returns, and bank statements. He compiled a list of ships lost between 1492 and 1520.

1492:   *Discoverer:* Columbus; *model of ship: nao; name: Santa María; location:* bay of Caracol, Hispaniola

1494:   Columbus; caravels; *Maríagalante* and *Gallega;* La Isabela Bay, Hispaniola

1495: 1. Columbus; caravels; *San Juan* and *Cardera*; La Isabela Bay, Hispaniola

2. Juan de Aguado; four ships; names unknown; La Isabela Bay, Hispaniola

1498: John Cabot; four ships; names unknown; North America

1499: Alonso de Ojeda; caravel; name unknown; Jacmel Bay, Hispaniola

1500: Vicente Yáñez Pinzón; two caravels; names unknown; Bahamas

1501: 1. Gaspar Côrte-Real; caravel; name and location unknown

2. Cristóbal Guerra; caravel; name unknown; Pearl Coast, Venezuela

1502: 1. Miguel Côrte-Real; caravel; name and location unknown

2. Rodrigo de Bastidas and Juan de la Cosa; four ships; models and names unknown; Bahamas; caravels, *nao,* pinnace; *San Antón, Santa María de Gracia,* third and fourth names unknown; Cape Tiburón on Hispaniola, Cape Canongia on Hispaniola, third and fourth locations unknown

3. Francisco de Bobadilla; nineteen ships off Hispaniola

4. Alonso de Ojeda; caravel; *Santa Ana;* Margarita Island

1503: 1. Alonso de Ojeda; caravel; *Magdalena;* southeast Caribbean

2. Columbus; caravels; *Gallega* and *Vizcaína;* Río Belén in Panama and "near" Portobelo in Panama

3. Gonzalo Coelho; four ships; models and names unknown; probably South America

1504: 1. Columbus; caravels; *Santiago de Palos, Capitana;* Saint Ann's Bay, Jamaica

2. Cristóbal Guerra; caravel; name unknown; near Cartagena, Colombia

3. Juan Luis Guerra; one ship; model and name unknown; Gulf of Urabá, Colombia

1505:   1. Juan Luis Guerra; model, name, and location unknown

2. Juan de la Cosa; five ships; models and names unknown; Gulf of Urabá, Colombia and southern coast of Jamaica

1508:   more than twenty ships off Santo Domingo, Hispaniola

1509:   1. Bernardino Talavera; model and name unknown; Jagua Bay, Cuba

2. Several ships off Santo Domingo, Hispaniola

1510:   1. Francisco Pizarro; pinnace; name unknown; Cape Saint Antón, Cuba

2. Sebastián de Ocampo; model and name unknown; Jagua Bay, Cuba

1511:   1. Juan de Valdivia; caravel; name unknown; Pedro Bank, south Jamaica

2. Rodrigo de Colmenares; model and name unknown; Cuba

3. Diego de Nicuesa; pinnace; name unknown; western Caribbean

1516:   Juan Díaz de Solís; model and name unknown; Messiambu, Brazil

1517:   Francisco Fernández de Córdoba; brigantine; name unknown; Champotón, Mexico

1519:   Hernán Cortés; three caravels and seven smaller ships; Veracruz, Mexico

1520:   1. Diego de Camargo; two caravels; names unknown; near Veracruz, Mexico

2. Miguel Díaz de Aux; model and name unknown; near Veracruz, Mexico

3. Alonso Álvarez de Pineda; two ships; models and names unknown; Pánuco, Mexico
4. Pánfilo de Narváez; model and name unknown; Veracruz, Mexico
5. Hernán Cortés; three ships; models and names unknown; Veracruz, Mexico
6. Ferdinand Magellan; model unknown; *Santiago;* Río de Santa Cruz

The list contains more than one hundred shipwrecks. Whether they went down in the high seas or while anchored in protected bays, all have been at the mercy of the destructive forces of nature for nearly five centuries.

This list would seem to preclude the possibility that someone other than Columbus abandoned his ship in the bay off Nombre de Dios. Nobody went there before Columbus, and nobody went there until years after he had left. Diego de Nicuesa, an adventurer and excellent sailor, was the next captain to sail into the bay, roughly a decade after Columbus. Nicuesa stayed and founded the village of Nombre de Dios. The wreck therefore could have once been part of Nicuesa's fleet, though it seems highly unlikely that he would have left cannons and anchors behind. That would have been wasteful and ill-advised.

Another possibility was that the wreck off Nombre de Dios is that of a ship built in the New World. Were that so, it would have set sail from Santo Domingo and never been registered in European shipping registers. It could have been one of those moonlighting vessels that operated without official authorization from the Spanish crown. The ocean seas were full of fare dodgers—pirates and captains looking to avoid paying taxes. This could explain why no other ships were posted in the registries under the heading "sank off the coast of Panama." Perhaps this ship never officially existed.

This is a problem that underwater archaeologists constantly face. Until they can clearly identify a ship—or, as Felipe Castro from Texas A&M put it, "When we find the captain's driver's license"—everything remains conjecture. Donald Keith has seen the wreck off Nombre de Dios, as has his Tallahassee colleague Roger Smith. The last sixteenth-century wreck that Smith worked on was the Pensacola Bay Wreck, a galleon that Smith likened to "a kind of furniture truck." The ship measured ninety-seven feet in length and was thirty-one feet wide. Smith's team found a large number of weapons, tools, and trade goods; they were able to establish that it had to have sunk in 1559, when an enormous hurricane raged off the coast of Florida. Four Spanish ships had been en route to build a settlement in Pensacola Bay. They had priests on board, as well as women and horses. All four ships went down. Smith and his team speculate that the wreck they found was either the *Jesús,* the fleet's flagship—commanded by Diego López, who drowned in the 1559 hurricane—or the *Saint Andres,* the second-largest ship in the fleet. But the "driver's license," the ultimate piece of evidence, remains missing to this day.

Should underwater archaeologists fail to find proof positive of identity, they do the best with what they have. They compare weapons, structural details, and salvaged artifacts with data from other wrecks, which enables them to estimate the year the ship sank, even its name and history. If they find cannons with stone balls and wood without metal fittings, they know that the wreck is old. Donald Keith knows every wreck from the Age of Discovery. He has seen them all. "The perfect wreck is fully equipped, sank in a protective harbor, and has never been plundered," he wrote. The problem is that there is no perfect wreck. None of the more than one hundred ships on Keith's list has ever been found. Put another way, not one of the previously discovered wrecks has ever been identified as belonging to the discoverers. These wrecks lie on reefs and sandbanks, usually in shallow water. The currents and marine life quickly destroy anything wooden, but the warm and salty waters of the Caribbean also speed the process of encrustation that protects anything made of stone and metal.

Underwater archaeologists see hundreds of wrecks during their professional careers, but only three, possibly four, wrecks truly fire their imagination. At Texas A&M they call them "the wrecks of your lifetime." Given that the conservation, preservation, and analysis take ten years or more, three or four wrecks amount to thirty or forty years in an archaeologist's career. The wreck from Nombre de Dios, whether or not it turns out to be the *Vizcaína*, "could definitely become the wreck of my life," said Filipe Castro. In the same way that the Molasses Reef Wreck without question became the wreck of Donald Keith's life. He wrote his doctoral thesis about it, as well as a book and several articles.

In 1982 Keith received an invitation from the government of Turks and Caicos to study a wreck found on a six-foot-deep coral reef in the southeast of the islands. Keith and his team quickly realized that this was something special. They saw harquebusiers, the typical fifteenth-century firearm and forerunner to the musket. A few were still being used in the early sixteenth century but only rarely. The divers also found many cast-iron cannonballs dating back to the late fifteenth century, a mound of ballast stones measuring thirty-five by ten feet and weighing thirty-five tons, as well as ceramics of Spanish origin. The researchers applied inductive reasoning, drawing conclusions about provenance from the artifacts discovered on board. They found padding material between the planks and long wooden dowels inserted at an angle to connect the ribs to the keel. This method of construction was typical of Basque ships. The hull was made of oak, connected by iron studs and thick wooden pegs. They found pots and bowls, plates, and containers for olive oil—all from Spain. But there was no jewelry, no trading goods, and no glass. Everything served a practical purpose; there had been no need for decorative accessories. They found two small anchors, presumably for immediate use, as well as a huge anchor below deck and many tiny anchors for the small boats. They also found the kind of bombards and versos researchers had become familiar with from other Spanish ships. Faced with the threat of pirates and rebellious natives in the New World, typical weaponry in the early sixteenth century consisted of two bombards, two particularly strong versos, called *versos dobles,* and fourteen smaller versos.

The team from Texas A&M concluded that they had found a Spanish caravel from the late fifteenth or early sixteenth century. The reconstructed hull revealed that the ship measured around sixty-five feet. Possibly it was from the Age of Discovery. Or it was one of the first slave ships. Vicente Yáñez Pinzón had traveled through this region, but so had Ponce de León. Archaeologists often face the problem of being unable to find the last piece of the puzzle because it simply no longer exists. The answer may lie close at hand, but the question remains whether the team from Texas A&M would ever find it. The same question faced those working on the wreck in Nombre de Dios.

The world has been discovered, and the Age of Discovery is long past. "Only archaeology comes close to this era, in a dual sense," said Donny Hamilton. "Archaeologists can really decipher many of the mysteries surrounding the Age of Discovery. Archaeologists understand the discoverers and their era. Ships, for example, never transported just goods; they always conveyed ideas. That is why archaeologists tend to feel a bit like discoverers themselves. And that is why I became an archaeologist."

Entering the nautical archaeology department at Texas A&M can seem humbling. Artifacts from the Uluburun Shipwreck are displayed outside room 128, the Old World Laboratory. The wreck was discovered in 1982, and the project was finally completed in 1994. The Uluburun Shipwreck, found on a 130-foot-deep precipice off Turkey, is the oldest wreck ever fished out of the water—it is estimated to be thirty-three hundred years old. Archaeologists found oil canisters, a kind of fishing hook, knives, swords, a bronze statue, and a golden goblet. The ship did not feature a distinctive keel, nor did it carry any ballast stones. The load served to stabilize the ship. Somewhere around 2 percent of the hull, no more than a few wooden fragments, could be salvaged.

For Cemal Pulak, who has worked at Texas A&M since 1980, the Uluburun Shipwreck was the ship of his lifetime. Pulak and his colleagues, the underwater archaeologists at Texas A&M, work in an ochre-colored three-story building in the middle of the huge campus. Corridors that smell like a hospital lead to classrooms, a ship's model shop, and the offices of the Institute of Nautical Archaeology (INA). This institute is also headed by Texas A&M's Nautical Archaeology Program. Although INA does exactly the same work, it is a private institute, enabling it to raise funds. This frees it up administratively. Depending on the objectives and issues involving a particular project, the two organizations can decide which one would be the most appropriate to oversee operations, Texas A&M or INA.

Donny Hamilton heads both departments. His offices are some 160 feet apart, which means he spends a lot of time walking between the two because he tends to forget where he might have left some vital piece of paper. It also means that the two departments work closely together and share tasks. Before he explained how he planned to approach the wreck off Nombre de Dios, Hamilton wanted to show us something. He led us to the Conservation Research Laboratory, a fifteen-minute walk away. It consists of a simple white building with a wooden roof. During the Second World War, it served as a firehouse; today it constitutes the hub of Hamilton's work. This is where the "nonsexy part" of underwater archaeology takes place, the conservation and preservation. This aspect of the job can take five, eight, or even ten years.

Several large rainwater tanks stand outside in the courtyard. Because of rising water costs, every gallon collected saves Hamilton money. The smaller tanks and tubs house cannons. Tubes lead into the bubbling and hissing tanks. The golden rule of conservation is that artifacts remain in a constant wet state, to prevent encrustations from hardening further. The iron in the cannons can only be conserved by electrolytic rust removal, to prevent it from oxidizing and disintegrating. Iron is far more brittle and unstable than wood. Buried under a layer of sand, wood can be preserved for a thousand years; iron lasts for two hundred. Wood is relatively easy to conserve with an alcohol-and-sugar solution, but iron rusts in water, and if it is brought on land, it rusts all over again. That explains why often only the handles and shafts of axes and hammers are found on wrecks, but not the heads.

Forklift trucks transport the heavy artifacts to a warehouse where Hamilton's colleague Peter Fix has reconstructed the hull of a wreck called *La Belle*. He can heave the ship out of water at the push of a button. Inside there are dozens of file cabinets, "even the smallest piece gets its own index card," explained Hamilton. Careful organization is yet another one of the golden rules of archaeology; otherwise one can easily forget which piece of wood or which clay handle belongs to which ship.

Web cameras transmit live broadcasts on the Internet, and there are plenty of workbenches for people like Helen C. Dewolf, associate professor at the Archaeological Preservation Research Laboratory. "I love every single piece of wood. You have to love it, otherwise you'd go mad." Drills and rulers, glue and books are everywhere, and charts and graphs and maps line the walls. Classical music plays in the background, and the Cuban flag as well as the Stars and Stripes hang from the ceiling. In the back there is an X-ray machine behind a sign reading: "Caution! Radiation Area."

This is where Donny Hamilton and Filipe Castro planned how they intended to work on the wreck off Nombre de Dios. Hamilton began with a caution. "Some of the things down there have become so entangled that they have grown into one massive block that can't be moved. We have to use a jackhammer."

"And that," added Castro, "is always dicey because you can't prevent smaller pieces from being destroyed." Hamilton explained the procedure. "You have to divide the huge chunk as carefully as possible and then x-ray the smaller pieces in the lab. Then we begin working with chemicals to try and loosen all the deposits."

Castro outlined the seven stages of their work.

1. The wreck would be salvaged in chunk-sized pieces and then loaded up and taken to Texas. First the cannons

and anchors, and then the ballast stones and shards, and finally the hull. Larger chunks would be divided into smaller pieces. Everything is photographed and analyzed, and every discovery is recorded.

2. The coarser deposits are removed using hammers, chisels, and drills; and the finer deposits are then separated using knives and tweezers. Everything is photographed, measured, and recorded.

3. Electrolysis in the tanks and tubs begins. This is a long process. In the case of cannons, it can take up to a year. Every day the artifacts are fished out of the water and deposits are removed by hand, and then the artifacts go back into the bubbling water.

4. Chemicals help in the conservation process. Finally, the artifacts reach the stage where they shine and glint. They are photographed and measured again.

5. This is the most exciting part of the work: the hull is reconstructed inch by inch. What angle did the beams and ribs form? How were they attached? How were the pegs and dowels driven through which holes?

6. "And then the artifacts are ready to be transported back to Panama," said Castro, "where they will hopefully have built a museum to house the exhibition."

7. Models of the ship will be built at Texas A&M; examination papers and doctorates will be written as well as articles and books. Many publications will be written if the wreck off Nombre de Dios does turn out to be the *Vizcaína*.

"But presumably it will take awhile before we know," Castro added.

When Wolfram zu Mondfeld first saw the underwater photographs of the wreck off Nombre de Dios, he was nervous. It was as if he had spent thirty years waiting for something, only to suddenly see it and then be forced to believe that it was worth the wait. Mondfeld has spent thirty years investigating the ships used by the discoverers, the caravels. Neither a historian nor an underwater archaeologist, he nonetheless knows as much as there is to know about these ships. He specializes in them at the German Museum of Technology in Berlin and has built many of the ship's models exhibited there. So far model builders have been driven to despair by these caravels. Mondfeld spends hundreds of hours gluing and filing in an attempt to reconstruct every last anchor capstan, to make it as true to the original as possible, right down to the smallest peg. His models are built to a scale of 1:50, and while that may be small—a caravel of this scale measures less than one and a half feet from bow to the stern—he cannot afford any inaccuracies.

That, of course, poses a problem, given that nobody knows exactly what these ships looked like. Caravels, which did more to change the world than any other ship, have disappeared almost without a trace. There is no wreck from which to copy the design plan. There are no design plans from which to reconstruct a caravel. The constructional drawings have been lost—if they ever existed at all. So far no researcher has ever been able to find more than a few planks belonging to a caravel. These have been either from the Caribbean or Africa's western coast, not even from where they were originally built, in the waters off the Iberian Peninsula. Mondfeld needs the facts. Like so many others, he has studied old engravings, paintings, and coins to get a sense of what these ships could have looked like. But even under a magnifying glass, these images reveal only a few details.

Using submarines, divers have located Roman galleys in the Mediterranean; treasure hunters have plundered sunken Chinese porcelain junks; and archaeologists have dug Viking dragon ships out of the silt of the Schlei River and the Roskilde Fjord. Only the search for the caravels, which are a much more recent phenomenon than the galleys or dragon ships, has remained unsuccessful. Echoing something Filipe Castro had said, Mondfeld complained that they knew more about the ships used by the Vikings than about the ships used to discover the New World. The same questions asked by historians and archaeologists for generations continue to be asked. How was the hull constructed? How stable were they? How much wind and waves could they endure? What were their chances in rough seas? Where did they stow the anchors? How were the cannons mounted? Researchers know that caravels were highly maneuverable and fast; that they had a low draft, making them ideal for expeditions into shallower waters. But how low was the draft? The question is, what could men like Columbus, Magellan, Vespucci, Ojeda, or Cortés do with these ships and what could they not do? Where could they have sailed to, and what destinations were beyond their reach?

That was why Mondfeld became fascinated by these underwater pictures from the Caribbean. "This find is a sensation. That is a caravel lying there. And that means we will be able to document a ship like that for the very first time." Mondfeld has yet to see the wreck himself. But the images and the sketch maps drawn up by the divers seem clear enough to him—clear enough for him to risk giving the ship a name. "The *Vizcaína*. This could be the *Vizcaína*." In Mondfeld's eyes, one of the stronger pieces of evidence was that the planks of the wreck lay directly in the sand. He could see immediately that there were no lead plates. Lead plates would have signified that this ship did not date back to Columbus's time. Lead is imperishable. It never rusts and never crumbles, and it is far too heavy to be washed away by the currents. If there was no lead there now, then there never had been any lead on the ship.

Mondfeld claimed that the royal decree issued in 1508 about employing lead sheathing to deal with shipworm tilted things toward Columbus. This ship must have left Spain prior to 1509. "Just this once, it was a good decree, a sensible decree. Ships were very expensive at the time. Even the wood was incredibly expensive. The Spaniards were forced to laboriously import timber from the north." This is why Mondfeld believes that following the decree, ship's owners and captains were probably very quick to nail inch-thick lead plates to their hulls.

Mondfeld admitted, however, that there might be alternative explanations for the lack of lead sheathing. The ship could have belonged to a careless captain or to a ship's owner lacking the necessary means to pay for the lead plates. It could have belonged to an adventurer who cared little for royal decrees or to pirates, who cared little about anything. Were any of these the case, the ship could be a lot younger. Nonetheless, Mondfeld remained convinced. At the very latest, by the time Columbus returned from his fourth voyage, every sailor must have known "that there was a sea monster living over there that could eat ships faster than they could be built." Everyone in Spain would have known that the *Teredo navalis,* which grows to be as thick as a thumb, could sink ships, and destroy valuable cargo. Setting sail in an unprotected ship would have made no sense.

Furthermore, lead plates offered additional advantages that would have made immediate sense to any sailor. They could protect a ship when it ran aground on a reef. They even protected against coral, which could slice a hull open in shallow surf. Lead was tremendously useful as ballast, which helped ships stay upright even in high waves and kept them from capsizing. Without ballast, no sailing ship would have ever gotten out of the harbor in one piece. Prior to the 1508 decree, the Spaniards hauled blocks of stone into the hulls of their ships—a cheap solution and a bad one. After 1509 the stones were thrown overboard and the holds emptied. Sailors were able to store more provisions on their way to the New World and bring more treasure back home. Sheathing the hull in lead conferred too many advantages for Mondfeld not to believe that the wreck off Nombre de Dios dated to Columbus's time.

Mondfeld also examined the cannons protruding from the wreck carefully. "Banded wrought-iron cannons," he announced without hesitation. Salt water and iron are incompatible, particularly in the humid heat of the tropics, where sailors could watch rust form. When Columbus set sail on his fourth voyage, cast-bronze cannons were state of the art, according to Mondfeld, but they were also expensive. Due to the cost, some Spaniards had been forced to continue using banded wrought-iron cannons. "These cannons were antiquated but they were cheap." The wrought-iron versions functioned abysmally; they were little better than slingshots that thundered and smoldered. They were built by blacksmiths, who bundled iron rods together, then pulled iron rings over the rods and welded them as best they could. "Very often, these cannons posed a greater danger to the ship than they did to the enemy. Sometimes they simply exploded."

And even if the cannons fired true shots, the balls never flew very far. "A few hundred meters at most," said Mondfeld. This was due to a flaw in construction—the seal between the powder chamber and the forged muzzle. When loading, the cannoneer would first push a cannonball into the muzzle from the back. Then he would press in a stopper, usually a cloth scrap or anything that happened to be lying around. His helpers would insert a powder chamber, an iron box full of gunpowder. Although the powder chamber extended into the muzzle, it was funnel shaped and the sailors would usually wedge it in from behind with a peg or dowel. But there was seldom a tight seal between the chamber and the muzzle, and the explosion often fizzled out to the side, leaving no more than a feeble puff to blow the cannonball out of the muzzle.

Antiquated or inadequate weaponry was another useful indication, in Mondfeld's view. Columbus had limited financial means for equipping his ships. He had been forced to economize. He had not been anticipating a battle at sea, and the antiquated cannons would suffice to impress the natives with a show of force. Mondfeld claimed that this was in keeping with the fourth voyage—like the position of the cannons on the wreck. "Normally, the cannons would have been spread out along the railing." Therefore, they should have been spread out along the mound of the wreck. But off Nombre de Dios, many of the cannons had been found lying in a heap. "It is very likely that they were just piled up on deck. And that would support the Columbus theory, for, after all, the *Vizcaína* didn't just sink; she was abandoned on purpose."

Mondfeld even believes that he can reconstruct the final moments of the *Vizcaína*. "They probably roped two ships together side by side in the bay. And then they off-loaded everything they needed, leaving all they could spare on the *Vizcaína*, even the cannons. Then they probably hacked holes into her hull and cast off. She was so full of wormholes that a sharp kick would probably have been enough to sink her. And they probably had to sink her in order not to reveal all their technology to the Indians."

That certainly sounds plausible. Mondfeld finds it hard to believe that the ship could have belonged to anyone but Columbus. The only person he can think of is Rodrigo de Bastidas, the notary from Triana, near Seville, who obtained a license from the Spanish crown authorizing him to discover lands that Columbus had missed on his first voyages. Armed with his license, Bastidas immediately set sail in two ships. The document is housed at the Archivo General de Indias in Seville.

Bastidas had accompanied Columbus on his second voyage. His plan was to trade with the natives and return to Spain a wealthy man. He did accumulate riches, in what is now Venezuela and Colombia, and he sailed north along the Panamanian coast. It is highly probable that he came to Nombre de Dios and Portobelo. His ships were also plagued by the *Teredo navalis,* and his crew was forced to careen the ships en route; in the end, it was all hands to the pumps. "As far as we know," explained Mondfeld, "Bastidas managed to bring his ships home in one piece." According to Donald Keith's list, however, either he or Juan de la Cosa lost four ships.

Filipe Castro's office at Texas A&M is filled with books, sea charts, and world maps, but he spends most of his time traveling. "The best moments in my career are when you slip into your diving gear and get ready to discover a new wreck," such as when he visited the site in Nombre de Dios in 2003.

"What a wreck. There must have been about twenty-six by ten feet of the hull still left. That's a dream for us. The wreck is in exactly the spot Columbus is said to have lost the *Vizcaína*. But we have to be careful about hypothesizing. From an archaeological point of view, this is like hitting the jackpot—if the wreck turns out to be a caravel from the first thirty years of the sixteenth century. And yet everything seems to speak in favor of that."

The term "caravel" first appeared in Italy in the eleventh century and was applied to fishing vessels. In the twelfth and thirteenth centuries, the caravel had disappeared, for this was the age of the cog. The cogs were followed by what are known as *cocas,* small merchant ships. "They had a large, square sail, which enabled them to sail downwind at high speed, and a triangular sail that made the ship very maneuverable," explained Castro. The disadvantage was that the sails were rigged quite close to the bow, concentrating the forces there and making the ship hard to control. Over time the masts moved toward the back, particularly the mainmast. Europe's sailors developed the ships we are still familiar with today. The model called the *nao,* first mentioned in 1409, was a ship with a mainmast and space for additional sails at the bow and stern. With the *nao,* the caravel returned to Spain and Portugal, although it was used far longer in Spain.

Castro explained that the technology we take for granted in shipbuilding today was first developed around 1450. Instead of timbering one plank to the other, shipbuilders designed a frame, a kind of skeleton, and the planks were aligned to fit the form of the frame. "We assume that caravels were built in much the same way, but we don't know." That is one of the things the team hopes to discover in Nombre de Dios.

After several dives Castro believes that the wreck off Panama was a vessel with a capacity of fifty tons. The shape of the planks would fit, but the anchors are extraordinarily large. He was surprised by the thickness of the planks, measuring nearly two and a half inches. Given the measurements taken underwater, Castro concluded that they were dealing with a ship that measured fifty-nine feet from bow to stern, stood at forty-nine feet above the waterline, and measured thirty-nine feet at the keel. "We will know for sure at some stage." The question is what does Castro believe? "Wishful thinking and false theories can ruin an archaeologist's career," he replied, sidestepping the issue. "Of course, I would love to salvage one of Columbus's ships—that would be spectacular. I'll wait and see."

Sitting in his INA office, Donny Hamilton was exasperated that nothing was happening in Panama. The government had yet to give its okay, and Nilda Vázquez's company was still jealously guarding the salvaged cannons. "They haven't even drawn a sketch." Were the archaeologists allowed to bring just one cannon to their laboratory for a few weeks, they would know more quickly. Hamilton and Castro wrote e-mails and made phone calls to Panama, but nothing came of it. Nobody returned their calls or when they did, were noncommittal. The old battle between science and business, archaeologists and treasure hunters, was under way.

Texas A&M planned to begin work on the wreck off Nombre de Dios in the summer of 2004. They have already searched for the *Gallega* in Belén and found nothing; they were in Saint Ann's Bay and searched for the *Capitana* and the *Santiago de Palos* and found nothing. These expeditions cost around a quarter of a million dollars each. This time, however, things are different. This time there was a wreck. What remained was for it to be identified. The problem was that this wreck lay in the sovereign territory of a country with its own turf battles and its own ways of doing business.

Castro had drawn up a timetable, estimating that the project would take ten years:

> 2004: *Build a laboratory and commence with analysis and conservation of the artifacts; careful survey at the discovery site*
> 2005: *Conservation and study of the artifacts; begin archaeological recovery*

*2006: Conservation and study of the artifacts; complete
archaeological recovery*
*2007/2008: Conservation and study of the artifacts by a joint
team (local and Texas A&M)*
*2009–2012: Conservation and analysis of the artifacts by the local
team*

"We have to be very careful because we might have to conduct a third salvage season to protect the wreck," added Castro.

Hamilton was impatient and had wanted things to begin immediately. He shared Castro's views on the *Vizcaína,* basing it on the discovery of a large number of bombard cannons. "They have not yet been found on any other ship in the New World, for they were not commonly used after 1500. That probably means that this is a very early ship."

Hamilton has been at Texas A&M for about thirty years. Originally, he had been interested in prehistoric archaeology— land-based rather than underwater. But at the time, he had a wife and children to support and no job. "I would have taken on anything just to make money," he admitted. He was offered a job at the Conservation Research Lab, and when George Bass, a kind of father figure for underwater archaeologists, founded the Institute of Nautical Archaeology in the mid-1970s, he offered Hamilton a position. Today, of course, Hamilton is head of the department. He has fifty students in his program, although he himself never studied what he now teaches. "He can simply do it," said Castro. "Sometimes people can be geniuses." Hamilton dislikes talking about himself, preferring to speak about his team and the twenty or thirty projects they are currently working on. "We are by far the best in the world. We have two or three times more artifacts than all the other institutes together." There are a number of places considered to be first rate in underwater archaeology: Flinders University in Australia, the University of Southampton in England, East Carolina University, and Florida State University. Not one of them has the reputation of Texas A&M.

Reputation, however, counts for nothing when things in Panama are not moving forward. While Texas A&M has a plan that would involve researchers and students from Brazil, Mexico, and Panama, and that would lead to the transfer of the ship to a museum in Panama, there are people in Panama who believe they could make the deal of a lifetime with this wreck. "I've already been offered artifacts on sale from the Vizcaína," wrote Warren White in an e-mail from Belén; this seems ironic, given that he was the one to announce the discovery of the wreck.

In the meantime, analysis continued—and not without its frustrations. In April 2003, in Berlin's Rathgen Research Lab, Dr. Christian Goedicke examined four ceramic shards taken from the wreck. Using a method known as thermoluminescence, which measures how long the ceramic shards were exposed to environmental radiation since being fired, Goedicke came to the following results: "Sample number 1: 1449 ± 31 years; sample number 2: 1606 ± 22 years; sample number 3: 1450 ± 34 years; sample number 4: 1561 ± 25 years."

Scholars and researchers found these results exasperating. Samples 2 and 4 were clearly too young for a wreck dating back to the early sixteenth century; samples 1 and 3 were unusually old. One theory being put forward by researchers currently working on the project is that shard samples numbers 2 and 4 did not match the very old weapons and the unsheathed wood. It could be that these shards had washed up when Nombre de Dios turned into a busy harbor after 1510. It could also be that the ballast stones or other artifacts had altered the environmental radiation to which the shards were exposed. Secondly, shards number 1 and 3 could have originated from containers that had been reused. The only certainty is that no European ship could have anchored here in the mid-fifteenth century. Because the four samples vary so greatly in age, the ultimate conclusion is that they reveal only little.

In May 2003 Juan M. Ramírez, director of the Agriquem Laboratory in Seville, using a complicated chemical process to examine food particles left on the salvaged shards, concluded that the residual particles were olive oil, originating from south Andalusia.

In June 2003 Wolfram zu Mondfeld viewed all the data and reviewed the theories regarding the wreck and composed an impassioned summary. "If Señor de Bastidas did not leave a ship behind in exactly this place, then the wreck we are dealing with off Nombre de Dios is the *Vizcaína*, abandoned by Columbus on his fourth voyage. It would be a scientific mortal sin not to examine this wreck more closely!" He also mentioned the weaponry on board the ship. "Stone cannonballs were not in use after the early sixteenth century." Ten stone balls had been found on the wreck. With reference to the weaponry found, Mondfeld wrote, "The high number of cannons indicates that this armament is not from one ship but that cannons from more than one ship were sunk here."

In November 2003 Beta Analytic, Inc., in Miami examined another piece of wood from the wreck. The protocol stated that the C14 analysis "went according to plan. There was sufficient carbon available for an accurate measurement." There was a high probability that the wood samples dated to a period between 1530 and 1550. The finding was significant and dealt a blow to anyone hoping the wreck might be the *Vizcaína*. A ship that sank in 1503 could hardly have been built from timber taken from a tree that was felled between 1530 and 1550. Professor Pieter Meiert Grootes from Kiel analyzed the same sample and confirmed the result. "You have to take values that don't suit your theory just as seriously as values that confirm your dream—anything else just wouldn't be scientific," argued Filipe Castro. "You can't build an entire house on just one tiny piece of wood," said Grootes. "Of course, mistakes are possible when measuring these samples. And if you go back five hundred years, then you have to include a margin of error of about thirty or forty years." In the case of the *Vizcaína*, thirty or forty years would be vital.

Salvage work in Nombre de Dios continued to be delayed into 2004. Nilda Vázquez and her treasure-hunting company were unwilling to begin. They wanted money. The Panamanian government and their appointed archaeologist, Carlos Fitzgerald, either opted not to get involved or were unable to assert their authority. Nothing was happening. Filipe Castro sent e-mail after e-mail. When he finally managed to get Vázquez on the phone, she told him that a Florida-based company belonging to treasure hunter Kim Fisher had told her this wreck was worth millions. Gassan Salama was obviously "convinced that he could change the laws, make masses of money, and find dozens of wrecks," Castro complained. George Bass, the man who had founded INA, wrote, "I've been in the business for forty-three years and have never heard of a country that derived any financial advantage from collaborating with treasure hunters. On the other hand, museums based on the work of underwater archaeologists in Turkey, Cyprus, Israel, England, and Sweden, to name only those I have visited, have all become major tourist attractions that have brought their governments admission fees and created revenue from taxi rides, hotel stays, flights, and restaurants, et cetera."

Nilda Vázquez and Gassan Salama continued to hold the keys to the freshwater tanks where the artifacts found on the wreck are stored. Nobody in Panama seemed to have the power to force them to hand them over. Castro continued to make his pleas. To Salama he wrote:

> We plan to bring a team to Nombre de Dios and draw up a comprehensive map of the discovery site, then salvage the cannons, draw another sketch, map out the ballast and salvage it, and then describe the hull. Then comes the tough part: We will decide whether it is possible to salvage the hull, taking a protocol of each piece of wood and creating a 3D model of the rest of the hull. Then we can ascertain whether your museum has the means to exhibit the hull, and decide how we can salvage and conserve the wood and reconstruct it in a museum. . . . Then we can begin constructing replicas to be sold in a future museum and for presentations in touring exhibitions.

In mid-January 2004 Castro flew to Panama City for a summit meeting with Vázquez, her son Ernesto, Governor Salama, and the diver Karl Vandenhole. The participants asserted that their only goals were to further research, advance science, and benefit the population of Panama. Everyone agreed that Texas A&M would be an excellent partner for this project. Everyone asserted that they were willing to put aside their egotism and work constructively toward completing it. Gassan Salama added that, naturally, it would be impossible for him to forgo the opportunity of selling off artifacts found on the wreck.

And therein lies the root of the problem. Nobody wants to touch an archaeological project that is scheduled to last a decade and cost millions without the assurance that the artifacts will not turn up on eBay and then disappear without a trace.

Negotiations broke down. Castro flew back to Texas. The case dragged on for weeks and months, then years. Time and again, he flew down to Panama, conducted talks, and waited for negotiations to continue. Time and again he was told, "We know you do serious work" and "Nobody wants the treasure hunters to sell cannons," but he never received permission to begin salvaging the wreck. Ultimately, Castro spoke or wrote to everyone involved. Now he can do no more than wait.

Then there were the rumors—such as, for example, that the wreck had disappeared. Divers went to look and found the wreck still there, unscathed. Then Nilda Vázquez's authorization expired; everybody hoped this meant that the archaeologists could finally and immediately commence salvage operations. But Panama's Supreme Court is considering the case and it is uncertain when or whether the judges will hand down a ruling.

On September 19, 2005, Texas A&M received a fax from Reinier Rodríguez, the new director general of INAC:

> After reviewing your "Proyecto de Arqueología Subacuática Playa Damas" submitted on May 11, 2005, we regret to inform you that we will be unable to issue the permits to dive, explore, and excavate the site.
>
> The Panamanian Supreme Court has provisionally suspended all activities at the Playa Damas site due to a lawsuit

presented against the salvage contract held between the salvage company that worked there and the Direction of Cadaster and Patrimonial Assets of the Ministry of Economy and Finances. Thus, while the Supreme Court Justices come to a final decision, it is impossible to conduct any kind of research at Playa Damas. However, we remain very interested in maintaining a fruitful and amicable relationship.

The wreck that has been lying in the bay off Nombre de Dios for five hundred years will lie there for a while longer.

CHAPTER 10

Conclusion

Christopher Columbus could be both remarkably clever and astonishingly dense. He was driven hard by his hopes and dreams yet unable to let go of his misprisions and unwilling to correct his mistakes. The combination led him to make some grotesquely bad decisions. He returned to Spain, expecting that everyone would be anticipating that very moment. He looked forward to being invited to the royal courts to relate his adventures. But nobody wanted anything to do with Columbus. The king and queen regarded the Lettera Rarissima as the final proof that he had gone over the edge.

On November 8 or 9, he returned to Seville, where he learned that Isabella was holding court in Segovia. Shortly afterward she fell ill, and on November 26, 1504, she "passed to a better life," wrote Fernando. This was more than simply a sad occasion for Columbus—it was politically fatal. Isabella had understood and sponsored him for years; she had accepted him for what he was. Now there was nobody left.

Columbus was a wealthy man. He had brought back gold from his fourth voyage. Moreover, he still had the gold that had survived the hurricane off Santo Domingo, and—surprisingly enough—he also had a coffer of gold that had been sent to him by Governor Ovando. Nonetheless, Columbus railed against his fate. He was consumed by self-pity. The only thing that interested him was his "tenth, eighth, and third."

The contract Columbus signed with the crown in 1492 granted him 10 percent of all the removable assets found in the newly discovered lands—his "tenth." King Ferdinand, however, only paid Columbus a tenth of the fifth belonging to the crown, amounting to 2 percent rather than 10. Columbus had been promised an eighth of the profits from all merchant ships traveling from the Indian colonies—his "eighth." Ovando and the others, however, were unwilling to hand over anything they considered to be theirs, certainly no more than the coffer of gold that rightfully belonged to Columbus. A passage in the Capitulations stated that, like the grand admiral of Castile, Columbus was entitled to levy a 33.3 percent tax on all trade in his jurisdiction—his "third." This would have meant that Columbus would have been the only one to profit from the discovery of America, which was of course unrealistic. He might have realized that no monarch would or could be that generous. Anyway, these agreements were based upon future trade with India, not America.

Columbus rented a house in Seville. While he found "relief from his many hardships and exertions," as Fernando wrote, the discoverer was unable to find peace of mind. After a lifetime of adventure, he could not resign himself to spending his remaining years in a state of repose. In a noble gesture on his part, Columbus sent letters urging and begging the high treasurer of Castile to settle the accounts of those sailors who had accompanied him on his High Voyage. Centuries later researchers assumed that his efforts were in vain, that it had been an "abortive attempt," and that "most of the survivors who came home with the Admiral arrived penniless," as Morison noted.

Consuelo Varela, however, has documented that the opposite was true. Columbus's entreaties were successful, if not for his own personal gain, then at least for his crews. Little by little, the sailors received their wages. Varela found the first payment instruction, the "Primera carta-nómina" for the equipment on the four ships. The crews' wages were paid with a disbursement signed by the crown in Segovia on May 28, 1505, ordering the payment of 326,852 *maravedís* and 4 *cornados*. There was a payment list, the "Primera nómina de pago" dating back to August 5, 1505, which listed twenty-five members of the crew who had received a total of 623,573 *maravedís*. In addition, there was a second payment order signed on November 2, 1505, instructing the paymaster Sancho de Matienzo to disburse a total of 673,858 *maravedís* to the thirty-eight men who had remained on Hispaniola. As a result, there was also a second payment list, dating to August 8, 1506, that mentions thirty-eight men who received a total of 475,393 *maravedís*. This was far less than had been instructed, but there was always a little shrinkage in these matters.

As the months passed, Columbus realized that he had come to the end of his voyages. He was fifty-three years old and a sick man. He knew that he could not realistically be reinstated as viceroy and governor of Hispaniola. He concentrated his efforts upon saving his reputation, protecting his legacy, and ensuring his sons' future. He was particularly proud of Diego, who had married Doña María de Toledo, a blue-blooded cousin of the king, and been accepted into the highest circles of Spanish society. Diego had set his sights on securing his father's rights and titles. He wanted to become a governor in the New World. Unlike his father, however, he never spoke openly of his goals. He simply smiled and advanced. On November 21, 1504, Columbus wrote Diego:

> *Very dear son,*
>
> *I was very much pleased to hear the contents of your letter and what the King our Lord said, for which you kissed his royal hands. It is certain that I have served their Highnesses with as much diligence and love as though it had been to gain Paradise, and more, and if I have been at fault in anything it has been because it was impossible or because my knowledge and strength were not sufficient. God, our Lord, in such a case, does not*

require more from persons than the will. At the request of the Treasurer Morales, I left two brothers in the Indies, who are called Porras. The one was captain and the other auditor. Both were without capacity for these positions. . . . They rebelled on the island of Jamaica, at which I was as much astonished as I would be if the sun's rays should cast darkness. I was at the point of death, and they martyred me with extreme cruelty during five months and without cause. Finally I took them all prisoners, and immediately set them free. . . . These records and the Notary are coming on another vessel, which I am expecting from day to day. . . . I had a chapter in my instructions in which their Highnesses ordered all to obey me, and that I should exercise civil and criminal justice over all those who were with me: but this was of no avail with the Governor, who said that it was not understood as applying in his territory. He sent the prisoner to these Lords who have charge of the Indies without inquiry or record or writing. . . . It is not wonderful to me that our Lord punishes. They went there with shameless faces. Such wickedness or such cruel treason were never heard of.

I wrote to their Highnesses about this matter in the other letter, and said that it was not right for them to consent to this offence. I also wrote to the Lord Treasurer that I begged him as a favor not to pass sentence on the testimony given by these men until he heard me. Now it will be well for you to remind him of it anew. I do not know how they dare to go before him with such an undertaking. I have written to him about it again and have sent him the copy of the oath, the same as I send to you. . . . I commend myself to the mercy of all, with the information that my departure yonder will take place in a short time.

I would be glad to receive a letter from their Highnesses and to know what they order. You must procure such a letter if you see the means of so doing. I also commend myself to the Lord Bishop and to Juan López, with the reminder of illness and of the reward for my services.

Done in Seville, November 21

On December 27, 1504, Columbus wrote to Nicoló Oderigo, the Genoese ambassador to the Spanish court.

> *Learned Sir,*
>
> *... I arrived here very sick. At that time the Queen, my Lady, died without me seeing her, and rests with God. So far I cannot say what will become of my affairs. I believe that her Highness has provided well in her testament, and the King my Lord fulfills very well. ...*
>
> *The Admiral of the Ocean Sea
and Viceroy and Governor of India*

Columbus was mistaken in his assumption. Isabella had made no mention of Columbus in her testament, thus forcing Columbus to further pursue matters. On February 5, he wrote to his son Diego:

> *Very dear son,*
>
> *Diego Méndez left here Monday, the 3rd of this month. After his departure I talked with Amerigo Vespucci, the bearer of this letter, who is going yonder, where he is called in regard to matters of navigation.*
>
> *He was always desirous of pleasing me. He is a very honorable man. Fortune has been adverse to him as it has been to many others. His labors have not profited him as much as reason demands. He goes for me, and is very desirous of doing something to benefit me if it is in his power. ... See what he can do to profit me there, and strive to have him do it; for he will do everything, and will speak and will place it in operation, and it must all be done secretly so that there may be no suspicion. I have told him all that could be told regarding this matter, and have informed him of the payment which has been made to me and is being made. This letter is for the Lord Adelantado also, that he may see how Amerigo Vespucci can be useful, and advise him about it.*
>
> *His Highness may believe that his ships went to the best and richest of the Indies, and if anything remains to be learned*

more than has been told, I will give the information yonder ver-
bally, because it is impossible to give it in writing.
    May our Lord have you in his Holy keeping.
            Done in Seville, February 5.
    Your father who loves you more than himself.

By the spring of 1505, Columbus had recovered sufficiently to
travel to the court in Segovia by mule. The aim of the journey
was to fight for what he believed was his share of the profits. In
advance of his arrival, he sent a letter to the king in which he petitioned not for himself but for Diego, entreating that his son be
appointed to the government of which he, Columbus, had been
so wrongfully deprived. "This," he wrote, "is a matter which con-
cerns my honor; as to the rest, do as your Majesty may think
proper; give or withhold, as may be most for your interest, and I
shall be content. I believe the anxiety caused by the delay of this
affair is the principal cause of my ill health."

King Ferdinand welcomed him warmly, giving every appearance of royal pride in his nation's most famous mariner. He
promised to appoint a mediator to avoid troublesome legal proceedings. Columbus mistrusted the royal mediators and therefore
rejected the offer, arguing that the contracts and the issue of his
rights and titles were clear, rendering negotiations unnecessary.
Presumably, King Ferdinand could only smile indulgently before
he made a second attempt. He indicated that Columbus would
receive a beautiful house and enough money if he would simply
relinquish his claims to these dubious titles and shares. Columbus
refused. Morison concluded that in his pride Columbus wanted
everything or nothing. Now that it had become clear what riches
lay in the New World, "the King wished to regain absolute control over them," claimed Fernando.

Then as now, court proceedings could be drawn-out affairs; when
a judge had to take the wishes of the king into consideration,
they could take even longer. The court was moved from Sala-
manca to Valladolid, and though he was plagued by arthritis, Co-

lumbus followed. His condition worsened; soon he was unable to leave his bed. Realizing that this would be his final resting place, Columbus drew up his last will and testament. In anticipation of the outcome of the legal proceedings, he distributed his money and his shares among his two sons and other relatives. He also decreed that a chapel be built in Hispaniola where prayers for his soul were to be said every day.

When Columbus heard that Doña Juana, daughter of King Ferdinand and the late Queen Isabella, had arrived in Spain and asserted her claim to the throne, he took heart, hoping to receive from her the justice her father had denied him. He sent his brother Bartolomeo to Doña Juana, who would go down in history as Joanna the Mad.

On May 19, 1506, Columbus was so ill that he was barely able to speak or move. Having drawn up his testament on August 25 in Segovia, he had it ratified on May 19, 1506. Columbus wrote:

In the name of the Most Holy Trinity, who inspired me with the idea, and afterwards made it perfectly clear to me, that I could navigate and go to the Indies from Spain, by traversing the ocean westward; which I communicated to King Ferdinand and to Queen Isabel, our sovereigns; and they were pleased to furnish me the necessary equipment of men and ships, and to make me their admiral over the said ocean, in all parts lying to the west of an imaginary line, drawn from pole to pole, a hundred leagues west of the Cape Verde and Azore islands; also appointing me their viceroy and governor over all continents and islands that I might discover beyond the said line westward; with the right of being succeeded in the said offices by my eldest son and his heirs for ever; and a grant of the tenth part of all things found in the said jurisdiction; and of all rents and revenues arising from it; and the eighth of all the lands and every thing else, together with the salary corresponding to my rank of admiral, viceroy, and governor, and all other emoluments accruing thereto, as is more fully expressed in the title and agreement sanctioned by their highnesses. . . .

And as we hope in God that before long a good and great revenue will be derived from the above islands and continent, of which, for the reasons aforesaid, belong to me the tenth and the eighth, with the salaries and emoluments specified above… wherefore I have concluded to create an entailed estate (mayorazgo) out of the said eighth of the lands, places, and revenues, in the manner which I now proceed to state.…

Diego, or any other inheritor of this estate, shall distribute the revenue which it may please our Lord to grant him, in the following manner: Of the whole income of this estate, now and at all times, and of whatever may be had or collected from it, he shall give the fourth part annually to my brother Bartolomeo Columbus, Adelantado of the Indies; and this is to continue till he shall have acquired an income of a million maravedís… From the revenues of the said estate, or from any other fourth part of it, (should its amount be adequate to it,) shall be paid every year to my son Fernando two millions, till such time as his revenue shall amount to two millions.… Diego or Bartolomeo shall make, out of the said estate, for my brother Diego, such provision as may enable him to live decently, as he is my brother, to whom I assign no particular sum, as he has attached himself to the church.…

He was sounding the same familiar notes. At issue were his third, his eighth, and his tenth. Columbus was nothing if not persistent—even obsessed, egocentric, narcissistic. Finally, mercifully, his testament finally drew to a close. Columbus finished:

And I direct [Diego] to make provision for Beatriz Enríquez, mother of Fernando, my son, that she may be able to live honestly, being a person to whom I am under very great obligation. And this shall be done for the satisfaction of my conscience, because this matter weighs heavily upon my soul. The reason for which it is not fitting to write here.

Written on August 25, 1505, in Segovia.

Christoforus.

Columbus then listed the names of people whom he owed money: "Principally the inheritors of Gerolamo del Porto, the father of Benito del Porto, chancellor in Genoa, twenty ducats or the corresponding value" (twenty years previously Columbus and his father, Domenico, had borrowed thirty-five Genoese lire from Gerolamo del Porto, equivalent to twenty Spanish ducats); "a Jew who used to live near the Jewish Gate in Lisbon half a mark of silver to pay for a priest to pray for his soul...." It seems beyond a doubt that Columbus was plagued by a guilty conscience. It is not known, however, whether the nameless Jew was ever found or whether anybody ever even searched for him.

Columbus's life drew to its close on May 20, 1506. The Admiral of the Ocean Sea and viceroy and governor of India lay on his bed in Valladolid. No bishop attended him; no messenger came from the king, no representative of the court. In the days that followed, there would be no mention in the official chronicles of his death or of his burial. His two sons were present, Diego and Fernando, as were his youngest brother, Diego, and two friends, Bartolomeo Fieschi and Diego Méndez. They summoned a priest, who read Mass and administered last rites. "In manus tuas, Domine, commendo spiritum meum" (Into your hands, O Lord, I commend my spirit).

———

Remains of the Age

Monuments can sometimes have the opposite effect of their original intent—due either to physical grotesqueness or by seeming grotesquely out of place. El Faro a Colón, the Columbus Memorial Lighthouse, has both of these effects.

Finished in 1992 to commemorate the five hundredth anniversary of the discovery of the Americas, it is now an abandoned ruin of epic proportions, measuring 820 feet long, 328 feet wide, and 164 feet high. It was originally conceived in the form of a gigantic cross; it bears greater resemblance to a futuristic battleship. It was to have become Santo Domingo's most famous landmark: the largest lighthouse in the world. Powerful searchlights were added to project a gigantic cross that could be seen as far away as Puerto Rico. In 1992 it was illuminated from the side; vertical sheets of light shone up into the sky. The problem was that whenever the searchlights went on, power to the rest of Santo Domingo shut off. El Faro a Colón has not been illuminated in some time.

Before long the money necessary to maintaining the bronze and marble ran out; the paint on the monument's exterior began to look blotchy and muddy. The inscriptions emblazoned on the massive marble slabs—quotes from Pope John Paul II and Aristotle—are still decipherable, however. The words "CRISTÓBAL

COLÓN Gran Almirante del Océano" appear repeatedly. When it was built, the citizens of Santo Domingo failed to comprehend why their president would spend millions on this monument. They continue to ignore it. The parking lots are empty. A few joggers run along the gravel paths outside.

The monument houses permanent exhibitions, symbolizing the various nations affected by the discovery of the Americas. The United States, for example, is represented by newspaper articles detailing the events of September 11. Argentina sent wooden figurines made by the writer Jorge Luis Borges. Chile contributed some silver jewelry. Paraguay coughed up a flag. Nobody seems to want to enter the thing, whose interior has the feel of a mausoleum. That is exactly what it is, for the monument also houses the lead box containing the mortal remains of Columbus. The sarcophagus sits in the center, where the two crossbeams intersect, and rests on two marble plinths, bearing the Castilian coat of arms, the date 1492, and crosses on the front and back. The thirty-foot baldachin above the tomb bears the inscription "A Cristóbal Colón, Descubridor de América" in gold lettering. It is a gaudy piece of work, decorated with little flowers, turrets, and roaring lions. The tomb is guarded by a soldier wearing a white uniform. "Here lies Christopher Columbus," he whispered.

"Of course Columbus lies here," insisted the historian Tristán Colente. "He lay in the cathedral for centuries, and in 1992 he was moved here. Where else should he be?" The issue regarding the exact location of Columbus's remains is not as simple as Colente claimed. Indeed, finding his remains has turned into something of a challenge; researchers are currently attempting to solve the mystery by using the most advanced forensic techniques available.

For years Doña Anunciada Colón de Carvajal, the historian and Columbus descendant, has been trying to solve the mystery behind a particularly bizarre episode. She has written a substantial book on the subject, *Cristóbal Colón—Incógnitas de su muerte* (The mystery behind the death of Christopher Columbus). It is a weighty tome—the appendix alone weighs several pounds. The

length and breadth attest to there being many mysteries surrounding Columbus's remains, most of them due to the fact that
Columbus's body traveled nearly as widely as the man himself.

Initially, Columbus's relatives had him buried in Valladolid at
a cost of 50,000 *maravedís,* an amount they managed to swindle
out of a Genoese bank (they were taken to court and lost). Three
years later Columbus's remains were exhumed, taken to Seville,
and laid to rest at the Carthusian monastery Santa María de las
Cuevas on the river island of La Cartuja. In 1537 the Colón family decided that their famous ancestor should be laid to rest in the
place he had always wanted to be buried, on Hispaniola. Columbus's bones were transported to the New World along with those
of his son Diego and buried for a third time in the cathedral of
Santo Domingo. There they probably lay until 1795. That year
Spain was forced to cede the eastern part of the island to France.
Under no circumstances did the withdrawing Spaniards wish to
place Columbus's body under foreign rule. They took what they
thought to be his bones and brought them to their nearest colony,
Cuba. Columbus was then buried in Havana. This was his fourth
burial, but by no means his last. Cuba gained independence in
1898, forcing the Spaniards to leave. Once again they retrieved his
bones and brought them back home.

At this time what remained of his remains fit neatly into a
lead box the size of a child's coffin. The Spaniards built a monument to surround this lead box in the cathedral in Seville, consisting of four larger-than-life statues bearing an oversize coffin.

By this point a controversy had already begun brewing, for in
1877 workers restoring parts of the cathedral in Santo Domingo
came across a lead box, located to the left of the altar. The box
bore the inscription "Don Cristóbal Colón." This is the box now
housed in the bronze coffin of the Columbus Memorial Lighthouse in Santo Domingo. Since the discovery of this second box,
there have been disputes among scholars and heated discussions
among nations as to who possesses the real Columbus. If the box
in Santo Domingo is real, whose remains did the Spaniards take

back to Havana? And whose remains now lie in the cathedral in Seville? One theory is that they are the remains of his son Diego.

As if matters weren't complicated enough, in 1960 an expert from Yale opened the lead box in Santo Domingo and discovered remains belonging to two separate skeletons, neither complete. Again, one theory was that the bones of the father and the son had gotten mixed up. The governing bodies in the Dominican Republic were not pleased by the results of this analysis and have since denied foreign scientists access to the lead box.

Anunciada Colón has spent years researching the truth and looking for historical documents but has yet to find conclusive evidence. She is currently working with historians and scientists from the University of Granada, in an effort to bring an end to the old dispute. The team includes experts in DNA analysis. This genetic analysis, said Dr. José Antonio Lorente, a specialist in forensic genetics with the university's Department of Legal Medicine, "should provide the answer to the key question of whether the remains in Seville are authentic or not."

To answer this question, Lorente needed comparative genetic material, ideally from bone fragments belonging to Columbus's mother, which no longer exist. Alternatively, the material could come from one of Columbus's brothers. Anunciada Colón believes she knows where the remains of Diego Colón are buried. Diego—easily confused with Columbus's son of the same name—was probably the youngest of the three Colón brothers and certainly the least forceful, as was proved when his brother made him head of the council governing the town of La Isabela on the island of Hispaniola in April 1494. In 1495 Diego returned to Spain, where he was allowed to settle wherever he wanted—a singular honor at the time. Diego did not remain in Spain for long. He returned to Hispaniola, where Royal Commissioner Francisco de Bobadilla had him arrested and sent back to Castile. He traveled back and forth between continents for a few years, always living well off the money left to him by his brother. He had a house and several slaves and died in Seville in 1515.

Diego Colón was buried in a crypt at the monastery Santa María de las Cuevas. Centuries later a British business entrepreneur named Charles Pickman had the monastery converted into a ceramics factory. His workers walled up part of the crypt and used the rest of the space as a warehouse. Pickman's descendants located the old crypt behind the wall in 1930, but the vault wasn't opened until 1950. Inside they found a skeleton, the coffin that had contained it having long since disintegrated. A forensic scientist confirmed they were the remains of a man around five feet six inches tall who had died between the ages of fifty and sixty-five—several centuries earlier. This gave rise to the theory that while the bodily remains could belong to Diego Colón, they might also be those of his famous brother, Christopher, for the remains of the discoverer had also been interred in the monastery for a certain time.

The directors of the Pickman factory stowed the Colón remains in a zinc box, which they exhibited in one of their offices. When the entire factory was relocated to another site in Seville, the metal box was also moved. There, in the new factory building, was where Anunciada Colón came across the small coffin, noting the unusual location in her book. The box was removed and buried in the garden of the factory, where it remained for a few years. In 2002 Anunciada Colón had the box unearthed for comparative DNA analysis. In June 2003 she was present when scientists from the University of Granada opened the monument in the cathedral of Seville. Inside they found two metal boxes, one of which was said to contain the remains of Columbus's son Fernando. The other was said to contain the bones that had been rescued from Havana in 1898. "We thought we would find only a handful of dust," said Marcial Castro, head of the team of historians in charge of the investigation, "but there were plenty of bones."

The three boxes were brought to Granada under police escort, where Lorente's DNA specialists began comparing the skeletons to determine which belonged to Columbus, his son, and his brother. The results were due out in a year's time.

One reason the investigation has taken so long was because Castro and Lorente were also attempting to illuminate another mystery. Were they not such respected scientists, one might dismiss the whole thing as sheer nonsense. At issue is the "Spanish theory." Advocates of this theory believe that Columbus was not born in Genoa but was the illegitimate son of a Spanish prince called Carlos de Viana, who lived on Majorca. They claim that the discoverer was born there in 1461 and received his name from his mother, Margarita Colón, descendant of a Jewish family from Felanitx on Majorca. There is no evidence to support this theory, and the counterevidence—the documents from Genoa that mention Christopher Columbus—seems to be overwhelming. But the prince of Viana is buried in Tarragona, and DNA specialists from the University of Granada had removed bone fragments. While analyzing other samples, they felt they might as well test the validity of this theory.

Fernando Colón, Columbus's illegitimate son and greatest biographer, became a renowned scholar and collector of rare books. He later achieved fame for his correspondence with Erasmus of Rotterdam. He died childless.

Diego Colón, Columbus's legitimate son and his principal heir, achieved what his father had always wanted: entrée into the world of the nobility. After his marriage to Doña María de Toledo, her cousin King Ferdinand appointed the young Colón governor of Hispaniola in 1509. The couple lived in Santo Domingo, and Diego died in 1526.

Luis Colón, Diego's only legitimate son and the discoverer's only recognized grandson, became the "black sheep of the family," according to Consuelo Varela. His mother contrived to have the titles Duke of Veragua and Marquis of Jamaica bestowed on him, as well as a perpetual annuity of 10,000 ducats. He was appointed governor of Hispaniola, a post he held for eleven years between 1540 and 1551. He was, however, relatively unsuccessful, losing all of his important battles in the New World. One of his defeats also cost the life of his half-brother Francisco, Diego's illegitimate son. Luis married in 1542, married again in 1546, and then married a third time ten years later. The problem was that none of his wives had died by the time he remarried and divorce was not common in those days. He was arrested for polygamy and sentenced to five years in prison. He escaped and found a new mistress, whom he also married, much to the amazement of his wives numbers one through three. Eventually, Luis was banished and died in exile in Algiers in 1572.

The Colón name has survived over the centuries, and the family is now among the most prominent in Spain. Cristóbal Colón XX, Duke of Veragua, is currently the head of the family and bearer of the name and title. As tradition dictates, he became an officer in the Spanish navy. Later he became a businessman, though he has remained a passionate sailor. Like his sister, the historian Anunciada Colón, he loves nothing so much as the ocean.

————

The fact that the continent discovered by Columbus was not called Columbia was not only due to Amerigo Vespucci. The former assistant to Gianotto Berardi the slave trader turned up on the coast of what would later be Venezuela a few years after Columbus. When Berardi's company went bankrupt as a result of the immense costs of Columbus's second voyage, Vespucci took over the liquidation proceedings for the company. He also helped to equip Columbus's ships for the third voyage. The Admiral always considered Vespucci to be a good friend.

After 1499 Vespucci felt the urge to sail the ocean seas. While his traveling was limited to his being a passenger on a ship belonging to another discoverer, or to his being the navigator or captain of a ship that was part of a larger fleet, Vespucci was a magnificent storyteller—and just as magnificent a liar. He invented entire expeditions and sent vivid letters to acquaintances and dignitaries, describing journeys to Brazil, for example, as if he himself had been the principal man on board. To his credit, Vespucci quickly realized that he was dealing with a "New World." As a result, one of his texts was entitled *Mundus Novus*—a novel idea at the time.

Whereas Columbus wrote mostly dry descriptions of his discoveries, Vespucci emphasized the racy details. He described the Indian women as being "very lustful." They would "cause the private parts of their husbands to swell up to such a huge size that they appear deformed and disgusting." He also claimed that the men cohabited with anyone they pleased, even with their mothers and sisters. European readers avidly devoured these texts. Vespucci's letters were quickly copied, translated, and circulated throughout the old continent. Martin Waldseemüller, a young cartographer from Lorraine, read one of these texts, and apparently it aroused a consuming interest in him. When he published a world map together with a new edition of a book by Ptolemy, he wrote an accompanying text. "A fourth part has been discovered by Americus Vespuccius. I do not see what right any one would have to object to calling this part after Americus, who discovered it, and so to name it the Land of Americus, or America." The new continent was therefore named for the former errand boy to a slave trader. Delighted by his idea, and because "America" had such a nice ring to it, Waldseemüller immediately entered this name onto his map in capital letters. The book was published in 1507, a year after Columbus's death. Most other cartographers copied Waldseemüller's invention.

Estimates state that when Columbus first set foot in the New World, some fifty thousand Arawak Indians called Taínos lived on the Bahamas. Many were killed or died from diseases introduced by the Europeans. The rest were carried off into slavery and transported to Spain, Cuba, or the island of Hispaniola, a fate that cost thousands of lives. A hundred years after Columbus's arrival, the Taínos from the Bahamas were virtually wiped out. Today there is nobody left who can claim to be their direct descendant.

Other indigenous tribes and nations in Central America suffered the same fate when the Spanish conquistadors advanced into the region.

On Friday, March 15, 1493, Columbus wrote the final entry in his log of the first voyage of discovery: "I hope in Our Lord that it will be the greatest honor to Christianity that, unexpectedly, has ever come about." In the years that followed, the priest Bartolomé de las Casas, for one, was tormented by the murder of natives he had been forced to witness. When he recopied Columbus's log, ultimately preserving it for posterity, he added his own comments. This grim closing commentary is missing from many editions of the log, but the original lies in the National Library in Madrid:

> *Note here, that the natural, simple and kind gentleness and humble condition of the Indians, and want of arms and protection, gave the Spaniards the insolence to hold them of little account, and to impose on them the harshest tasks that they could, and to become glutted with oppression and destruction. And sure it is that here the Admiral enlarged himself in speech more than he should, and that what he here conceived and set forth from his lips, was the beginning of the ill usage he afterwards inflicted upon them.*

TRANSLATOR'S NOTE

In addition to the books and articles listed in the bibliography, I have relied upon the following sources for English-language versions of the primary texts that are quoted in the text.

Cohen, Jonathan: The Naming of America: Vespucci's Good Name in: Encounters, Vol. 7, S. 16–20 ff., cited at: http://muweb.millersville.edu/~columbus/data/art/COHEN-01.ART

Columbus, Christopher: The Four Voyages: Being His Own Log-Book, Letters, and Dispatches with Connecting Narratives, J. M. Cohen, ed. and trans. Penguin Classics, New York, 1992

Dunne, Oliver and James E. Kelly, eds.: The Diario of Christopher Columbus's First Voyage to America, 1492–1493 (American Exploration and Travel Series), University of Oklahoma Press, Norman, OK, 1989

Hale, Edward Everett: The Life of Christopher Columbus from His Own Letters and Journals, cited at: World Wide School, http://www.worldwideschool.org/library/books/hst/biography/TheLifeofChristopherColumbusfromhisownLettersandJournals/toc.html

Irving, Washington: The Project Gutenberg EBook of The Life and Voyages of Christopher Columbus, Vol. 2, cited at: http://www2.cddc.vt.edu/gutenberg/etext05/7col210.txt

Judge, Joseph: The Columbus Landfall at Samana Cay in: National Geographic Magazine, cited at: http://muweb.millersville.edu/~columbus/data/art/JUDGE-01.ART

Keen, Benjamin, trans. and annotator: The Life of the Admiral
    Christopher Columbus by His Son Ferdinand, Rutgers
    University Press, Piscataway, NJ, 1992
Narrative of the Third Voyage of Columbus as Contained
    in Las Casas's History, in: American Journeys
    Collection, Wisconsin Historical Society,
    http://content.wisconsinhistory.org/cgi-bin/
    docviewer.exe?CISOROOT=/aj&CISOPTR=4215
Olsonand, Julius E. and Edward Gaylord Bourne, eds.:
    Christopher Columbus, Journal of the First Voyage of
    Columbus, in: The Northmen, Columbus and Cabot,
    985–1503: Original Narratives of Early American History.
    Charles Scribner's Sons, New York, 1906, cited at:
    http://www.mith2.umd.edu:8080/eada/html/
    display.jsp?docs=columbus_journal.xml&action=show
Taviani, Paolo Emilio: Christopher Columbus: Genius of the
    Sea, in Halian Journal, Vol. 5, No. 5/6, 1991, S. 5–37 ff.
Thacher, John Boyd, trans.: The log of Christopher Columbus's
    First Voyage to the New World, in: Christopher Columbus:
    His Life, His Work, His Remains. G. P. Putnam's Sons,
    New York and London, 1903, cited at: http://www.
    gutenberg.org/dirs/4/1/1/4116/4116-h/4116-h.htm
Wilford, John Noble: Dominican Bluff Yields Columbus' First
    Colony, in: The New York Times, November 27, 1990, S. C1,
    C6 ff., cited at: http://muweb.millersville.edu/~columbus/
    data/art/WILFORD3.ART
Young, Filson: Christopher Columbus and the New World of
    His Discovery, J. B. Lippincott, London 1906
Young, Filson: Christopher Columbus and the New World of
    His Discovery, 2nd ed., E. Grant Richards, London, 1906

SELECTED BIBLIOGRAPHY

Athearn, Robert G.: *The American Heritage New Illustrated History of the United States, Vol. 1: The New World*, Dell Publishing, New York 1963

Axtell, James: *After Columbus, Essays in the Ethnohistory of Colonial North America*, Oxford University Press, New York and Oxford 1988

Bass, George F. (Ed.): *Ships and Shipwrecks of the Americas: A History Based on Underwater Archaeology*, Thames and Hudson, New York 1996

————: "Splendors of the Bronze Age," *National Geographic*, Vol. 172, No. 6, December 1987, p. 693 ff.

Cedeño Cenci, Diógenes: *The Panama Canal Strait Sought-after by Christopher Columbus in the Route of the Storms*, Edición del Círculo de Lectura de la USMA, Panama 2001

Colón de Carvajal, Anunciada and Guadelupe Chocano: *Christobal Colón—Incógnitas de su muerte 1506–1902*, Consejo Superior de Investigaciones Cientificas (CSIC), Madrid 1992

Colón, Fernando: *The Life of the Admiral Christopher Columbus by his Son Ferdinand*, Rutgers University Press, New Brunswick 1958

Colón, Hernando: *Cuarto Viaje Colombino: La Ruta de los Huracanes 1502–1504*, Edición de Luis Arranz Márquez, Dastin, Madrid 2002

Cornell, Jimmy: *World Cruising Routes*, International Marine, McGraw-Hill Professional, New York 2002

Culver, Henry B.: "A Contemporary Fifteenth-century Ship Model," *The Mariner's Mirror*, Vol. 15, 1929, No. 3, p. 213 ff.

Deagan, Kathleen and José María Cruxent: *Columbus's Outpost among the Taínos, Spain and America at La Isabela, 1493–1498,* Yale University Press, New Haven and London 2002

————: *Archaeology at La Isabela, America's First European Town,* Yale University Press, New Haven and London 2002

Edwards, Clinton R.: "Design and Construction of Fifteenth-century Iberian Ships," *The Mariner's Mirror,* Vol. 78, 1992, No. 4, p. 419 ff.

Granzotto, Gianni: *Christopher Columbus,* Doubleday, Garden City, NY, 1985

Hapgood, Charles H.: *Maps of the Ancient Sea Kings: Evidence of Advanced Civilization in the Ice Age,* Souvenir Press, London 2001

Jane, Cecil (Ed.): *The Four Voyages of Columbus: A History in Eight Documents,* Dover Publications, New York 1988

Kamen, Henry: *Spain's Road to Empire: The Making of a World Power 1492–1763,* Penguin Press, London 2002

Keith, Donald H. and Toni L. Carrell: "The Hunt for the Gallega," *Archaeology,* January/February 1991, pp. 55–59

————: "The Molasses Reef Wreck." Dissertation, Texas A&M University 1987

Keegan, William F.: "Riddles of Columbus," *Archeology,* January/February 1992, p. 59

Komroff, Manuel: *The Travels of Marco Polo,* Liverlight Publishing, New York 1953

Morison, Samuel E.: *Admiral of the Ocean Sea,* Little, Brown and Company, Boston 1942

————: *The European Discovery of America: The Northern Voyages,* Oxford University Press, New York 1971

————: *The European Discovery of America: The Southern Voyages,* Oxford University Press, New York 1974

Peter, Karl H.: *Wie Columbus navigierte,* Koehlers Verlagsgesellschaft, Herford 1972

Phillips, William D. Jr. and Carla Rahn Phillips: *The Worlds of Christopher Columbus,* Cambridge University Press, New York 1993

Pulak, Cemal: "The Uluburun Shipwreck," *The International Journal of Nautical Archaeology*, 1998, pp. 188–224

Sale, Kirkpatrick: *Christopher Columbus and the Conquest of Paradise*, I. B. Tauris & Company, London 2006

Smith, Roger C.: *Vanguard of Empire. Ships of Exploration in the Age of Columbus*, Oxford University Press, New York 1993

Sokolow, Jayme A.: *The Great Encounter: Native Peoples and European Settlers in the Americas, 1492–1800*, Sharpe, Armonk, NY, 2002

Taviani, Paolo Emilio: *Christopher Columbus: The Grand Design*, Orbis, London 1985

van Nouhuys, J. W.: "The Model of a Spanish Caravel of the Beginning of the Fifteenth Century," *The Mariner's Mirror*, Vol. 17, 1931, No. 4, p. 327 ff.

Varela, Consuelo (Ed.): *Cristóbal Colón: Textos y documentos completos*, Alianza, Madrid 1982

Vaughan, H. S.: "The Nodal Caravels of 1618," *The Mariner's Mirror*, Vol. 3, No. 2, p. 171 ff., 1913

Venzke, Andreas: *Christoph Kolumbus*, Rowohlt Taschenbuch-Verlag, Reinbek bei Hamburg 1992

Wassermann, Jakob: *Columbus, der Don Quichote des Ozeans: Eine Biographie*, dtv, München 1992. First published 1929 by S. Fischer, Berlin.

Wiesenthal, Simon: *Sails of Hope: The Secret Mission of Christopher Columbus*, MacMillan, New York 1973

Wilford, John Noble: *The Mysterious History of Columbus*, Knopf, New York 1991

Wilson, Samuel M.: *Hispaniola: Caribbean Chiefdoms in the Age of Columbus*, The University of Alabama Press, Tuscaloosa and London 1990

ACKNOWLEDGMENTS

This book has been a team effort, for it evolved along with a television program and a documentary film. In the sixteen years of collaboration between *Der Spiegel* magazine and Spiegel TV, there has probably never been an occasion for a greater feeling of mutual trust. The credit in this case goes to Marc Brasse, author of the documentary and head of the television crew, and his researcher and underwater cameraman Karl Vandenhole. Thanks also go to cameraman Bernd Zühlke, sound engineers Pascal Capitolin and Philip Fleischer, as well as Claudia Moroni, the ZDF, and Arte.

We would also like to express our gratitude to journalists Heinz Egleder and editorial director Katharina Lüken, without whose help this book would have been full of mistakes. We thank the scientists who have facilitated this project from the outset and have embraced it as their own: Filipe Castro, Donny Hamilton, Consuelo Varela, Juan Gil, Stuart Schwartz, Roger Smith, Carlos Fitzgerald, Karl-Uwe Heussner, and Pieter M. Grootes. Thanks also go to Udo Ludwig, Ulrike von Bülow, and Jürgen Dahlkamp as well as our German editor, Julia Hoffmann. They were the first critical readers. We would like to thank Klaus Keppler, Diógenes Cedeno Cenci, Björn Kraft and Warren White, Andrea Krüger and Kirsten Beitz, Christa von Holtzapfel and Ulrike Preuss, Margarete Hüttenberger, Renate Bohlmann and Heidi Miketa, Cornelia Pfauter, Bibiana Menniken, Reimer Nagel and Lutz Diedrichs, Brigitte Müller, Michael Neher, Matthias Schmolz and Sabine Krecker and Cora for asking so many questions.

We are particularly grateful to our *Spiegel* colleagues Heiner Schimmöller, Alexander Jung, Olaf Ihlau, Hans Hoyng, and

Christian Neef for their support in the editorial office as well as to the editor in chief Stefan Aust, his assistants Martin Doerry and Joachim Preuss, and the editor in chief of Spiegel TV, Cassian von Salomon, without whose curiosity projects like this would not happen.

For the English-language edition, we thank our translator, Annette Streck, and our editor, Tim Bent.

INDEX

———————

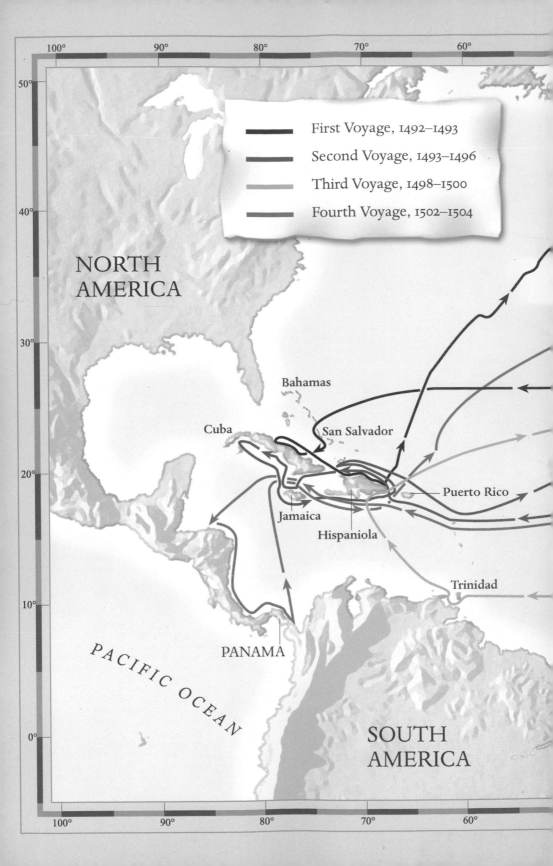

First Voyage, 1492–1493
Second Voyage, 1493–1496
Third Voyage, 1498–1500
Fourth Voyage, 1502–1504

NORTH
AMERICA

Bahamas

Cuba   San Salvador

Jamaica   Puerto Rico

Hispaniola

PANAMA   Trinidad

PACIFIC OCEAN

SOUTH
AMERICA